THE UNIVERSITY OF NORTH CAROLINA
SESQUICENTENNIAL PUBLICATIONS

A STATE UNIVERSITY
SURVEYS THE HUMANITIES

THE UNIVERSITY OF NORTH CAROLINA SESQUICENTENNIAL PUBLICATIONS

Louis R. Wilson, DIRECTOR

CHRONICLES OF THE SESQUICENTENNIAL

THE UNIVERSITY OF NORTH CAROLINA, 1789-1835:
A Documentary History

THE CAMPUS OF THE FIRST STATE UNIVERSITY

THE GRADUATE SCHOOL: RESEARCH AND PUBLICATIONS

THE GRADUATE SCHOOL: DISSERTATIONS AND THESES

STUDIES IN SCIENCE

STUDIES IN LANGUAGE AND LITERATURE

A HUNDRED YEARS OF LEGAL EDUCATION

A STATE UNIVERSITY SURVEYS THE HUMANITIES

SECONDARY EDUCATION IN THE SOUTH

IN SEARCH OF THE REGIONAL BALANCE OF AMERICA

STUDIES IN HISTORY AND POLITICAL SCIENCE

LIBRARY RESOURCES OF THE UNIVERSITY OF NORTH CAROLINA

RESEARCH AND REGIONAL WELFARE

PIONEERING A PEOPLE'S THEATER

UNIVERSITY EXTENSION IN ACTION

BOOKS FROM CHAPEL HILL

A STATE UNIVERSITY SURVEYS THE HUMANITIES

Edited with a Foreword

BY

LOREN C. MacKINNEY
Professor of Medieval History
CHAIRMAN OF THE EDITORIAL BOARD

NICHOLSON B. ADAMS
Professor of Spanish

HARRY K. RUSSELL
Associate Professor of English

CHAPEL HILL
THE UNIVERSITY OF NORTH CAROLINA PRESS
1945

Copyright, 1945, by
THE UNIVERSITY OF NORTH CAROLINA PRESS

Van Rees Press, New York

FOREWORD

As THE UNIVERSITY OF NORTH CAROLINA reaches its hundred and fiftieth anniversary, it takes stock of its past, present, and future in the educational world. The Division of the Humanities offers the present volume as a contribution to this larger enterprise. The Division includes the Departments of Art, Classics, Comparative Linguistics, Dramatic Art, English, General and Comparative Literature, Germanic Languages, Journalism, Music, Romance Languages, and the following departments which also belong to other divisions: Education, History, and Philosophy.

The Division of the Humanities offers a much wider range of subjects than were included in the so-called "humanities" of the past: the ancient "liberal arts" of Cicero's day, the "human learning" (the trivium and quadrivium) of the Middle Ages, the Roman and Greek classics of the Renaissance, or the belles-lettres of the early modern times. Widely inclusive as our Division is, its faculty claims no monopoly of humanistic or liberal studies. The validity in the concept of the humanities lies in the humanistic *ideal*, not in a group of traditionally humanistic *subjects*. We believe, however, that these subjects offer especially rich opportunities for the development of the humanistic ideal. We also believe that every course in a university can appropriately embody this ideal, and can thus inculcate attitudes and habits of approach characteristic of informed and mature persons.

The humanistic ideal unifies and inspires all divisions of a university, and invigorates the work of scientists, artists, specialists, professional men, and workers of all sorts. The humanistic ideal is timeless; it has been appropriate in every age, and it is appropriate in ours. Man has justified his humanity and realized his highest capacities in proportion to his attainment of the widest humanistic perspective. The humanistic ideal involves a broad view of man's struggle to place himself in his environment, and it offers a noble tradition to guide him in his development. It informs and enriches his attitude and his behavior toward the world about him, makes him an understanding member of society, and helps him to realize his highest capabilities as an individual.

Such an ideal is important for a world that has become, in recent years, dangerously materialistic and mechanistic, and which has stressed technical progress more than cultural values. It is obvious that, in order to maintain their integrity in this complex world, young people must learn how to live as well as how to earn a living. If we agree that man cannot live by bread alone, we accept the idea that education which is solely vocational is partial and deficient. Necessary though specialized training is, there must be something beyond, something that touches the spirit as well as the body, something that exalts the dignity of man's personality. It is this which the humanistic ideal should and can supply, by emphasizing the development of the whole man, inclusive of special skills, whether mechanical, industrial, artistic, or professional. We hold that educating students into maturity and citizenship in a complex world is the most important obligation of a university. No department or division alone can discharge this obligation. Every element in the curriculum should make its fullest contribution to this primary and all-inclusive end.

The purpose of this volume, then, is to show that the humanities are not merely a group of academic subjects, but that they represent an ideal which can permeate all human activity. In accordance with this view, we have brought together natural scientists, social scientists, and professional men, as well as men of letters, to collaborate in setting forth past experiences, present problems, and future aspirations in humanistic education. We believe that the following essays indicate how the humanistic ideal can touch and illuminate all fields of human thought, including specialized research, the professions, and the life of the average citizen in the modern world.

The Editorial Board, representing the Division of the Humanities, offers sincere thanks to those who have contributed to this volume. The editors and the present chairman of the Division, Howard R. Huse, wish at this time to pay tribute to the first chairman of the Division, our honored colleague, William Morton Dey, who guided the Division in its early years and helped to inspire it with a vitality and a co-operative spirit of which we hope this volume is an expression; and to the second chairman of the Division, the late Gustave Adolphus Harrer, who furthered the development of the Division with the same high degree of success that he achieved in all his devoted service to the University.

L. C. M.
N. B. A.
H. K. R.

Chapel Hill, N. C.
May, 1945

CONTENTS

	PAGE
Foreword	v

PART I

THE HUMANITIES AT THE UNIVERSITY OF NORTH CAROLINA 1795-1945

1. THE HUMANITIES AT THE UNIVERSITY OF NORTH CAROLINA, 1795-1945, A HISTORICAL SURVEY   3
   Wallace E. Caldwell, *Professor of Ancient History*

PART II

THE HUMANITIES AND THE HUMANISTIC IDEAL IN THE FIELDS OF UNIVERSITY EDUCATION

2. HISTORY   33
   James L. Godfrey, *Assistant Professor of History*

3. LITERATURE: THE BEAST IN MAN   41
   George C. Taylor, *Kenan Professor of English*

4. LITERATURE: THE CREATIVE IN MAN   56
   Paul Green, *Professor of Dramatic Art*

5. PHILOSOPHY AND RELIGION: THE HUMANITY OF MAN   68
   Helmut Kuhn, *Associate Professor of Philosophy*

6. LANGUAGE STUDY   81
   Howard R. Huse, *Professor of Romance Languages*

7. MUSIC   92
   Glen Haydon, *Professor of Music*

8. THE FINE ARTS   102
   Clemens Sommer, *Associate Professor of the History of Art*

		PAGE
9.	THE SOCIAL SCIENCES Howard W. Odum, *Kenan Professor of Sociology*	108
10.	EDUCATION AND PSYCHOLOGY John F. Dashiell, *Kenan Professor of Psychology*	118
11.	THE BIOLOGICAL SCIENCES: THE SCIENCES IN THE HUMANITIES Robert E. Coker, *Kenan Professor of Zoology*	129
12.	MATHEMATICS AND THE PHYSICAL SCIENCES Archibald Henderson, *Kenan Professor of Mathematics*	144

PART III

THE HUMANITIES AND THE HUMANISTIC IDEAL
AS VIEWED BY PROFESSIONAL MEN

13.	MEDICINE George L. Carrington, M.D., *Class of 1913, Head of the Alamance General Hospital, Burlington, North Carolina*	163
14.	LAW A. A. F. Seawell, *Class of 1889, Associate Justice of the Supreme Court of North Carolina*	172
15.	BUSINESS Thomas C. Boushall, *Class of 1915, President of the Morris Plan Bank of Virginia and Chairman of the Committee on Education of the United States Chamber of Commerce*	184
16.	JOURNALISM: THE HUMANITIES AND THE COMMON MAN Gerald W. Johnson, *Professor of Journalism, University of North Carolina (1924-1926), Editor and Author*	192

PART IV

THE FUTURE OF THE HUMANITIES IN STATE UNIVERSITIES

17. THE FUTURE OF THE HUMANITIES IN STATE UNIVERSITIES   205
   Norman Foerster, *Professor of English, University of North Carolina (1914-1930), Director of the School of Letters, University of Iowa (1930-1944)*

Part I

THE HUMANITIES AT
THE UNIVERSITY OF NORTH CAROLINA
1795-1945

Chapter I

THE HUMANITIES AT THE UNIVERSITY OF NORTH CAROLINA, 1795-1945, A HISTORICAL SURVEY *

Wallace E. Caldwell

To WRITE THE history of the humanities at the University of North Carolina is in large measure to write the history of collegiate education in Chapel Hill. Certainly during the first period of the University's history, the administration of President Joseph Caldwell (1804-35), it seems doubtful that the Faculty would have understood or accepted as valid any distinction between the humanities on the one hand and mathematics and the sciences on the other, nor would they have acknowledged the idea of competition between them. Together these made up the essentials of a liberal education. The first and for a brief time the only professor in the University, responsible for the whole range of university education, was entitled "Professor of Humanity."

The professors who succeeded him and came to form the University Faculty were with few exceptions trained as preachers, even the great scientists Olmsted and Mitchell. Following the practice of the time, Elisha Mitchell called his field "Natural Philosophy" and asked the Trustees for money with which to buy philosophical apparatus. The academic discussions which took place in those early days dealt not with the relative merits of the humanities and the sciences, but with the advantages of a "liberal" as against a "useful" education. A useful education seems to have been thought to comprise Eng-

* The material for this paper is drawn from Kemp P. Battle, *History of the University of North Carolina* (2 vols., 1907-12), from the minutes of the Board of Trustees and of the Faculty, and from published letters and addresses. Gratitude for assistance is due Professor R. D. W. Connor, Miss Mary L. Thornton, Librarian of the North Carolina Collection in the Library, and Mr. Benjamin H. Wall, former graduate student and instructor in the Department of History.

3

lish and such sciences as might be applied to agriculture and engineering.

Though the advocates of this program delivered their chief attack on the classical languages, their real enemy was the whole philosophy of liberal education.

> May this hill be for religion as the ancient hill of Zion; and for literature and the muses, may it surpass the ancient Parnassus!

With these words spoken at the laying of the cornerstone of Old East in 1795, Dr. Samuel E. McCorckle launched the new university on its career. The classical tradition of university education would seem to have made a good start. Yet at the outset the advocates of usefulness were in control. Even Mr. McCorckle had followed them in a program which he presented to the Trustees in 1792. His program called for "the study of languages, particularly the English, the acquirement of Historical knowledge, ancient and modern, the study of Belles letters [sic], Mathematics and Natural Philosophy. Information in Botany to which should be added a competent knowledge in the theory and practice of Agriculture best suited to the climate and soils of this state. The principles of Architecture."

At the actual opening of the University in 1795, however, this plan was modified. A literary curriculum was established for the study of English, Latin, Greek, mathematics including book-keeping, natural philosophy, astronomy, logic, moral philosophy, principles of civil government, history and belles-lettres. Provision was also made for a scientific curriculum, for the study of the sciences and the English language, an early forerunner of the Bachelor of Science program. This entire program was placed in the hands of the "Professor of Humanity" and a tutor in mathematics. The tutor, Charles W. Harris, a Princeton graduate of the class of 1792, was so pleased with the situation that on April 10, 1795, he wrote in a letter to his uncle, Dr. Charles Harris:

> There is one class in Natural Philosophy & Geography & four in languages. The constitution of this college is on a more liberal plan

than any in America, & by the amendments which I think it will receive at the next meeting of the trustees, its usefulness will probably be much promoted. The notion that true learning consists rather in exercising the reasoning faculties, & laying up a store of useful knowledge, than in overloading the memory with words of a dead language, is becoming daily more prevalent. It appears hard to deny a young Gentleman the honour of a College, after he has with much labour and painful attention acquired a competent knowledge of the Sciences; of composing & speaking with propriety in his own language, & has conned the first principles of whatever might render him useful or creditable in the world, merely because he could not read a language 2000 years old. Tho' the laws at present require that the Latin & Greek be understood by a graduate—they will in all probability be mitigated in this respect. These old forms, "which have been sanctioned by time but not by utility" ought to be dispensed with.

The amendments promised in this letter were embodied in an extensive plan of studies, the work of William R. Davie, which was adopted by the Trustees in 1796. This provided for a preparatory school and for a series of University professorships. In the preparatory school, English, Latin, and French were to be taught, with Greek optional. It was further provided that "any language, except English, may be omitted at the request of the parents." In the University the President was to teach rhetoric and belles-lettres. There were to be five professorships, devoted to moral and political philosophy and history; natural philosophy, astronomy, and geography; mathematics, chemistry, and the philosophy of medicine; agriculture and the mechanic arts; and languages. Only for study under the professor of languages was Latin to be a prerequisite. Anyone who could pass examinations in English and arithmetic was to be allowed to study under any of the other professors. All who completed a selected program were to receive degrees. There was thus no absolute requirement of a foreign language laid down for all recipients of degrees.

In a letter to Joseph Caldwell written in 1797 Davie stated:

A Bachelor's degree generally imports a knowledge of the learned languages as well as the sciences, to confer such a degree upon a person who understood neither Latin or Greek does not appear to be proper. The ruling or leading principle in our plan of education is, that the student may apply himself to those branches of learning and science alone which are absolutely necessary to fit him for his destined profession or occupation in life.

He, therefore, proposed that the Bachelor of Arts degree be given for proficiency in English, the sciences, and either Latin or Greek, and that a diploma certifying knowledge and progress in the arts and sciences be granted to one who omitted the classics.

The advocates of useful education were thus fighting a losing battle. From the very start the influence of Princeton was strong. Tutor Harris wrote early in 1796: "We imitate Nassau Hall in the conduct of our affairs as much as our circumstances will admit." In 1796 Joseph Caldwell was brought from Princeton to be Professor of Mathematics. In 1800 he was made Presiding Professor and in 1804 President of the University. Though a mathematician and a scientist, he was, as befitted his Princeton background and his ministerial training, a strong believer in the classics. Though none of the motions in the Board of Trustees bears his name, there can be little doubt that his was the dominant influence.

In 1800 the Trustees repealed their ordinance conferring the degree of Bachelor of Arts on those students "having passed an approved examination on the English Language and the Sciences," and set up a Latin requirement for admission to, and graduation from the University. In 1801 a choice of Greek or French was added. The triumph of the proponents of classical culture was complete when in 1804 on motion of Archibald D. Murphey Greek was made a *sine qua non* for admission and graduation. The committee of the Trustees reported that "they are of opinion the dignity of the University requires that the study of the Greek Language be again introduced, and that no student except such as are hereafter mentioned, be admitted to the Honors of the institution without a competent knowledge of the Greek language."

In an address delivered to the graduating class in 1827,

President Caldwell explained the establishment of the Greek requirement.

It is perhaps little known to some, while to others it may appear strange, that such an experiment actually made, is already upon the records of our University, and that it was continued with no small perseverance, to accommodate that portion of public opinion which decried the utility of these languages. And what was the result of this? No sooner did candidates begin to offer themselves for the highest honours of the institution, as having substituted the requisite portion of modern language for the ancient, than intelligent and enlightened members of the Board, making no pretensions to collegiate learning, and having no undue prepossessions in behalf of the prescriptive learning of the schools, after witnessing the collateral examinations of such as were versed in the ancient languages, and of others who had not enjoyed these opportunities, exclaimed under the severe disparagement of the comparison, against the continuance of a practice, of whose effects no previous exposition could have convinced them.

At the same time the Trustees made one concession to the modernists. They allowed students to enter the University with a deficiency in Greek, "it being at all times understood, that the students admitted under this disqualification will not be considered as candidates for the honours of the University." The lists of "irregular students" in the later catalogues indicate that many availed themselves of the privilege of attending the University without hope of a degree.

Thus established on what the President regarded as a firm basis, the University proceeded on its classical way, not, however, without an occasional glance, as it were, over its shoulder. When in 1817 the Trustees determined to create a chair of chemistry and appointed Denison Olmsted to it, the opinion was expressed that this act would be well pleasing to the agriculturists of the state. In the same year the cause of science in North Carolina was greatly advanced by the appointment of Elisha Mitchell to the chair of mathematics, though it must be remembered that this great scientist was also a theologian of merit and a firm believer in the program of liberal education. At the same time a chair of rhetoric and logic was established with S. K. Kollock as Professor, and President Caldwell became Professor of Moral Philosophy and Metaphysics.

The enlargement of the faculty was accompanied by an expansion in the curriculum. The program instituted in 1818 was presented to the Trustees by President Caldwell himself. It provided for studies in Latin, Greek, mathematics, and English during the first two years, advanced mathematics, English literature, rhetoric, natural philosophy, and sciences, moral philosophy and metaphysics, during the Junior and Senior years. The catalogue of 1824, however, shows that by that year courses in Greek and Latin were being taught in the Junior and Senior years. The same catalogue lists political economy among the courses given. The appointment of N. M. Hentz as Professor of Modern Languages in 1826 made possible the teaching of French and Spanish. After his departure in 1831 French was continued but Spanish was dropped.

Such is the record of the curriculum under the administration of President Caldwell. Of the men who taught in these formative years of the University little remains but their names and tales of disciplinary troubles with unruly students. The only measure of their success as teachers is the great part their students played in after life as leaders in politics, law, and business in the state. Fortunately, we have from President Caldwell an address delivered to the graduating class in 1828. After thirty-two years of service in the University he summed up in this speech his philosophy of education. Since this philosophy had been unquestionably the continuing dominant force through all these years, we quote his speech in part.

As the great objects of education here are to treasure up knowledge in the mind, to expand and invigorate the faculties, to discipline it to a pertinent, skilful, and efficient use of them, and above all to attach it if possible, inseparably to virtue, the occupations of the young are modelled to the accomplishment of these purposes.... The plan of business, or the whole system of mental culture, and the mode of initiation in literature and the sciences here practised, are determined, it is believed, to be the most eligible that can be framed, by the aid of all the accessible light and experience of past and present times, adapted to the instrumentality and present circumstances of this institution, to the state of our country, and to its other literary institutions. The ancient languages and classics of Greece and Rome, which the world has to the present day, continued to sanction as constituting the best basis of refined taste and correct knowledge in our own language, and in all the modern languages of Europe, are assiduously cultivated by the instructors provided for them.... But in the attainment of these distinguished languages of antiquity, it is the great and eminent object of our instruction, to use them as the key for unlocking and setting in full view before the young the treasures of knowledge, taste and genius, in the enlargement they had attained in these most interesting nations. If the student here acquire not these riches of Greek and Roman literature, it is assuredly not that the lecture of the instructor, must be deemed accountable for a consequence much to be regretted.

By a recent measure of the Board of Trustees, advantages of a character both literary and practical, have been secured to the education of the college. I allude to the provision for a competent attainment of such modern languages as are of the highest interest and value. The French must be important, as furnishing the most diffusive communication with the whole of Christendom. It is the language also of one of the most scientific, polished, and enlightened nations of the world. The Spanish is of peculiar interest to us, on account of the vicinage, and even the intimate relation, in some instances actually subsisting between us and those who speak it; and because with little abatement, the whole of this new continent, now independent of the old, is divided between them and our own people. This acquisition to our literature is further to be prized, as a greater augmentation to the learning of the student than could have been compassed by any other mode of appropriating the time and study necessary to their attainment. A knowledge of the ancient languages once acquired, becomes an instrument for gaining a prompt and easy access to most of the modern languages of Europe. Not to apply it to such a purpose, is to incur a forfeiture of privileges most cheaply secured. It is to disregard the laws of the wisest and most efficient economy in literature.... The basis then of a liberal education is correctly laid in a knowledge of language as the essential instrument of thought and reasoning, without which the researches and communications of science could be prosecuted within but very contracted limits. This is done upon the best models which the world has furnished for such a purpose. To us these models are eminently valuable, and peculiarly fitted, because our own language, not only in its scientific parts, but in all its comprehension, is most largely indebted for its copiousness and transparency, to the same Greek and Roman springs. The completion of an education consists of Mathematics, first pure in their various branches; then mixed, in Natural Philosophy, Chemistry, and Astronomy, succeeded or accompanied by Rhetoric, a rational Logic founded in the true Philosophy of the mind, Political Economy, and Ethics. With these are intermingled, through every part of the course the practice of composition, elocution, and the habit of explanation on every subject in the ordinary recitation to which the student is habitually called.

Meanwhile educational activities were not limited to the classroom. On June 3, 1795, there was organized a "Debating Society" for the "cultivation of lasting friendship and the promotion of useful knowledge." Significantly indeed, the first motion made and passed in this society was for the purchase of books. The first debate was on the question, "Is the study of ancient authors useful?" and the supporters of the classics won the argument. Within a year the society was divided, the new group being called the Concord Society. Classical influence again made itself felt. The names were soon changed from Debating to Dialectic and from Concord to Philanthropic, names which have been continued to the present time, usually abbreviated in common parlance to Di and Phi. From the beginning these groups played a part of great importance in the life of the University. In 1796, inspired apparently by their tutor of French, one William Richards, who had been an actor, the societies put on a dramatic performance. This essay into drama, precursor of the productions of the modern Carolina Playmakers, was not repeated. It did not meet with the approval of the Trustees, particularly of General Davie.

Following their first motion, the societies continued to assemble books until 1895 after which their two collections were merged with the University Library. Debates and declamations on all sorts of subjects, literary and political, occupied the time of their meetings, training the minds and the voices of the participants and preparing them for forensic work in later life. Orations including a salutatory in Latin were a feature of commencement. To the interest of this occasion the societies contributed by inviting distinguished speakers to address them. William Gaston, later Justice of the Supreme Court of North Carolina, directed his address in 1832 to a defense of University education. We quote in part:

> But not unfrequently is the question asked by querulous Students, why all this devoted attention to the dead languages, to mathematical theorems, philosophical experiments, metaphysical disquisitions and critical subtleties? In the world, no one talks Greek or Latin, and at the forum, or in the Legislative hall, we shall not be called upon to demonstrate the propositions of Euclid, or explain the phenomena of hydrostatics and optics. The motives of human action are better learned in that great practical school, the world, than by poring over the theories of metaphysicians; and all the rules of Quinctilian, Rollin or Blair, will never make a powerful reasoner or an eloquent orator. Why, then, shall we consume our nights and days in the acquisition of that which is to be of no practical utility hereafter, and which brings with it no immediate advantage, except the gratification of pride, a short-lived honor, a distinction at Commencement? Beware, my young friends, beware of the tempter. These are the suggestions of Sloth—the most insidious, persuasive and dangerous of deceivers.... Here are inculcated those elementary principles of science and literature, which experience has shewn to be best fitted to form the foundation of the character of the scholar and gentleman—those rudiments of instruction, which, omitted here, are rarely indeed acquired afterwards. Here are to be formed those habits of vigorous and continuous application—here, the capacities for improvement are to be cultivated and strengthened, so that every occasion and every employment without these walls may become subsidiary to further advancement in knowledge, ability, and usefulness.

Another address, that of Henry L. Pinckney of South Carolina, is worthy of a brief quotation, because it illustrates so well the influence of the classics on the oratory of the period and also presents another argument in support of liberal studies.

> Hitherto, you have lived like a band of brothers, now wooing wisdom in the philosophic grove, now roaming on the flowery

heights of Helicon, now mingling in the contests of the Athenian Assembly, or Roman Forum, and feeling the spirit of Liberty burn within your bosoms, as you caught the inspiration from the very altars of Antiquity. Hitherto, you have dwelt together, now sitting at the feet of Plato, as he sublimely unfolded the divinity of virtue, or hanging with rapture on the lyre of Pindar, as it poured forth the tide of Olympic song; and while you thus called up "antiquity from the old Schools of Greece", and communed with the spirits of the mighty dead, similarity of pursuits naturally engendered confraternity of feeling, and your hearts glowed, and still glow, for each other, with all the ingenuous warmth of youthful friendship. ...*You should by no means abandon your devotion to the Classics.* The mind, like the body, not only requires strength for usefulness, but decoration for effect. The massive pillars of a temple, however efficient without adornment, become objects of admiration to the tasteful eye, when they display the richness of Corinthian capitals, or are beautifully fluted with Ionic art. Continue, then, to drink deeper and deeper of the Pierian Spring. The study of the Classics not only disciplines the mind, but it supplies the orator with imagery, and the reasoner with illustration. He may be a good lawyer, who know nothing but law, or a good physician, who know nothing but medicine; but no man can be accomplished, in any liberal profession, who cannot command extensive resources in literature. Repudiate the new-fangled doctrine, that the Ancient Languages are dead, and should therefore be discarded. They are not only not dead, but will live until ancient literature shall be buried in oblivion: and, however conversant a scholar may be with modern literature, yet he, who neglects the ancients, does great injustice to himself, because it is unquestionable that almost all that is sublime in conception, or beautiful in description, or exquisite in pathos, amongst the moderns, may be traced, and not unfrequently, with the most palpable distinctness, to the hallowed fountains of antiquity. But, not to stray further in this seductive field, allow me to recommend *the advantages of History*. Were it only a barren chronicle of the births and deaths of monarchs, who were born, no one knows when, and died, no one cares how; or did it only record the revolting details of all the cruelties, and massacres, and wars, by which humanity has been disgraced and afflicted, in every country, and in every age; no one will dispute that the time would be idly occupied that might be devoted to its study. But it has far higher ends and purposes than these. If it tells of trifles not worth knowing, it also narrates events, and describes characters and actions, which will live forever in the memory of man, and which even now exercise an influence over the destinies of nations.

The administration of President Caldwell ended with his death in January, 1835. In the same year Governor David L. Swain was elected to succeed him. His administration is marked by a gradual extension of the University curriculum. At first this did not mean any relaxation in the basic requirements of Greek, Latin, and the English classics. Indeed one of the first acts of the new administration was to divide the professorship of ancient language into separate chairs of Greek and Latin. The catalogue announcements speak pridefully of the great advantage to the students to be derived from this advance. Modern languages suffered a brief decline. The professorship of modern languages shortly became a professorship of French. From 1843 to 1850 even this chair was lacking as Professor J. DeB. Hooper and his successor F. M. Hubbard were each entitled Professor of Latin Language and Literature and French. During the next decade, however, this modern branch of the humanities recovered its strength and expanded. In 1850 A. M. Shipp became Professor of French and History. In 1856 Hildreth H. Smith, Professor of Modern Languages, offered required courses in French and "volunteer classes" in German, Spanish, or Italian. The following year German was introduced in the Senior year as an optional substitute for Latin and Greek, with Spanish and Italian still on a "volunteer" basis.

President Swain gave a course to the seniors in international and constitutional law. Apart from this course his chief interest was in history. In 1844 he was instrumental in the development of the University of North Carolina Historical Society, whose purpose was to collect source materials and books dealing with the history of North Carolina and occasionally to listen to addresses by distinguished speakers at commencement. The catalogue of 1844-45 lists "Geography and History" as a single course in the second term of the Freshman year. After the appointment of Professor A. M. Shipp in 1849, history began to occupy a more important place. Professor Shipp was first Professor of English Literature and History; later, in 1850, he was entitled Professor of French and History. In 1853 history was listed for the first time as a separate department in the University. And in 1854 Professor Shipp was finally made Professor of History. Courses were given in Greek and Roman antiquities, in ancient, medieval and modern history "with special emphasis on English and American History." After the resignation of Professor Shipp in 1859, ancient history reverted into the hands of the professors of Greek and Latin, and the President, who had already added political economy to the list of his teaching subjects, took on modern history as well for the seniors.

In the meantime the University had broadened its offerings still further. In 1845 a professorship of law was established with William H. Battle as professor. Most of the students under Judge Battle had no formal connection with the University; a few undergraduates were given permission to attend his classes. Again in 1853 a "School for the Application of Science to the Arts" was established giving training in engineering and scientific agriculture. Those who entered this school, after a course of two and one half years, received the degree of Bachelor of Science. Regular students, however, were allowed to substitute the courses of this school for Greek and Latin during the first term and for these studies and international and constitutional law during the second term of the Senior year. The catalogue for 1857-58 offered seniors a choice of Latin and Greek or German or studies in the Scientific School. Such students received the Bachelor of Arts degree in regular course and the degree of Master of Arts at the conclusion of their scientific program.

This expansion of studies was a cause for much concern. A student writing in the *North Carolina University Magazine* in 1852 bewailed the tendency. "Among the many abuses with which our college system is pregnant none is to be more deprecated than the mania which possesses all institutions of this character in America for the multiplication of their studies more in amount than in thoroughness." He went on to point out that the old-fashioned education gave the leaders of the Revolution a maturity and strength of intellect. In 1857 Thomas Ruffin proposed to the Board of Trustees that a committee be appointed to investigate the curriculum with a view to its simplification. The committee was appointed but the minutes record no report.

The programs of President Caldwell's administration seem to the modern student arduous enough. That of 1856 was indeed a test of mental fortitude, as the following programs of study well illustrate.

The catalogue of 1825 reads as follows:

FRESHMAN CLASS

FIRST SESSION, commencing six weeks after the Thursday next succeeding the first Monday in June.
1. Sallust, the whole,
2. Adams' Elements of Ancient Geography, and Mythology,
3. Arithmetic, revised,
4. Graeca Majora. Cyropaedia,
5. Algebra,
6. English Grammar.

SECOND SESSION, commencing four weeks, reckoning from the Thursday next succeeding the first Monday in December.
7. Virgil, Georgics,
8. Cicero's Orations, seven Orations,
9. Graeca Majora, Anabasis, Herodotus, Thucydides, Polyaenus,
10. Algebra completed,
11. Gray's Memoria Technica,
12. English Grammar.

SOPHOMORE CLASS

FIRST SESSION, as before. July.
13. Graeca Majora. 100 pages,
14. Horace. Odes, and one book of Satires,
15. Caldwell's Geometry, four books,
16. Translation from English into Latin,
17. Rhetorick.

SECOND SESSION, as before. January.
18. Horace,
19. Homer's Illiad, four books,
20. Cicero de Officiis, or Tacitus,
21. Rhetorick continued,
22. Geometry completed, seven books,
23. Modern Geography, revised.

JUNIOR SOPHISTERS

First Session, as before. July.
24. Logarithms,
25. Plane Trigometry, in the volume of Geometry,
26. Day's Mensuration, Navigation and Surveying,
27. Simson's Spherical Trigonometry,
28. Vince's Conick Sections,
29. Graeca Majora, second volume,
30. Horace, or Cicero de Officiis,
31. Rhetorick continued.

Second Session, as before. January.
32. Fluxions [Calculus],
33. Mechanical Philosophy,
34. Chronology,
35. Graeca Majora, second volume.

SENIOR SOPHISTERS

First Session, as before. July.
36. Chemistry,
37. Moral Philosophy,
38. Rhetorick, and practical Elocution,
39. Logick,
40. Optics—Wood's,
41. Graeca Majora, second volume,
42. Quinctilian, or Tacitus.

Second Session, as before. January.
43. Chemistry completed,
44. Mineralogy and Geology,
45. Philosophy of Agriculture,
46. Metaphysicks,
47. Political Economy,
48. Astrology,
49. Graeca Majora, second volume,
50. Tacitus.

In the catalogue of 1856 the students' fare was as follows:

FRESHMAN CLASS

First Term.
Xenophon; Virgil; Cicero; Grecian and Roman Antiquities; Algebra; Science of Form.

Second Term.
Herodotus; Livy; Ancient History; Algebra; Geometry.

SOPHOMORE CLASS

FIRST TERM.
Homer; Demosthenes; Horace; French; English Composition; Trigonometry, Surveying, &c. Or Geometry and Conic Sections.

SECOND TERM.
Thucydides; Horace; Cicero; French; English Composition; Anal. Geom. and Diff. Calculus, Or Trigonometry, Navigation, &c.

JUNIOR CLASS

FIRST TERM.
Greek Tragedy; Juvenal; French; English Composition; History, Ancient and of Middle Ages; Chemistry and Mineralogy; Int. Calculus and Anal. Mechanics, Or Natural Philosophy.

SECOND TERM.
Greek Tragedy; Cicero; French; English Composition; Modern History; Chemistry and Mineralogy; Natural Philosophy; Astronomy.

SENIOR CLASS

FIRST TERM.
Mental and Moral Philosophy; Political Economy; Logic; Chemistry and Geology; Plato's Gorgias, and Cicero, Or Studies in the Scientific School.

SECOND TERM.
Logic; Chemistry and Geology; International and Constitutional Law, Plato's Gorgias, and Cicero, Or Studies in the Scientific School.

All the classes are required to attend Divine Worship in the College Chapel on Sunday forenoon, and in the afternoon to recite on the Historical parts of the Old and New Testaments.

In the first of these programs the careful integration of Latin, Greek, mathematics, and philosophy is to be noted. The second, containing still these elements of education, is made more complex by the addition of history, French, and international and constitutional law.

Thanks to the descriptions in President Battle's *History of the University of North Carolina*, some members of the Faculty who taught the courses under President Swain appear more clearly than do those of earlier times. He knew many of them personally as a student in their classes. Elisha Mitchell, eminent scientist, rigorous preacher, and doughty protagonist, seems to have made the greatest impression on him. Manuel Fetter, Professor of Greek, was, according to Battle, beloved of his students even though he insisted more on grammatical forms and rules and "Dictionary meaning" than on "grandeur of thought and beauty of imagery." J. DeB. Hooper, as Professor of Latin and French, though equally exacting, was always ready and able to point out the excellencies of style and thought. President Battle remarks that his pronunciation of French was said to have been formed from the teaching of books. His successor as Professor of Latin, Fordyce M. Hubbard, had an "extensive acquaintance with the Classics and English Literature. He had a keen eye for discerning their force and beauty." William Mercer Green, Professor of Rhetoric and Logic, was "a good teacher, as far as he went, but his heart seemed to be in his clerical duties more than in his department." Even his preaching seemed to lack fire and enthusiasm.

In spite of the heavily loaded curriculum, the students found time for other activities. Throughout the years of the Swain administration the Di and Phi societies continued their activities in debate and declamation. In their two libraries they possessed some six thousand books well distributed over the fields of knowledge. This was fortunate since in spite of gifts and occasional purchases the University Library was pitifully small, was never open to students, and was seldom used even by the Faculty. For a number of years the Trustees made no appropriation at all for the purchase of books. Yet in 1850 a building was erected to house the University Library.

The North Carolina University Magazine was launched in 1844 but died at the end of the academic year for lack of support. Larger numbers of students and greater interest resulted in another attempt which was successful from 1852 till war broke out in 1861. In its issues the students expressed themselves in prose and poetry on subjects grave and gay. One witty youth, delivering a Latin salutatory at Commencement, gave greetings among others to *"matronae virginesque quibus sit decor, quibus absit."* It was fortunate for him that the matrons and maidens who were not decorative could not understand his Latin.

The Civil War bore heavily on the University, as some of the faculty and most of the students left Chapel Hill to battle for the Confederacy. The remaining professors labored at great sacrifice to keep the institution alive through the war years. In 1867 elaborate plans were made for a complete reorganization of the curriculum on an elective basis. They were never carried out. A Board of Trustees appointed by the Reconstruction Government of the state accepted the resignations of President and Faculty and appointed others more acceptable in political affiliation.

The Reconstruction Trustees and Faculty made an attempt to carry on their program, which was in large measure a continuation of the offerings of the Swain regime with a proviso of free choice of studies for all students. Students were few; money was lacking and the legislature refused to support the institution. In 1870 the University closed its doors.

At a meeting of the Board of Trustees on July 23, 1868, Charles Manly, Secretary-Treasurer of the old board, had turned in his records with this fine summary which seems as it were an epitaph to the old University.

You may... trace her gradual but steady growth in reputation and influence, till through the noble and sustained efforts of her first President, Joseph Caldwell, and the still more extended and successful policy of her last President, David L. Swain, and the unremitting labor of her noble band of professors and teachers, she became the just pride of the State, distinguished among the most elevated institutions of the whole country. Here we see the scholastic footsteps of her thousand young men, pursuing the curriculum to the final goal of their Collegiate course. When leaving her academic grove her Alumni have gone forth to fill and adorn the highest places in the Nation. They fill the pulpit and Bar and

Bench and National Councils. You will find them in the highest offices in the gift of the American people, Governors, Senators, Ministers abroad and in the Cabinet at home, and in the Presidential Chair.

On September 15, 1875, the University reopened its doors. The story of the heroic efforts that resulted in this happy event has been told by others. It does not come within the purview of this study. The following year, 1876, Kemp P. Battle was elected president and continued in that office till 1891. Under his guidance the University again assumed a position of leadership in the state and region. At first the new curriculum showed marked similarities to the old. A classical course was established leading to the Bachelor of Arts degree. Greek, Latin, mathematics, rhetoric, and physics were required during the first two years. The third year was occupied with chemistry, French or German, mechanics, astronomy, logic, rhetoric, and modern history; the fourth with political economy, constitutional law, geology, mineralogy, psychology, moral philosophy, and English literature. Charles Phillips was Professor of Mathematics; J. DeB. Hooper returned to become Professor of Greek and French; George T. Winston was Professor of Latin and German; Adolphus W. Mangum, of Moral Philosophy and English Literature; A. F. Redd of Physics and Chemistry. President Battle after his appointment lectured on constitutional and international law and on political economy. Three-year courses were established in science and in agriculture, each leading to the degree of Bachelor of Science.

Whether because of the influence of President Battle, or of the example of recently founded Cornell, which Professor Winston had attended, or of the growing prestige of Charles W. Eliot, President of Harvard and champion of the elective system, or simply of the spirit of the times, whatever the cause and whether it was for better or worse, the University moved toward the elective system.

New influences were certainly at work. The omission of Latin and Greek and the choice of French or German in the upper classes of the new curriculum are noticeable. In 1877 a new step was taken in the establishment of a philosophical course, so called because it led to the degree of Bachelor of Philosophy. This program required Latin or Greek and French or German. The movement away from classical studies was completed by the creation in 1890 of a program prescribing two modern languages for which the degree Bachelor of Literature was awarded. This experiment was short-lived. The announcement of the literary course disappeared from the catalogue in 1894. Thence until 1905 the classical tradition continued, though somewhat weakened.

Meanwhile the catalogues show the gradual encroachment of the elective system. In 1883-84 three hours were elective in the Junior and Senior years; in 1885-86 nine hours in the Junior and six in the Senior year were open but with the limitation that three must be in a language. By 1891-92 these numbers had become eight and nine, with no restrictions. The elective system reached a climax in 1893-94 with seven hours in the Junior year and the entire fifteen in the Senior year elective. The year 1898 saw a reaction in the direction of a group system, for control over the upper-class electives.

Whatever the curriculum, the quality of the faculty during the last quarter of the nineteenth century kept instruction on a high level. In 1885 Walter D. Toy, as Professor of Modern Languages, began a long and distinguished career in Chapel Hill. Quiet, gentle, and scholarly, he was a great teacher of languages, of literatures, and of the thought and experience that lay behind them. In the same year Thomas Hume became Professor of English Language and Literature. One of his students characterized his teaching as difficult for the ordinary student but full of riches for the interested and able. In 1886 Eben Alexander became Professor of Greek. A great scholar, he attained such national recognition that he was sent as Minister to Greece, Rumania, and Serbia during the second administration of Grover Cleveland. Professor George T. Winston taught Latin until he was elevated to the presidency of the University, whereupon he took over courses in political and social science. He was distinguished for the breadth and depth of his knowledge and for the incisiveness of his thinking. His duties as Professor of Latin were assumed by Karl P. Harrington, a Latin scholar and teacher of great reputation. Kemp P. Battle, after his retirement from the presidency, became a much loved Professor of History in which field he introduced the seminar method of instruction. In 1890 Horace Williams as Professor of Mental and Moral Science started his work as an influential teacher of philosophy. During the absence of Professor Alexander the University was so fortunate as to secure the services of the distinguished Sanskrit and Greek scholar, H. C. Tolman. In 1893 E. A. Alderman became Professor of History and Philosophy of Education. He succeeded George T. Winston as President in 1897. His name looms large in the history of public as well as university education in North Carolina.

As in the earlier periods, so in this there were extracurricular activities, cultural in quality. The Dialectic and Philanthropic societies, revived in 1875, continued both their forensic activities and their purchases of books. The Historical Society was revived to stimulate investigation in North Carolina history. A Shakespeare Club founded in 1886 listened to learned papers on the work of the great English dramatist. At the same time a seminary of literature and philology began to hold sessions in which papers were presented on such topics as Lyric Poetry, Epic Poetry, the Alphabet, Sacred Literature, and the Supernatural in Literature. On January 20, 1893, the Philological Club held the first of the long series of meetings which have contributed greatly to the work and influence of the humanities in the University.

The most recent phase of the history of the University began during the administration of Francis P. Venable, who was president from 1900 to 1914. The number of students, already increasing at the beginning of the period, grew still more rapidly. With this growth came an increase in the number of buildings, in the size of the Faculty and therewith in the number, range, and quality of courses offered. One important curricular change must be noted. In 1905, under the pressure of modernity, the classical requirement for the Bachelor of Arts degree was at last abandoned. The catalogue offered three programs, one containing Greek and Latin, the second, two languages and history or three languages, the third, one language with electives. All three programs led to the Bachelor of Arts degree. The Bachelor of Philosophy degree was accordingly abolished. This set of requirements was modified in a conservative direction in 1907 by a provision requiring one year each of two languages. The Bachelor of Science degree was henceforth awarded for a four-year course in the sciences.

President Venable was an eminent chemist and his administration has long been properly celebrated for his work in expanding teaching and research in the natural sciences. Yet a study of the records indicates a concomitant though unnoticed growth in the fields of the humanities. George Howe, fresh from training in the University of Halle, became Professor of Latin in 1903. Charles W. Bain succeeded Professor Alexander in the chair of Greek in 1910. In 1905 a separate department of Romance Languages was established under Professor James D. Bruner. On his resignation in 1909 Professor William M. Dey was appointed professor and head of that department. The German Department, continuing under the guidance of Professor Toy, was enlarged in 1912 by the appointment of Kent Brown. The roll of the English Department for this period contains many distinguished names. Professor Hume served until his retirement in 1907. C. Alphonso Smith, orator, Shakespearian scholar, and man of letters, became Professor of English in 1902 and served as head of the department from 1907 until his resignation in 1909. He was succeeded by Edward Kidder Graham, already in the department and soon to rise to greater fame. In the year 1909 the distinguished name of Edwin Mims appeared in the President's announcement of appointments. The History Department was enlarged by the appointments of J. G. deR. Hamilton in 1906 and H. M. Wagstaff in 1907. When Professor Battle retired in 1907, Dr. Hamilton was made Alumni Professor of History and head of the department. Louis R. Wilson, appointed Librarian in 1901, labored long and successfully to raise the Library to a status befitting the expanding University. In 1907 a new library building was erected with the assistance of Andrew Carnegie. The roster of humanistic teachers of this period is one of which the University is justly proud. The quality of the work done by the University was recognized in 1904 by the establishment of a chapter of Phi Beta Kappa.

The records likewise show a healthy activity of extracurricular humanistic pursuits on the campus. The Shakespeare Club languished with the retirement of Professor Hume. However, a modern literature group and an Odd Number Club, the latter organized in 1905 by E. K. Graham to encourage creative writing, fostered literary interests. The Di and Phi societies continued their activities, but after 1895 their libraries finally were merged with the growing University Library, thus ending one phase of their work. The Historical Society and the Philological Club continued to function. The *Deutscher Verein* and the *Cercle Français* provided for the linguistic interests of the students. The appearance of a musical association in the catalogue announcement of 1907 is another evidence of the widening interests of the campus.

The expansion of the University thus begun in the administration of Dr. Venable, gained impetus from the inspiring but all too brief presidency of Edward Kidder Graham (1914-18) and continued to gain speed and range under the wise leadership of Harry Woodburn Chase (1918-30). Since 1930, in spite of depression and war, the University has maintained a high reputation in the nation for liberalism and scholarship under President Frank Porter Graham.

During this period (1914-45) two curricular changes of importance to the humanities have taken place. In a general reorganization of the University on the quarter system in 1918, the Faculty made important changes in the curriculum. Courses in history, English, mathematics, and science were prescribed for all freshmen and sophomores. In addition to these, underclassmen were required to take three courses in each of two foreign languages, classical or modern, above the entrance requirement of two years of high school study in each language. The earlier free elective system in the upper classes was modified by the setting up of major and minor subjects.

In 1935 after long discussion the curriculum was again revised. The first two years at the University were set up as a "General College," with the language requirement reduced to two years of one language. A choice was allowed in the Freshmen year between mathematics, Greek, and Latin. Two years each of English, social science, and natural science were required with one full year course as a free elective in the Sophomore year. The upper college was divided into the three divisions of the Humanities, Social Sciences, and Natural Sciences. A Division of Teacher Training was added later. The upper-college student selects a major subject in one of the divisions in which he takes from six to eight courses. He must also take from five to seven allied courses within the same division and from five to seven courses in the other divisions.

The Humanities Division contains the departments of the Classics, English, Germanic Languages, Romance Languages, Comparative Linguistics, General and Comparative Literature, History (which is also in the Social Science Division), Education and Philosophy (which have representation in all divisions), Journalism, Art, Dramatic Art, and Music. The activities of the Division are directed by a board consisting of representatives of all the member departments. William M. Dey, Professor of Romance Languages, was the first chairman of the Division and its Advisory Board. The task of organization which thus fell to his lot was brilliantly executed. Under his leadership the Division began to function well in the management of the duties assigned to it and in the promotion of the interests of humanistic studies on the campus. Gustave A. Harrer succeeded him as chairman in 1941 and served with great ability and devotion until his death in 1943. The present chairman is Professor Howard R. Huse, Head of the Department of General and Comparative Literature.

During the thirty-one years from 1914 to 1945, humanistic studies have kept pace with the natural sciences and the expanding social sciences in the University. The departments already existing have been enlarged and have widened their activities in undergraduate and graduate teaching and research. New departments have been added as opportunity, general interest and support, and student demand have warranted. The English Department was enlarged by the appointment of specialists in the varied fields of English language and literature, by the addition of professorships in American Literature, and by the establishment of courses in creative writing. In 1918 Frederick H. Koch became Professor of Dramatic Literature in the English Department. He straightway launched the Carolina Playmakers on a career distinguished for both the composition and the performance of dramatic productions. In 1924 Smith Building, originally constructed in 1850 as a library, later used as a Law School, was remodelled and equipped with funds obtained from a bequest by R. K. Smith and the Carnegie Corporation of New York into a well-equipped theater. In 1937 Dramatic Art became an independent department.

The Classics Department added a professor of Classical Archaeology and began to offer courses in Greek and Latin literature in translation. The German and Romance Language departments grew in size and in range of interests. As a result of the work of Sturgis E. Leavitt, Professor of Spanish, and W. W. Pierson, Dean of the Graduate School and Professor of Latin-American History, in the development of inter-American relations, the University was selected by the Institute of International Education as the site of an experiment. In 1941, Latin-American scholars to the number of 108 came to Chapel Hill to enjoy a "summer school" in our wintertime. Since that time, because of wartime exigencies, there have been smaller groups each year, who have come to the University to study and by their presence have added to the cultural riches of life in Chapel Hill. The creation of a department of general and comparative literature has brought professors and students in the various language departments together. Among the courses offered in this department are several in folklore by Professor Boggs of Romance Languages. To promote research in this important field a Folklore Council was established in 1937. The development of a program of comparative linguistics had the happy result of bringing to the University for two years, 1940 and 1941, the annual summer school of the Linguistic Society of America.

The Department of History has been enlarged by the addition of specialists in the fields of American history and by professors of ancient, medieval, and modern European history. The Southern Historical Collection of the University of North Carolina founded in January, 1930, under the direction of Professor J. G. deR. Hamilton and containing an ever-growing number of letters, diaries, plantation records, and other documents of priceless value, furnishes source material for the cultural as well as the economic and social history of the South.

The Philosophy Department, much enlarged, offered its services to all the divisions with such courses as Philosophy of the State, Foundations of Natural Sciences, Philosophic Ideas in Modern Literature, and Philosophy of Mathematics, in addition to the classic courses in the history, method, and theory of philosophy.

In 1919 a Department of Music was created. Since that year it has grown to occupy an important place in University life. While giving courses in the history and appreciation of music and musicology, and in musical composition, it has also developed and directed an orchestra, a band, glee clubs, and a choral society of students, faculty, and townspeople. In 1930 the Carnegie Library building, no longer used by the University Library, was converted with the generous aid of the family of John Sprunt Hill of Durham into a Music Building equipped with offices, class rooms, practice rooms and an ample auditorium for concerts and recitals. An Institute of Folk Music was created in 1931 to study the folk music of the state, particularly in the mountain areas.

The interest of President Graham and many members of the Faculty and the devoted labors and support of Mrs. Katherine Pendleton Arrington of Warrenton, N. C., resulted in the creation of a Department of Fine Arts in 1935. Person Hall, once the auditorium where degrees were conferred (the old Latin diplomas read *In Aula Personica*) later used by the School of Pharmacy, was rebuilt into a museum for the display and study of art. Provision was made here for the teaching of creative art, along with courses in the history and appreciation of art. Changing exhibits in the Person Hall gallery have brought to Chapel Hill a wide range of the products of artistic schools and periods.

The Library, greatly enlarged, was moved to new quarters in 1929 and a Library School on the graduate level was established in 1931. The Library is equipped with large reading rooms, a study room for "Reserved Books" in use by classes, and rooms for special collections with a catalogue of the author cards issued by the Library of Congress and one of the library of nearby Duke University. Present needs for enlargement in space, books, and staff are pressing. Yet it is a far cry from the little collection of books of the 1850's which "even the Faculty seldom used."

An Extension Division was established by the University in 1912 to provide University instruction to the people of the state. Its services have expanded to include lecture and correspondence courses, public forums, radio programs, community dramatics, art exhibits, photographs, lantern slides, and films, concerts and community musical activities, high school debating and athletic programs and library service. The Extension Library has also provided club or group programs dealing with literature, art, and music which have been of great value in the cultural upbuilding of the state.

To call the roll of the Faculty of the Humanities for this period would be well-nigh impossible. A few have already been mentioned. Among the many men of distinction are such humanistic scholars as Edwin M. Greenlaw, James F. Royster, Addison M. Hibbard, George Howe, Gustave A. Harrer, Norman Foerster, Howard Mumford Jones, Thornton Shirley Graves, and Paul John Weaver. Edwin M. Greenlaw, distinguished Spenser scholar, is worthy of special mention. As head of the English Department from 1918 to 1925, and Dean of the Graduate School, 1920-25, he played an important part in the expansion of his department and in the development of graduate study in the University. Many other humanistic scholars of eminence are at present in the service of the University.

With the expansion of the University, extracurricular activities on the campus have likewise grown along humanistic lines as well as in the scientific, journalistic, social, and athletic spheres. The University community benefits from lectures given by distinguished scholars and public men under the McNair and Weil Foundations. The McNair lectures which began in 1908 are financed by a bequest of the Reverend John Calvin McNair of the class of 1849, "the object of which Lectures shall be to show the mutual bearing of Science and Theology upon each other and to prove the existence and the attributes, as far as may be, of God from Nature." The fund provides for the publishing of the lectures. The families of Mr. Sol Weil and Mr. Henry Weil of Goldsboro, N. C., have established a foundation for the Weil Lectures on American Citizenship. In addition to these the Young Men's Christian Association sponsors an Institute of Human Relations which has held biennial conferences, bringing distinguished speakers to the campus. Visiting scholars give occasional lectures and a movement is under way to secure funds for the provision of regular lectures in the field of the humanities.

Chapel Hill has become also the center of organizations of state-wide importance which have little or no official connection with the University. Among these are the Archaeological Society of North Carolina and the State Symphony Orchestra. The Archaeological Society was organized to do research in the Indian culture of North Carolina. It has carried on explorations and excavations and published many articles in its bulletins. Its museum collection is deposited in the University. The State Symphony Orchestra was organized under the direction of Lamar Stringfield and has been directed in recent years by Benjamin F. Swalin. It is composed of musicians from all parts of the state and gives annual concerts in many centers, including Chapel Hill.

The University Press, established in 1922, has become, under the management first of Louis R. Wilson, then of W. T. Couch, not only an instrument of service to the Faculty in the publication of works of research, but also an institution of national importance.

The Di and Phi societies, somewhat altered in structure, still meet, though with the decline of public interest in debating they are not as prominent nor as powerful as they once were. The *Daily Tar Heel* (published biweekly during the war period) and the *Carolina Magazine* are written and edited by the students.

The Philological Club continues to provide meetings of interest to Faculty and advanced students. Interested undergraduates were members of German, French, and Spanish clubs until the war interrupted their activities. Musical organizations —the symphony orchestra, the band, the glee clubs, the choral club, and a chapter of Sinfonia, the national honorary musical fraternity, have helped to make music a vital force on the campus. A student organization provided also musical entertainment of a lighter variety, its tunes sometimes the product of student composition.

The humanities have had a great past at the University of North Carolina. For over a century they formed an integral part of a "liberal" education, being considered essential along with mathematics, the sciences, and philosophy, "best fitted to form the foundation of the character of the scholar and gentleman," as Judge Gaston phrased it. When they were subjected to the rigorous test of the elective system and to the insistent demands for modernization of the curriculum, though they lost in part their commanding position, yet they maintained their tradition with dignity.

More than this, they enlarged their departments and expanded their offerings. Today while proud of their traditional part in the University, they rely rather upon the consciousness that, as they present man in the varied aspects of his cultural life in the past and as they instruct and encourage youth in the creation of literary or historical prose, poetry, drama, music, and the arts, their offerings do now and will in the future continue to enrich the life of students and through them the life of the state and nation.

Part II

THE HUMANITIES AND THE HUMANISTIC
IDEAL IN THE FIELDS OF
UNIVERSITY EDUCATION

Chapter II

HISTORY

James L. Godfrey

THE RELATIONSHIP OF HISTORY AND THE HUMANITIES is obvious and close, yet any attempt to define and delimit this relationship involves one in the danger of becoming ensnared in the verbal bog that in recent years has characterized so much of our writing on educational topics. Both subjects are heavy with those accretions of age that so frequently cover over essential forms; each suffers distortion from pressure of the revolutionary period in which we live and the tendency of our times to force and fashion all things in its unstable mould. History, in a broad sense, has become all things to all men, while the humanities are torn between definitions in terms of subject and in terms of spirit.

It is not the purpose of this essay to deal with this area of conflict and confusion, but to explore the terrain for landmarks common to history and the humanities and recognizable as such by men who have passed that way before and who may again be searching for the familiar in a land that has grown strange and forbidding. This is not a work of criticism, nor is it written with observance of the *punctilio* that surrounds university publications and productions of scholarship. It is, rather, for thoughtful persons who have become distressed by the growing separateness of fields of knowledge and discouraged by the forces and interests that have dethroned man and exalted things. And, as becomes a historical analysis of the problem, it is a word of hope written in the belief that we are entering upon a generation more improved in human understanding and emotion than any that has gone before it.

For our purposes history may be described as a method, an attitude (both preceding and following the collection of materials), and an extensive and partially organized body of information. To go further and attempt the definition of the quality and degree of these three attributes of history would be to tempt a disagreement that should be avoided. It is believed that no reasonable and informed person would deny that history is at least the three things claimed for it.

It is also contended that, in similar spirit, the humanities may be considered as a series of subjects such as literature, history, philosophy, the classics, languages, and the fine arts. Originally the term referred to the distinction between secular (*humanus*) and religious learning. During the Renaissance classical Latin literature was the chief concern of the humanist; to this was added the Greek language and literature and something of classical mathematics and science. In later times the term humanities came to denote the group of subjects, dominantly classical in spirit, which have been mentioned. In their modern and more significant form, however, the humanities are not only subjects but attitudes, and today more attitudes than subjects. These attitudes are concerned with the quality and peculiar nature of man, and are directed toward an understanding of man in all of the attributes that distinguish him from the other animals. This expansion of definition may be questioned, but the present trend is clearly toward its acceptance. A combination of the old and the new definition would mean that literature, philosophy, and the other humanistic subjects, in certain of their aspects, such as concern for the morphology of language or technique of thought, cease to be humanistic, while the sciences, previously outside the humanities, may now be included insofar as they concern themselves with the increasing importance of the human element in their disciplines. This recent amplification of meaning leaves the humanities still identified with the original subjects but has opened a realm in which all subjects may participate in achieving the goal of the humanities, which must be the understanding of the nature of man.

In terms of these definitions the main problem for this paper is obviously a demonstration of the ways in which the method, attitude, and content of history may enrich the humanities, and conversely some conception of the manner in which history draws from the storehouse of the humanities. It would be impossible to find a subject better suited for this demonstration, since history, a member of the humanities, is also a member of the social science group. It is peculiarly a bridge subject across which ideas conveniently make their way.

The method of history is concerned, in large part, with the "literature of evidence." This literature makes up the bulk of the materials to which the historian may turn in his efforts to recreate and to understand the life of the past, but almost any historical remains may be considered by the historian if in them can be found any aid to depiction or interpretation. The treatment accorded these materials has as its sole purpose the establishment of facts that may answer three questions: What happened? How did it happen? Why did it happen? The testimony once taken is joined with the depositions of other records, and the correlation represents the finished form of history. The quality of history varies with the skill and judgment of the men examining the evidence and drawing up the record. Questions of veracity and meaning, and problems of control and arrangement are vexations. This method and these difficulties are at the center of historical writing, but they are not the exclusive possession of the historian. There is scarcely a field of scholarship that does not from time to time utilize this method. All fields of knowledge must deal with the past, and the method of the historian—the control of records—and the purpose of the historian—the establishment of fact—become a part of every discipline.

Not only is this true in a segment of the work of the original humanities and in those subjects capable of humanistic interpretation, but this segment is at present increasing in scope and importance. If the signs of the time are read aright, almost every discipline, both before and during the present war, is enlarging its concern with the human relationships of the material upon which it works. The pure sciences are increasingly busied with their own histories, which can but mean an accentuation of those elements of human sacrifice, devotion, and genius upon which the sciences have fed and flourished. More and more the scientist is conscious that the ideas and products of his laboratory affect human life and institutions. If this is so in scientific fields, which are humanistic only by attitude, how much more does it characterize those subjects that are humanistic by their very nature.

There is a growing tendency to restore man to a position nearer the center of interest and to enhance his value as the object of all concern. Although this will call upon all existing forms of investigation for some contribution, inevitably the processes associated with the historical method will enjoy a modest primacy. Should man become, as Protagoras would have him, the measure, rather than the measurer of things, then the past becomes the richest source from which the mind, spirit, and nature of man can be illuminated. This does not deny the validity of the present or the importance of the future; rather it guarantees both, by placing them in their proper order and rank in the human adventure. It insures the fruitfulness of both present and future by rooting them in the firm strata of human experience.

This would be much, though not all, that could be expected of history. The growing use of the historical method in other disciplines promises to alleviate the grievous burden of separateness now existing in the intellectual world. The day when a man could hope to participate in the secrets of all branches of knowledge is long since gone, but the development, through the historical method, of a running account of our fields of knowledge, provides a public portion of each field that can be acquired by specialists in other fields. In addition to this valuable service, the increased use of the historical method tends to make for unity in knowledge by introducing in the several disciplines the same method of selecting and treating materials, thus providing a basic weave upon which the individual pattern appears with reduced confusion. All in all, the historical method represents an extensive and invaluable process for the study of man and his problems. This in turn, adds to the humanistic element in all subjects.

While no one would be inclined to deny the existence of a technique of investigation known as the historical method, it is not certain that all would admit the pertinence of that orientation which we refer to as the historical attitude. Some of the objection, however, might be removed by the explanation that the historical attitude is not intended to mean an identity of position on the part of historians as they view the wide ramifications of their subject. All that is implied is that historians in general have the historical attitude in that they are interested in man in his meaningful existence through time. There can, of course, be no history outside the limits of the human boundary or beyond the concept of the time process.

Within these simple, fundamental restrictions the entire range of human experience is open to historical investigation. Historians, as such, have occupied themselves, though unequally, with every phase of human activity concerning which there are records. To this, however, must be added numerous other examples, greater in bulk and not less worthy in quality, that are classified under other disciplines yet are essentially historical in method and attitude. It is unfortunate that the term "history" should be reserved for the works of those professionally called historians who deal usually with political, economic, social, or military records, and too frequently denied the works of others in art, literature, and science, for example, whose writing is of the same essential character.

From this broader consideration of the extent of historical scholarship certain conclusions can be drawn that should clarify, to a degree, the relationship between history and the humanities. The two terms have become so closely associated that a blending is inevitable. History should be thought of as that portion of the humanities dealing with man in those circumstances in which the duration of time becomes an important factor and in which the historical method is the principal technique. History-within-the-humanities and the humanities *per se* are concerned with what may for lack of a better term be called the whole man. If they, advancing along a broad front, could close their ranks and prevent disorder and lagging, the composite effect of combined efforts should result in a reasonably complete portrayal of human society.

Such an even advance has been impossible in the past and may not occur in the future. At present the excessive concern with the economic man and with the materialistic interpretations of human activities have presented us with an imposing array of documents, but one that through its quantity and quality has overemphasized the economic side of life and caused a distortion in our understanding of men and events. In most of the world today decisions are being made in non-economic terms and man is responding out of a range of motives that go horizontally from the most selfless to the most selfish and vertically from refined rationality to the mysteries of the subconscious. The attempt to interpret man solely or principally on the basis of economic determinism has failed, and all similar attempts that concentrate upon such a narrow portion of human nature will fail. The only hope for any large degree of success in achieving this interpretation resides in multiple investigations directed from every point of the human compass. This in turn implies a concerted and orderly effort on the part of all disciplines.

Distortion due to overemphasis is not the only danger. The historical attitude implies the obligation to accept the evidence resulting from the proper practice of the historical method and from that evidence to draw appropriate conclusions. The securing of evidence involves skill and patience, its interpretation demands balance and judgment. There are thousands of chances of error and the margin of accuracy is narrow. He who avoids excessive intellectual commitment to one approach, such as that of economic determinism, must at the same time avoid the danger of exaggerated emotional attachment, such as that involved in sentimental humanitarianism. The position of the humanities and the humanist in modern life has been greatly weakened by the widespread belief that both could be classified with the humanitarians of the moist eye and the swelling heart. The real humanist is, above all, engaged in the task of understanding man, so that through such understanding he may achieve knowledge and wisdom. The true humanist, knowing the compound of good and evil in man, becomes a balanced humanitarian of the mind as well as the heart. He cannot sidestep by any emotional commitment the fundamental obligation of rigid historical method and of common sense.

In pursuing the relationship of history and the humanities, the historian finds that his historical attitudes, involving the experiences of man in time, bring within his scope much of the writing and thinking of the humanities. It denies the validity of the single approach or single interpretation, it forbids a disabling emotional attitude, and it demands intellectual balance.

To the method and attitude of history may be added the content or informational aspect of history, the written and partially organized record of man's past. In this vast literature, drawn from every field of intellectual activity, the complete story of mankind is presented, in so far as it has been possible to overcome the complexities of human experience and explain the deviousness of human motives. This information is essential to understanding, for here, within the all-inclusive record, is embodied the principle of continuity, without which human existence becomes but a jumble of idiotic occurrences. Here, too, one finds that the principle of vitalism, involving as it does the possibility of conscious choice and thus endowing the actions of man with purpose, introduces dignity into, and multiplies the complexities of, human existence. Continuity inclines the course of events toward unity, vitalism leads to diversity. Here is posed the essential paradox—unity within diversity, continuity embraced by vitalism—of history and of the humanities.

It is not to be inferred that the historical portion of humanistic studies can arrive at any definitive solution of the problem of the blending of unity and diversity in human affairs any more than physics can definitively solve the problem of energy, or medicine unravel and abolish the mysteries of death. What is suggested is that it should be possible for all disciplines to continue to move from the periphery of their problems toward the center. Each move is a gain even though none will ever make the final assault into the exact center of knowledge beyond which anything else would be a recession.

In this continuing approximation the concerting of energies and the exchange of information will become increasingly important. It is fortunate that a portion of all the humanities is history and that history as such is interested in and has drawn from its sister subjects. This cross-fertilization enriches all and must become more rather than less prevalent. It is important that the non-humanities be brought more and more into this exchange relationship and it is suggested that history serve as a common medium in much the same way that gold served the international community a generation ago. The professional historian and those using the historical method in the other disciplines would serve as bankers intervening to modify the ravages of inflation and deflation in the several parts of the world of the intellect. There would arise, all the way round, an enlarged responsibility and opportunity for the communication of information and for a more orderly advance upon the central objective. In this merger, leading to an increased understanding of man in all of his complex relationships, the existing content of history would play an important part. Its role would become even more significant as the professional historian, already interested in these cross-currents, gives an increased attention to the varied aspects of civilization. Perhaps we can never again produce universal scholars, but we can and will have scholars of broader interests and greater humanistic fervor who will neither be indifferent to history in its broader aspects nor doubt that the proper study of history is man, and that the proper study of man involves history.

The modern university has reached the point in its educational development where diverging lines give indications of converging, and where diversity may yield for a time to unity. There will be no abandonment of any important outpost of learning in the newer sciences, nor any disruption of the long communication lines of the older disciplines. In the army of the mind the insignia differ but the uniform is the same. What is needed is a re-emphasis of objectives and an improvement in staff work. Each has done his part in the melee; each must continue his part as the battle settles into more clearly defined lines. All will share in the gains that will bring for the humanist renewed confidence, for the historian a brighter page, and for the scientist a richer participation.

Chapter III

LITERATURE*

THE BEAST IN MAN

George C. Taylor

LITERATURE is in part the record of what man has said about man. A realization of the full humanistic value of this record depends upon our acceptance and use of what has been said about the evil as well as the good in man's nature. The good has often been taken as the sole province of humanistic literature, but the idea that man, although the gentlest of animals, is capable of reverting with celerity to the beast, has also been developed by representative literary men during the last two thousand years. In this essay, because of limitations of space, it is possible to consider only the latter idea.

At first sight it might appear that the discussion of this apparently simple idea would result in monotonous repetition of conventional literary commonplaces passing more or less unchanged from age to age, from literary genius to literary genius. The theme, however, abounds in rich variety. In recent years, for instance, few writers handle the theme with the fierce intensity of a Swift or a John Wesley. Few apply the idea to man in general, with which this discussion is concerned. Class, national, and race hatreds result today in much indiscriminate and loose throwing about of accusations in which the other fellow, the other class, the other nation, constitutes the human beast. The conception is employed temperately by a Pascal or a Mumford; fiercely by a Swift. It is used to point up a complete and hopeless pessimism in Schopenhauer or to show how

---

*Acknowledgments of indebtedness will not appear as the writer is conforming to the editorial policy of the volume. It is impossible, however, to avoid mentioning the writer's use of many of the translations to be found in *The Documents of Primitivism* edited by Lovejoy and Crane and the recent translations of Pico della Mirandola by Miss E. L. Forbes and of Pomponazzi by W. H. Hay.

by controlling the beast man is made a god, as in Plato or the Renaissance humanists. No great Renaissance thinker soft-pedals the matter as do our leading thinkers of today. Great scientists (exclusive of the social scientist) are generally realistic as to the beast in man.

It has been said that "politics makes strange bedfellows." Even stranger bedfellows are to be found as one follows our theme. In the works of an obscure New England naturalist of 1825 and in Aldous Huxley's *Ends and Means* (1942), man is said to be the only animal who sinks to a level below the beast in organizing to exterminate his own kind. Other such coincidences will appear as we trace the idea.

It is well to start with Plato, for his development of the conception is influential on later thinkers. In *The Republic* he writes as follows:

> Those then, without experience in sound sense and excellence of character but associating always with feastings and the like, are borne downward and back again up to the middle, and wander in this way throughout their lives. Having taken no thought of the true upper, they never look up towards it, nor are they ever borne upward to it. They are never really filled with true being, nor have they ever tasted of pure and steadfast pleasures; but like cattle, looking always downward, bent to earth and over their (festive) tables, they eat and gorge and reproduce and out of greed for things of this kind they kick and butt and slay each other with iron horns and hooves because of their insatiability since they (can) never satisfy with the unreal the unreal and untrue part of themselves.

Almost as important is the observation in Book IX of *The Republic:*

> In saying this I have been running into a digression, but the point which I desire to make is that in *all of us,* even in good men, there is a lawless wild-beast nature, which peers out in sleep.

It is to be observed that in Plato the beast in man is associated as much with sensuality as with fierceness. So also later with Pico della Mirandola, and Milton in *Comus*. Plato also stresses the killer instinct as an outgrowth of man's overindulgence in beastly desires. The sensual and the cruel go together likewise in many writers after Plato—"Lust hard by hate" is Milton's way of putting it. Plato's third point is that man actually turns into different kinds of beasts through inordinate pleasures, as illustrated by Circe's victims in Milton's *Comus*. Plato also holds that the rational faculties by keeping control over the passions can (as Shakespeare later put it) *"make a man a god."*

Aristotle has two important passages concerning the beast in man. No one emphasizes more strongly than he the fact that, when man turns beast, he is much worse than a beast because he is endowed with discernment. In the *Treatise on Government* Aristotle says:

... in this particular, Man differs from other animals, that he alone has a perception of good and evil, of just and unjust....

... without law and Justice he would be the worst of all, the most cruel, the most lustful, and most gluttonous being imaginable....

In the *Ethics* he writes, "A bad man would produce ten thousand times as much harm as a brute." Greek and Roman writers carry on the theme with slight variations.

Two of them, who greatly affected the most representative thinkers of the Renaissance, will be noticed first—Seneca and Plutarch. Certainly no thinker was ever in a more favorable position to observe at first hand the general beastliness of human beings than the tutor of Nero. The excerpts from Seneca which follow present phases of the idea which continue to the present time. One of the most fundamental is the fact that the pull in human nature is down to the beast, whereas the rise above that level demands effort. Practically all theologians to and including Milton assume this and even Bacon affirms that "Evil to man's nature is a natural motion, good a forced motion." Seneca's opinion is found in his *Letters to Lucilius*.

Men, gentlest of the animal races, aren't ashamed to revel in shedding each other's blood, to wage wars and hand them on to their posterity to wage, though even the dumb wild beasts live at peace among themselves....

We take easily to the baser, because on that road guidance and companionship are unfailing; besides, the process is automatic, needing neither companion nor guide.

Plutarch's contribution to the theme is found in *Gryllus* as follows: "For I do not believe there is such a difference between beast and beast in reason and understanding and memory as between man and man." This expression was changed by Montaigne 1600 years later into the most devastating development of the idea perhaps to be found in literature.

Among the other Roman writers who used the theme, Ovid, in the *Metamorphoses*, presented the idea that the discovery of metals brought about man's deterioration.

After this, a third race, of bronze, succeeded, more savage than its predecessors and prompter to (take up) bristling arms, yet not utterly wicked.

Lucretius, in *De Rerum Natura*, emphasizes gold and its corrupting effect through pleasures. It was the discovery of bronze, however, that led to the beastly tendency of man to kill his own kind.

After this, property was invented and gold was discovered, which easily robbed those who are strong and handsome of their honor.... Thus gloomy discord... added new terrors to warfare day by day. ... But they wished to do these things not so much in the hope to conquer, as with the desire to cause their enemies to mourn.

Horace writes similarly in the *Satires:*

For even before Helen woman had been a shameful cause of war; but those who snatched a fickle love, in the manner of beasts, perished by unknown deaths, slain by a stronger rival, as a bull in a herd.

In the *Natural History*, Pliny emphasizes not so much the killer instinct as the softening sensualities of man's nature:

In the race of man there are sexual perversions among the males ... every kind of crime against nature.... How much more wicked are we in this matter than the wild beasts!... But, by Hercules, most of man's evils come from man.

Polybius, on the contrary, in his *History* sees the beast in man, the killer.

> But the Cynaetheans... engaged instead in warfare... to such a degree that they became so bestial that nowhere in the Greek cities were there impieties worse or more continuous.

The history of theological writing shows an acute awareness of man's natural beastliness, his "forced motion" up to God. From Philo Judaeus, the great Jewish Neo-Platonist, through Origen and Augustine to Du Bartas and Milton, the theory seems to be as follows: Adam and Eve, created relatively perfect, had an unquenchable thirst for knowledge, useless as well as usable. Hence the erroneous exercise of free will and the consequent fall of man. Thereafter, the drag is down; only by a forced motion do we lift ourselves above the level of the brute, with capabilities of becoming gods.

Aside from theologians there are outstanding individuals in the Middle Ages who demand attention. Chaucer's simple analysis of the nature of man is an adaptation of Boethius. In *Boece* he writes:

> And if he be ploungid in fowle and unclene luxurie, he is withholden in the foule delices of the fowle sowe. Than folweth it that he that forleteth bounte and prowesse, he forleteth to ben a man; syn he ne may nat passe in-to the condicion of god, he is torned in-to a beeste. Man is a resonable two-foted beest.

In similar fashion, Pico della Mirandola:

> Whatever seeds each man cultivates, those seeds will grow to maturity and bear in him their own fruit. If they be vegetative, he will be like a plant. If sensual, he will become brutish. If rational, he will issue as a heavenly being....
>
> If you see one blinded by the vain illusions of imagery, as it were of a Calypso, and, worn down by their gnawing allurement, delivered over to his senses, it is a beast and not a man that you see.

Pomponazzi (on the *Immortality of the Soul*) continues the Pico tradition concerning man's sensuality, thrusting him down:

... wherefore men are not called gods, but godlike or divine. But man can not only make himself equal to the beast, nay he may excell the beast: for there exist some men far crueller than any beast as Aristotle says.

Roger Bacon, like Pomponazzi, emphasizes the beastliness of man's sensuality:

We know, therefore, that thru-out the whole universe self-indulgence in men fights against the natural dignity of men. And therefore man becomes a brute animal and more than a brute.

It is during the Renaissance that we find the most remarkable instances of general acceptance of the theme that man throws back to the beast. During this period the idea is expressed with rich variety of literary effects and with emphasis on those seeds referred to by Pico which if cultivated make man a god. The pendulum swings violently back and forth from beast to god, from god to beast. Montaigne, Shakespeare, Bacon, and Spenser never rise to greater literary heights than in the handling of this theme. It is only with Hobbes that we find the sinister emphasis (as with Machiavelli) on the beast rather than the god in man. Milton, though conscious of the beast, continues to emphasize the potential god in man through his exercise of free-will.

Machiavelli is, of all writers examined, most insistent on the beast in man. To such an extent does he push the theory that he fails to recognize the natural good in man. He also stresses (in *The Prince*) the old tradition of man, the natural beastly killer:

It is therefore necessary for a prince to know well how to use the beast and the man. The one without the other is not durable. Whoever desires to found a state and give it laws must start with assuming that all men are bad and ever ready to display their vicious nature.

Montaigne leads all others in his emphasis on the weakness and imperfection of man, as distinguished from his evil tendencies. Unlike many others Montaigne includes himself in the imperfect group. He asserts man's cocksureness, presumption, pride, his assurance as to his own constitutional make-up, the inadequacy of reasoning faculties to lead him to definite conclusions, his low cunning and his natural cruelty. Montaigne has such a high opinion of the intelligence of animals that the beast-in-man in his works differs from that of other Renaissance thinkers. Nor does he emphasize the tradition, running from Plato and Aristotle through Pico and Pomponazzi to Milton, that voluptuousness makes man a beast. Montaigne thanks the gods for every pleasure he has had; hence he has been denounced as a voluptuary even to our own day. What horrifies Montaigne most about man is his inordinate cruelty and his stupidity. But he does admit that man is of a higher order than other animals, in his assertion that "There is a greater difference between many a man and many another man than between many a man and many a beast." Francis Bacon, though he cites Montaigne, does not follow his conception of the imperfection of man. Without stressing man's cruelty as bestial, he refers to the beast-god concept of preceding centuries: "He who delighteth in solitude is either a wild beast or a god." Furthermore, Bacon places himself squarely on record, in his essay on *Human Goodness,* to the effect that "Good to man's nature is a forced motion, evil a natural motion."

The beast in man is mentioned by Donne in his elegy to Herbert, which begins:

"Man is a lump where all beasts kneaded be

. . . . . .

All which was man in him is eate away."

Shakespeare is so rich in examples of the beast-in-man idea that it has been found necessary to prepare a separate article on the subject for the current issue of *Studies in Philology.* We shall cite here only a few outstanding instances. Hamlet, Lear, and Timon, disillusioned beyond all others, analyze man often and in so doing reduce him to the beast and lower:

"A beast would have mourned longer," says Hamlet to his mother; and to himself,

> What is a man
> If his chief good and market of his time
> Be but to sleep and feed? a beast, no more.

The expressions reflect the idea of overindulgence in pleasure which was emphasized two thousand years before. In Lear, the beast is savage and cruel; in Timon it appears in all man's activities.

For purposes of enlightening our own day, Hobbes is the most brilliant and convincing analyst of the idea. Had the modern borne in mind what Hobbes had to say, he would not now have been caught off guard by one of the most beastly throwbacks in the history of man. Hobbes is similar to Machiavelli in his emphasis on the natural selfishness of man. Unlike Machiavelli, however, he recognizes the powerful forces of good in man's nature and suggests a better organization of society. Along with the beast in man, without idealistic rhapsodizing, he sees the moral potentialities of his nature. In the *Leviathan,* and *The Philosophical Elements of a True Citizen,* he writes as follows:

> All men in the state of nature have a desire and will to hurt, but not proceeding from the same cause, neither equally to be condemned. For one man, according to that natural equality which is among us, permits as much to others as he assumes to himself... But the most frequent reason why men desire to hurt each other, ariseth hence, that many men at the same time have an appetite to the same thing.

> ...no arts; no letters; no society; and, which is worst of all, continual fear, and danger of violent death; and the life of man solitary, poor, nasty, brutish, and short.

Milton, although an extreme idealist, was realistic as to natural man. "God of our Fathers, what is man?" he asks. And his reply is that through the Fall of Adam we are naturally beastly. He is first cousin to John Bunyan, who exclaimed as he saw condemned felons passing to be hanged and quartered, "There but for the grace of God, goes John Bunyan." Milton, however, uses the beast in man as a condition from which it is possible either to sink to the sub-brute or to rise to the perfect man capable of becoming a son of the Sons of God. In the literary convention by which Circe's victims actually become beasts through sensuality and inordinate pleasures, Milton's *Comus* preserves the Platonic and Aristotelian tradition.

The year 1623, which saw the appearance of Shakespeare's first folio, saw also the birth of Pascal, who made one of the wisest comments ever contributed to the subject.

It is dangerous to make man see too clearly how nearly equal he is to the brutes, without showing him his greatness. It is also dangerous to make him see too clearly his greatness without his baseness. It is still more dangerous to leave him in ignorance of both. But it is very advantageous to represent to him both.

Pierre Bayle, in his *Dictionnaire historique et critique*, follows Pascal in using this theme. Of "Pope Ottoboni's" death he wrote: "Ce qu'on a dit des bêtes que jamais elles ne font plus dangereuses que quand elles mordent en mourant." More graphic still is his comment on Ovid: "L'homme est fait d'un Dieu et d'une Beste, qui sont attachés ensemble."

Some of the master satirists of the eighteenth century manifest a literary consciousness of the brutal and stupid potentialities of man. One of Fielding's most delightful digressions in *Tom Jones* deals with the

principle which distinguishes men from brutes, a principle however under which men fail to operate and thus failing become beasts.... This active principle may perhaps be said to constitute the most essential barrier between us and our neighbors the brutes; for if there be some in the human shape who are not under any such dominion, I choose rather to consider them as deserters from us to our neighbors.

Pope in his *Essay on Man*, referring to the original age of pastoral perfection from which man degenerated, says:

> Ah! how unlike the man of times to come!
> Of half that live the butcher and the tomb;
> Who, foe to Nature, heard the gen'ral groan,
> Murders their species, and betrays his own.
> But just disease to luxury succeeds,
> And every death its own avenger breeds;

> The Fury-passions from that blood began,
> And turned on Man a fiercer savage, Man.

One of the most effective uses of the beast idea in eighteenth century English satire is found in Robert Gould's *Satire on Man:*

> What beast beside can me so slavish call as man?
>
> .   .   .   .
>
> Whisks him about, as whirlwinds do the dust,
> And dust he is, a senseless clod,
> That swells and yet would be believed a God.

Outstanding among English writers of the period with reference to the idea is John Wesley. Like some moderns he applies the beast concept to historical personages whom he dislikes, to Catholics and Turks, but finally to all of us. He also quotes the melancholy reflections of Cowley: "Man is to man all kinds of beasts.... The civilest methinks of all nations are those whom we account the most barbarous." Among other quotations is the following, evidently from Swift: "If a creature pretending to reason can be guilty of such enormities the corruption of that faculty is far worse than brutality itself"; and a reference to "the absolute want both of common sense and common humanity, which runs through *the whole* race of mankind." [Italics mine.]

Emanuel Kant's reflections on men and beasts introduce an amazing concept. In his *Anthropology* he suggests that "orangoutangs might acquire not only human form but also the organs of speech and the use of intelligence." Elsewhere he writes that he was "thinking many things with the clearest conviction which he would never have the courage to say"; which, according to Fritz Paneth, was that the orangoutang was a throwback from man. If Kant does not think this, Shakespeare's Apemantus does, and without the aid of Darwin: "... the strain of man's bred out into baboon and monkey."

Swift, stigmatizing man's degradation, ends with cruelty and employs the beast figure: "Cruelty is a cur of the same litter."

In the first quarter of the nineteenth century a New England naturalist, Richard Harlan, M.D., of Philadelphia, in a treatise entitled *Fauna Americana*, presented the following description of the species *Man:*

Characteristics of the species are those peculiar to the genus. Inhabits all parts of the earth, disputing for territory: uniting together for the express purpose of destroying their own species.

About twenty-five years later Nathaniel Hawthorne, in *The Scarlet Letter*, describes an old custom-house inspector as a human being with no troublesome sensibilities.

The original and more potent causes, however, lay in the rare perfection of his animal nature, the moderate proportion of intellect and the very *trifling admixture of moral and spiritual ingredients;* these latter qualities indeed being in barely enough measure to keep the old gentleman from walking on all fours.

Hawthorne's *The Marble Faun* is a more explicit portrayal of man as a beast. He suggests, for example, that:

Perhaps it is the very lack of moral severity, of any high and heroic *ingredient* in the character of the Faun, that makes it so delightful an object to the human eye... the coarser animal portion of his nature might eventually be thrown into the background, though never utterly expelled.

My colleague, Professor Engstrom, calls my attention to the fact that, in Europe at this time, Anatole France was exploiting the idea as follows in *The Opinions of Jérome Coignard:*

I have noticed in the varied chances of my life that men are evil beasts; one can only control them by force and cunning. But one must be measured and not offend the small amount of good tendencies which mingles with the evil instincts in their minds.

It is noteworthy that in this passage France, like Pascal, warns against over-emphasizing the beast in man. Professor Engstrom also suggests that Baudelaire in *The Voyage to Maxine du Camp* sings a song of despair equal to that of Bertrand Russell; unlike Russell, however, he places the blame for man's unhappiness not on his environment but on his stupid nature:

Jabbering humanity, drunk with its genius,
As crazy now as it was in the past,

Crying to God in its raging agony:
"O master, fellow creature, I curse thee forever!"
And then the least stupid, brave lovers of Lunacy,
Fleeing the gross herd that Destiny pens in,
Finding release in the vast dreams of opium!
—Such is the story, the whole world over.

Meanwhile Browning, in *Rabbi Ben Ezra*, writes: "I myself might have been a brute." He also creates brutal literary characters of fascinating psychological interest. In *Caliban upon Setebos* he actually pictures the dumb gropings of the half-beast-half-man. At about the same time, Tennyson, invoking the theory of evolution, gives us the best known phrase of the English-speaking world on the subject:

Though Nature, red in tooth and claw
With ravine, shrieked against his [God's] creed—

. . . . . .

No more? A monster then, a dream,
A discord. Dragons of the prime,
That tare each other in their slime,
Were mellow music matched with him [man] (*In Memoriam*).

In *Locksley Hall Sixty Years After* Tennyson records the lowest note of his hopelessness as to a mankind which sixty years before he had dreamed would establish "the Parliament of man, the Federation of the world."

Set the maiden fancies wallowing in the troughs of Zolaism—
Forward, forward, aye, and backward, downward too into the abysm!
Do your best to charm the worst, to lower the rising race of men;
Have we risen from out the beast, then back into the beast again?

Following Tennyson's "red in tooth and claw," Kipling prefaced his *Barrack Room Ballads* with the memorable verses:

We are very slightly changed
From the semi-apes that ranged
India's prehistoric clay.

After 1900 humanists become far more timid in their appraisal of man's nature. The blame for man's miseries is placed not on man, but on a society, or, as in Bertrand Russell's *Free Man's Worship,* on a universe with cards stacked against mankind.

That Man is the product of causes which had no prevision of the end they were achieving... the outcome of accidental collocations of atoms; that no fire, no heroism, no intensity of thought and feeling, can preserve an individual life beyond the grave.

Lewis Mumford's *The Condition of Man* exemplifies the recent moderate approach to the subject.

Every fresh emergent that man has made always runs the risk of being dragged back to the norm of his animal past; that is the "original sin" whose burden he can never escape.... Even man's cunningest efforts to escape nature's dominion may recoil against him: has he not, at this moment of apparent triumph over nature, seen himself slip helplessly back from freedom to automatism, from civilization to barbarism?

James Harvey Robinson, in *The Mind in the Making,* refers to the beast in man as follows:

In all our reveries and speculations, even the most exacting, sophisticated, and disillusioned, we have three unsympathetic companions sticking closer than a brother and looking on with jealous impatience—our wild apish progenitor, a playful or peevish baby, and a savage.

Ernest Albert Hooten in *The Twilight of Man* plays dangerously though at times humorously with the idea.

Racialism as a political doctrine is today the most potent catalyst wherewith evil and misguided men actuate the baser elements of the human animal to predatory and bestial behavior.

Humanitarianism... these sentiments, divorced from reason and applied without judgment to those who lack the intelligence to comprehend them and to reciprocate them, nourish vipers.

Aldous Huxley, in *Ends and Means,* clearly conscious of the brutal side of man's nature, repeats the idea of man's peculiar impulse to organize for the slaughter of his own species.

Technological progress has merely provided us with more efficient means for going backwards....

War is a purely human phenomenon. The lower animals fight duels in the heat of sexual excitement and kill for food and occasionally for sport.... Similarly, fights between hungry dogs or rutting stags are like pot-house quarrels and have nothing in common with war, which is mass murder organized in cold blood. ... Man is unique in organizing the mass murder of his own species.

Additional examples of the extraordinary survival of the idea are to be found in Nordau's *Degeneration,* Schwarzschild's *World in Trance,* Wylie's *Generation of Vipers,* and Richet's *Idiot Man.* Nordau, quoting from Nietzsche's *Zur Genealogie der Moral,* sees at the beginnings of civilization "a beast of prey, a magnificent blond brute, ranging about and lusting for booty and victory." His conclusion is that "progress is the effect of *an ever more rigorous subjugation of the beast in man.*"

Schwarzschild writes similarly:

The core of the tragedy [of the peace of Versailles] was that this whole sect of idealists, including Wilson, had no idea of the nature of man and of peoples; no understanding of the real forces moving the machine of history....

He quotes Clemenceau as follows:

There is no parallelism between the development of science and the development of mind. Human beings are like apes who have stolen Jupiter's thunder. It's easy to foresee what will happen one of these days: they will kill one another to the last man.

Richet, Nobel Prize winner and benefactor of mankind, attacks the nature of man savagely:

Humanity is like a sultan who has two wives. One is young, beautiful and healthy, radiantly graceful and sweet.... To her husband she gives pleasure, mirth and serenity. She is Science. The other wife is a dirty old hag, abject, blear-eyed, a walking skeleton. She has only a few scanty tufts of grey hair thick with vermin, toothless jaws and fetid breath.... Even from afar she stinks. She is War.

And yet, nevertheless, she is the favourite wife of this egregious fool.... Oh, men of taste! how will you judge this sultan? Intelligence yoking itself with stupidity—so might we sum up human evolution.

The very title of Wylie's *Generation of Vipers* indicates the intensity of his attack:

I have said that the scientific method and the Christian church have failed to lift man out of savagery....

I mean that man, except for his possible fatal accretion of machinery, has really advanced almost not at all in the last one thousand years.

The blame for Armageddon lies on man.

Hitler's use of the idea has affected millions, and still affects them. He once said:

I will free the German nation from a thousand years of domestic action. I want to see in the eyes of our youth the gleam of the beasts of prey. A youth will grow up before which the world will shrink back.

In conclusion we may turn with comfort from these recent unhappy estimates of man to repeat the reflection of Pascal which not only comprises some of the wisest words ever uttered on the subject but also represents the balanced humanistic viewpoint at its best:

It is dangerous to make a man see too clearly how nearly he is akin to the brutes, without showing him his greatness. It is also dangerous to make him see too clearly his greatness without his baseness. It is still more dangerous to leave him in ignorance of both. But it is very advantageous to represent to him both.

Chapter IV

LITERATURE
THE CREATIVE IN MAN

Paul Green

I

I BELIEVE THAT life is like a tree forever growing, and man is part of that life. And though he must continue to be a man as long as he exists, still he has the power to become unlike himself and ruined and beastly if he will. Nothing is protected in its *status quo ante* against the possibilities of its own future and flux and undoing, neither God nor fate, nor man. Change is forever taking place, and there is no abiding of things as they are. In any particular thing or conglomerate of things every tomorrow brings its process of differentiation and further varying. *Panta rei*, says the weeping philosopher.

Panta rei, everything flows. And if the particulars, the conglomerates which make up the sum of the whole, are eternally changing, so is the whole which they constitute. Then where is permanence to be found beyond change? Where is truth with her verities to be sought for?

Permanence might be expected in a realm where impermanence does not appear. Naturally. We might find it in the opposite of these particulars, the whole of things perhaps. Now the opposite of things is no-things, or nothingness. But this is a state identical with the state of death—this opposite. Then it seems death is the permanence, the nothingness we seek. But does not death, this nothingness, also suffer change even as the particulars and conglomerates in life? It does.

Then there is no permanence in death. For life will not let it be. It seizes upon the inert body-of-death, takes it apart piecemeal and speckmeal, plunders it, absorbs it, informs its own self with new vitality from it, uses it as the flame uses the wood, as the body uses the blood, as the rain the cloud, and as the sap uses the flower or the tree. But is not the wood the source of flame, the body the source of the blood, the cloud of the rain, and the flower and the tree the source of the sap? That too.

Each owes its being to the other. And insofar as one is a separate being it is so through the vitalizing process of causation flowing in and between them. Thus in this rich and mutual altruism life goes on. The inorganic feeds the organic, and the organic is everlastingly busy growing itself into full form, reproducing its kind, either better or worse and never the same, and giving its body into death in turn for the feeding and making of its kind that comes after it. The existence of one is the perpetuity of the other.

What humility! What sacrifice! And where is the law and the secular loose talk about the red dripping tooth and claw and the survival of the fittest, meaning the most cruel! Well, it depends upon who is seeking for what, and why, and how, as to the findings that result. For there is in nature a basic co-operativeness and beneficence which heals and helps even as a cool spring does a panting thirst. That too. And children know it. And all childlike people who have not been contaminated by the fad of analysis and dead learning and the tools and methods of pragmatic insolence and pride—they know it well and joy in it. And this co-operativeness, this beneficence, this changing activity of life into death and death into life is a process—the process of creation.

A wise man said, "Except a corn of wheat fall into the ground and die, it abideth alone." And he also said, "Greater love hath no man than this that a man lay down his life for his friend." And another said, "How are the dead raised up? And with what body do they come? Thou foolish one, that which thou soweth is not quickened except it die." And still another said—a voice of antiquity, ever-vital and ever-creative and spilling out its enrichment for man—he said, "And now abideth faith, hope, charity, these three; but the greatest of these is charity."

The world process is creative, both as to particulars and as to the whole! That is the truth, that is the permanence we require.

II

But this is an old and obvious truth to us—or it should be. We have heard it from Samson and his riddle of the bees and honey, from the weary wanderer and the riddle of the Sphinx. We heard it from Plato in his metaphysic of mortality and immortality and darkness and light. Plotinus and Origen told us the same. And so did the great and learned doctor of the thirteenth century, persuading us afresh to the freedom of the will, moral responsibility, intellectual love, and the salvation of souls. And before him his own master Aristotle spoke out his intuition and seeing of the nature of virtue and the good life in a world of practical affairs.

And the same refrain was told to his love in later centuries by Petrarch, him whom many a scholar holds as "the first modern man" and who no doubt would have felt surprised and lonely in his century if he had known he was to be that. And before him was Dante with his epic of endurance and attainment, and before him Boethius. And later Erasmus, and the great Jew of Amsterdam, and the sickly Bacon, and much later the heavy plodding-footed Hegel and the healthful aristocratic Goethe—all said the same.

These and a thousand others like them have risen up along the path of literature and life and affirmed this truth. They have stood as witnesses for the great process of creativeness, of life like a tree forever growing, of a mighty river forever flowing. But their words and their works have too often been in vain, most often have been in vain. We have not heard them.

III

For we teachers and scholars, caught in a scientific dispensation, find it impossible to accept life as a miracle of creativeness and growth. We are conditioned to believe that anything smacking of a miracle is perforce somehow mystic, medieval, sentimental, vaguely subjective and therefore unsound. It is the old scholasticism back again. And we fetch out our common-sense curricula and scientific methodologies and put them to bear upon the matter as if it were an object to be measured and described under a microscope. And that's what we do—measure and describe, and set down findings. We categorize, catechize, cut up, analyze and compare and put appraisals upon the process of life and not only upon life but upon art and literature—which is worse. In place of life and art and literature, we thus substitute a method of derivation, matters of influence and style and types—whether of classic, romantic, realistic, naturalistic, expressionistic, or what not and on down to as many adjectival examples of labeling as we can dig out of our inkwells or typewriters, being therefore the more solid and scientific in our results, we say. So we believe, and so we teach others to believe.

IV

And these labels we schoolmasters make and try to paste on the creative process of life are forever peeling off in the turn and twist and scouring of time. They will not stick. How could a label stick on a flowing river, or a stamp on shaking gay green leaves? But our activity continues. As soon as one label wears out or peels off or is blown away in contrary winds of doctrine or passes out of fashion we have another and more scientific one ready for the pasting. And much of the frustration in purposes and hindrances to man's development and joy occurs because of this confusion of labels and names which we are responsible for. They are seals stuck not so much perhaps on the body of the process of life and art itself as over the eyes of both the seeker and the seer.

Consider a term universally honored and respected by the schoolmen—to wit, nature's law. What confounding of wisdom and experience occurs in its name! A law of nature! The law! How it closes up the eyes of those who would look directly at the wonder and glory of the moon or the stars themselves but cannot see the object for the law which has it in thrall and makes it behave according to its will, the poor thing itself having no will. But there is in actual fact no law in nature, neither in the world of trees and men and growing things nor in the wheeling cindered stars. What we call the law is the way things act.

(But this sort of learning and this mathematical formulaizing are understandable and necessary in the world of things—science. Through them we are "able to do business" with our environment. But literature, art, are not sciences, not scientific. They are spiritual. Still we keep on trying to deal with them as sciences, as "things" even.)

Natural law then is but a label or word-concept which we apply to change. It is a product of man's mind, an attribute he has given, a reading he has taken and made fast in the books. Things change. Since they change the way they do change, we say they change according to the law of change, a causal sequence in time and space, and these last are two more labels or word-concepts. The truth is they simply change. It is their nature to change, their creative nature. And rather than being beholden to any law, the law as we describe it is beholden to them. They *create* the law. And potentially at any instant of "time" and any point in "space" an object may behave in a new way, a way it has never behaved before. It may turn into its opposite nothing, or a nothing may suddenly become a thing—as is happening all the time. The process then varies in itself but it cannot cease nor can it behave "unlawfully," that is, contrary to itself.

This is the essential mystery of the universe which consciousness perceives and can worship at but cannot penetrate and should not. For to do so it would have to become other than itself, other than the process, which it can never do. For consciousness, awareness—which is identical with the process—cannot be conscious of its own cessation. And if the cessation of consciousness has ever been witnessed it has never known it, and the witness himself became the embodiment of that which was witnessed.

And between this awareness, this conscious mind and the creative vital world, we educators place these misleading signs and tokens and distortions of meaning. And in doing so we are betraying our trust both as persons and as teachers. We betray our experience.

We are back at the old business of practicing the heresies of abstract medieval authority, except in this case the evil of abstraction is intensified. For we have made it of a lower scientific down-gazing earthly order, whereas in the old days of the wandering friar and hungry monk the gaze however blinded was upward and into a beneficent heaven.

V

But we scholars are tough-hided sinners and good party members. We will do anything in the name of our creed or cause. We are propagandists of the veriest sort, and the hapless quivering body of truth is inquisitioned, quartered and drawn on any class or feast day. We deny this, but still it is true. Look at the books we put out, the articles we print, our swarming midges of marginal footnotes, our journals, catalogues, compendia, our editions of volumes of art and volumes of literature, our flood of anthologies.

Everywhere we cut up life and the green creations of life into just such categories, movements, influences, currents, schools and the like, as mentioned above. And at any time we wish we will reach and take a living artist, or a dead one, lift him from the fireside of his creative activity, place him on the shelf and catalogue him. And any student or seeker for wisdom and joy from this artist may come as if to an idol in a temple, but shining big for him to see first of all is a huge label or card or notice which proclaims this artist as of such and such a type —not just an artist, but a certain kind of artist. And the emphasis is always on the kind and not the art itself. And the pity is that nearly every time the label or card or notice gives life the lie. As time well proves. But the confused young neophyte does not find that out for many years after, maybe never. And he stays away from the temple.

In a large and popular anthology of world literature now lying before me I notice Zola and de Maupassant have been labeled in heavy letters as being in the category of the Naturalistic School—whatever that means. The editor is following along in dog-leash obedience with hundreds of other editors who have preceded him, and uses several pages of *ad hoc* writing showing what is meant by naturalism and proving beyond a doubt and without rebuttal that these two authors, along with such others as Gorki and Dreiser, are condemned to this classification till hell freezes over and there's nothing to be done about it. Only as exponents and representatives, propagandists and exemplifiers of naturalism shall we know them.

I turn a wad of pages back in the same anthology and find that Aeschylus and Sophocles are representative of the classical period or school or age and nothing else. And from the editor's long and thorough essay on classicism, I am persuaded what vastly different creatures these four men were. In fact they were not four men. They were four propagandists—two for naturalism, two for classicism.

Again what a confusion of tongues we editors and scholars indulge in! Are there not blood and thunder and guts and organs of fecundity, liver and lights, tumors, thighs, stallions, procreation and abundant animal life in the stately "classical" drama and in Homer's epics even as in the "naturalistic" Zola and de Maupassant! Yes, plenty of them, plenty of "naturalism." In fact Aeschylus out-Zolas Zola. Open up the *Agamemnon* and read the scene where the wild and turbulent Cassandra sees the children of Thyestes sitting as gory phantoms above the doomed king's house. "See ye these infants sitting here on the palace like to phantoms of dreams?—Children just as if they had perished by the hands of their friend—their hands crammed with the meat of their own entrails, a piteous mess, of which their father tasted."

Or take another of his plays, *The Eumenides,* and read the scene, for instance, in the interior of the temple of Apollo where we can see and hear the shuddering and grotesque and wild snaky-headed women, hear their whimpering moanings, their scaly raspy movements and see rising from the ground the ghost of murderous and murdered Clytemnestra smoking with blood. Or turn to the golden and restrained, classic Sophocles and read how Oedipus tears out his own eyes, after having killed his own father and married his own mother and begot four children, half-brothers and sisters to himself. And think of the tragic queen Jocasta hanging from a rafter by the neck, dead of shame and grief. And consider sad and mellow Euripides with all his murders and betrayals and gods in the machine, and the story of his hysterical bloody Medea, mother and killer of children, her own. And pick up Homer and read of his devastations and lust and blood, the spearing and letting out of brains, the defilement of Hector's body, the eating of the dead by dogs, the hate and treachery and cunning, the quarrels among the gods, the bickering of Aphrodite and Athena, and the god of war himself running with cowardly howls over the plain, and then the crafty double-dealing of Odysseus. And so on, and so on. Only the label "time" has made them classical.

When we forget our tokens and labels and signs and hierarchy of pigeon-holing and think of the works, the stories and plays and poems, themselves, we find that they are part of that great creative process of life and men in life, and as such we can enjoy them, draw from them, be enriched and refreshed through them. Our learned findings of influences and kinds and types only get in the way and are a hindrance. They get between the appreciator and the object of his appreciation— that is, a really *felt* appreciation. And they are deadly for the creative artist. In fact a creative artist can only learn from a preceding work of art or master if he thinks of the painting as painting and the painter as a creative spirit, a technician working at a job, never giving a hang as to what school or movement he might belong to. And what is true of the creative apprentice is just as true if not truer of the student and critic. And if it is true of these why is it not also true for us teachers and schoolmen?

For do we not all live by the same bread of life?

Even as I type out these words my daughter is downstairs writing a paper for her scholarly professor on "Coleridge as Romanticist." What of Coleridge as just—poet? Or what of Coleridge's poetry—just that—with all its magic and music and exquisite imagination and delicacy of tone and touch and thought? Why not have her write about them? And why ever any such label as "Romanticist" to bring her nearer to him when it puts him farther off? Why not just let him be, and let all the others be and so let her receive them and their fire and glory and delight into her young soul? These should be the matter of interest, of concern and inspiration. But instead she has to be at the hard and blind and bull-headed behest of her professor searching her young noggin for secondhand words that will show she has surprised the secret out of the sage of Hampstead and henceforth will know the old loquacious, metaphysical boy for what he is—not a spirit and a miraculous soul but a type, an example of a movement writ down by us schoolmen as romanticism. It may take her years to recover from this damage and wrong filling of her mind, this wrong teaching which dries up her emotions and sterilizes her dreams. She may get contaminated by this jargon of analyzing and "sciencizing" and go out as a teacher of literature herself and help contaminate others. She may never be able to approach Coleridge again fresh and unprejudiced and pure as she should—approach him with an open heart in which the seeds and images of his beauty may thrillingly fall and as thrillingly grow. And so she will pass on to the next poet who stands in line as a representative of the movement, Wordsworth, and make the same tragic failure of missing the fragrance and breath of his glorious work, fail completely to feel the creative wonder of what he wrote.

VI

I remember one lonely Sunday on the farm when I was a boy. The day before in town I had met up with a bookpeddler and bought a copy of Shakespeare's *Hamlet*. And with the family gone off to church and the house silent and empty, I read the play. And as I read, I grew more interested and filled with suspense as to the people and their fate in the drama. And emotion became more and more packed up in me. And finally I came to the scene where poor piteous Ophelia enters with brains broken and mind deranged, speaking her little mad and anguished sayings—"There's rue for you, and here's some for me. We may call it herb of grace o' Sundays. O, you must wear your rue with a difference. There's a daisy. I would give you some violets, but they withered all when my father died. They say he made a good end." (Singing.) "For bonny sweet Robin is all my joy." And the tears gushed from my eyes, my heart opened with a yearning deep and wide, and I took her in to shelter her and wrapped my love around her. That day was a mark in my life. And because of that fresh wild appreciation, untrammeled and unprepared for by any professorial coaching as to influences and types and methods by which the play might have been derived to represent the Elizabethan age or something other than itself—because of that, *Hamlet* has stood solidly by me, a rich storehouse through the years, and has meant more to me than it otherwise could possibly have meant.

Another lonely hot Sunday on the farm I was lying in my sweaty little shed room reading the Bible, when I came upon the twelfth chapter of *Ecclesiastes*. I suddenly sat up in delight at what I read—the beauty of it thrilled me and put a stuffiness in my throat. I hurried out of the room and down the side porch into the kitchen where my sister was busy getting lunch. "Listen, Mary," I said, "listen." And I read, "Or ever the silver cord be loosed, or the golden bowl be broken, or the pitcher be broken at the fountain or the wheel broken at the cistern."

"That's wonderful," she said. And she stood by the stove, holding a little piece of firewood balanced in her hand, her eyes wide and thoughtful as she went on hearing the words over a second time in her mind. "Read it again," she said. And I did and for a while we shared the beauty and wonder of those lines and others in the chapter. And because of that experience, *Ecclesiastes* has always remained one of my favorite books. I thank my stars that I was not "prepared" for it by the usual teacher, say, of comparative literature, who talked of a preceding stoic philosophy and currents of Hebraic pessimism which brought the book to being. For it would have been marred before I got to it—as so many of the great works of literature were marred for me in precisely that way.

VII

Then what is the answer? What should we teach? How should we approach the subject? The answer is simple. Teach the subject itself, approach the subject itself, approach the subject directly and not put up labels and curtains that stand opaque and dividing between the seer and the seen. Get the student close to the object of his interest. Let him work at it too. Let him try his hand in practice. Let him experience the poem, or whatever it is, in the raw. Goethe says wisely enough, I think, in reference to literature, "He who does not take an active part in certain subjects knows them but half and superficially." And again in his *Conversations*, "A thing requires not only to be read and studied but to be done"—that is, done wherever one can. And there should be as little separation between creation and appreciation, between theory and practice as possible.

Some time ago a young actor was at my house trying out for a part in a play. The part he was interested in was that of a young pioneer woodsman. This actor was from the heart of New York and knew practically nothing of what a pioneer's life might consist of. The character in the play was supposed to be a hefty worker with an axe, and the soft-handed Brooklynite in reading the part showed that for all his two hundred pounds of hulk he didn't know what the feel of an axe was nor what the young pioneer really meant when the dialog spoke of "cutting trees and clearing land and sweating with the joy of it." So I took him out into my woods for a while to cut trees, talking the play the while. We cut and chopped and cut some more. Soon our coats were off, then our shirts, then our undershirts. And the sweat poured. The actor puffed and blew. In an hour or two his hands were blistered. But he liked it. And through these blisters something of the character's character entered into his body and spirit. And when we returned to the living-room after supper to go on with the reading, he read with a real and glowing difference.

And so it goes.

VIII

And here is this planet we call the earth. Its soil has been tilled for untold millenniums and yet its strength is not exhausted, nor will it be exhausted. Its generative and procreative powers remain undiminished. Treat it creatively, give it a little rain, a little sun, and spring and summer and teeming autumn with all their fruits and beauties pour themselves into the air again. So it is with man as with the earth.

For he is a quickened spirit, a self. He is neither scientist, pharisee, homo sapiens, classicist, romanticist, animal, nor humanist. He is a self, a living being, a personality, a soul. And he has his visions, his freedom of will and his ideals accordingly, and his essential nature is creativeness. There is in him a primal impulse and impetus towards the making of a truly beautiful and vital world. And however obscured, hindered, detoured by false doctrines and prophets, he will continue to strive towards that goal. But he needs help and that is the purpose of all teaching—to help him and help him creatively.... And through the blue depths of the sky the bird flies, but the tips of its wings are never stained in it! Moreover it is written that with faith a man thinks. Faithless, he cannot think. And he who worships the great King milks heaven and drinks it day by day, his food is never exhausted.

Peace to our souls!

Chapter V

PHILOSOPHY AND RELIGION
THE HUMANITY OF MAN

Helmut Kuhn

1. "The Proper Study of Mankind"

ONCE, IN BROAD DAYLIGHT, Diogenes of Sinope lit a lantern. "*Ἀνθρωπον ζητῶ,*" he said. The quest of Man, of all objects of inquiry the one most intimately known to man, has been one of the great preoccupations of philosophers throughout the ages.

Man as an object of human study belongs in various fields of investigation. The philosopher shares the theoretical interest in human nature with the biologist, the psychologist, the historian, and with many others. The humanities in their entirety help to throw light on its multiple manifestations. But all these lines of research converge towards philosophy. A comprehensive theory of man can be furnished only by a philosophical anthropology. Philosophy alone asks the radical question: "What is man?" And its answers alone, inadequate though they be, touch upon the root of what we are.

Literally translated, Diogenes' words read: "I seek *a* man." Many look like human beings but few are human, he suggests. In the philosophical inquiry, the theoretical interest in human nature springs from the practical concern over human destiny. To the original problem of the nature of man a fresh meaning accrues, taking research into a dimension beyond all merely factual investigations. The query is now: "What can man become?" or "What should he be?"

"The proper study of Mankind is *Man.*" This injunction, in Pope, is ushered in by a warning: "Presume not God to scan." But the Delphic "Know thyself," on which the poet comments, was originally not so understood. It meant: remember that you are not a god but only a man. And to be only a man meant to be mortal. Perhaps the ancient understanding of human self-knowledge is closer to the truth than Pope's couplet with its little fling at theology. Man calls himself "a mortal." In so doing he thinks he makes a more significant statement about himself than by applying to himself such terms as biped, carnivore, earth-dweller, or bread-eater. We must ask whether man in his mortality can understand himself except against the foil of immortality. The two questions, "What is man?" and "What ought he to be?" are capped by a third question with which philosophy as a science points beyond itself to faith: "Whose is he?"

In developing these three questions, philosophy defines its relations to other studies. Giving and taking, it maintains its character as *animi adversio humanissima ac liberalissima* (Cicero, *Pro Archia,* 7). For it is, we hold, the most human thing in man to be intelligently concerned about himself—his nature, his duty, and his ineluctable allegiance.

2. What is Man?

Man, for one thing, is a lump of matter in a material world. It is the business of the physicist to study the material world, and in discharging his duty, he incidentally enlightens us on ourselves to the extent that we are body. This solid flesh of ours, modern physics informs us, actually is a field of electric charges. We are, as Sir Arthur Eddington in his picturesquely paradoxical manner puts it, mostly empty space. Take this empty space away, and every one of us will be reduced to a tiny speck of matter. Observe this porous stuff of which we are made, and you will find it conforming to the universal pattern of behavior exhibited by material objects everywhere, on our planet or on some remote star. Formerly, physicists described this pattern in terms of causal determination. Today, they prefer to speak of statistically determined uniformities. But whether our vote go to rigorous determination or to its mitigated version, we as existent, as part and parcel of the material universe, must submit to what is good for our fellow-objects, the stone and the star. At the bar of the laws of nature, no human prerogative is acknowledged.

The realization of this fact, it is sometimes believed, must fill us with a sense of futility and abjectness. Popular writers on physics not seldom capitalize on the shock which it administers to a defenseless mind. I suggest (as others have pointed out before me, with particular force and clarity the late L. S. Stebbing) that this sentimental revulsion from certain findings of science is actually prompted by a confusion. Not the facts, but our fanciful ideas about them, frighten us. To say that, as a physical object, I am but a flimsy dynamic structure, with the ether-wind blowing through me, seems, at a first glance, a vivid dramatization of scientific data. In reality, it is a falsification. On the plane of physical abstraction, the ego is non-existent. In ascribing to a person the qualities of a microphysical object, we confuse the world of concrete experience with the context of physical abstractions. Looking at our reflected image in a mirror we recognize it as truthful. But we do not conclude from its flatness that we are planar beings rather than spatial ones. By the same token, we should not allow physics any competence in denying or attesting that central feature of the human personality which we call "freedom of will." The laboratory can neither obliterate nor restore personality. The frame of reference underlying mathematical physics simply excludes the concept of person just as it excludes such concepts as table or cowslip or alligator. The free-will debate stirred up by Heisenberg's indeterminacy factor was much ado about nothing. A nothing was made to seem something by victims of the "naturalistic fallacy." Mistakenly, the authority of physics was claimed for physicalism—a type of metaphysics no less perverted for lately professing libertarianism in the place of an outmoded causal determinism.

As material, man has his habitat on the solid parts of the surface of the globe, and the globe forms a part of the stellar universe. Modern astronomy has radically changed our conception of this universe. When the disciple of Hellenic-Medieval cosmology raised his eyes to the star-spangled sky, a spectacle both instructive and edifying disclosed itself to him. He discerned, so he thought, bodies composed of the finest of all material substances, called ether. These luminous bodies he regarded either as indestructible or as to be dissolved only by a divine decree. To him, they described perfect and harmoniously ordered circles in a dance that was to last eternally, as Aristotle believed, or from the beginning of things to the end of things according to the Christian view. In this sublime astral family, the earth was the humblest partner, compounded of the coarsest stuff. Yet it was placed in the center and honored above all stars by the presence on it of Man.

The modern observer puts upon the selfsame show a very different interpretation. He sees an immense host of incandescent bodies racing through space at a definable speed, their courses forming a highly intricate mathematical pattern. The sun, he holds, is one among a multitude of kindred stars, and the earth one of the sun's satellites. It would be otiose for him to regret the grand architecture of the geocentric heaven. With all its beauty it was, after all, not God's creation but man's fiction. In fact, it should not be too hard for us to reconcile ourselves to the facts as we now know them. Medieval cosmology expected the heavens to declare the glory of God in a language to be deciphered by astronomy. It is doubtful on philosophical grounds whether this was a reasonable expectation.

Let us imagine first a predominantly chaotic world, then a world unmistakably ordered towards a moral purpose. In neither of the two could human life be what it actually is. A disorderly world would prevent us from exercising reason, an unequivocally purposive world would rob us of our freedom. Were the decalogue written in the stars, clearly legible there for everyone, only consummate fools would break God's law. Modern astronomy reveals to us the same type of reality which we know from evidence gleaned in other fields. Ours is an ordered universe, a fruitful field for intelligent inquiry. But the factual order does not yield unambiguous information on the meaning of man's life. It continues a challenge to his reason. Even in his closest approach to metaphysical truth he cannot dispense with faith. In a universe so arranged, human life is the hazardous enterprise which we know. Its glory and its misery spring from the metaphysical twilight in which it is wrapped. Philosophy, almost from its inception, has been aware of this truth. Plato, the real inventor of the too-reassuring Aristotelian cosmology, offers his portrayal of the universe, in the *Timaeus*, not as science but as cosmogonic poetry, in his own words, as a "likely account." With him, we may rejoice in the fact that the heavens declare the glory of their Creator in a language other than astronomy.

Popularizers of modern science tend to take a different view. At their hands modern man, down-hearted though he is, must suffer another sermon on what is mistakenly styled humility. He is made to feel quite puny (think how big the stars are) and he is urged to blush at his domicile: the second-rate planet of a second-rate sun. The naïveté of these expressions which interpret the order of astronomic magnitude as an order of dignity is even more grossly at fault than the naïve dogmatism of Ptolemaic-theological astronomy. The happy and trusting child of the past has grown fretful and petulant. Failing to find the constellations an open book on moral philosophy, it denounces the macrocosm as an outrage on morality. As we take these teachings to heart, we will be torn between despondency and megalomania. While envying the big things, from the hippopotamus to the sun, for their sheer bigness, the human pygmy, a tragic clown, makes bold "to combat the cosmic process," as T. H. Huxley once put it.

The importance of the fact that man, as material, is a part of a material universe may be misinterpreted but it can hardly be exaggerated. It is fundamental. But only on pain of committing the error of physicalism can the sciences of the specific nature of this materiality (physics, chemistry, astronomy) prejudge the issue regarding human nature.

Man is matter organized into a living body. By so ranging ourselves alongside our fellow-animals, we approach more closely to what we actually are. With a few notable exceptions, such as the development of brain and skull, the upright posture, and the structure of the hand, man shares the characteristic features of his body with other living creatures, especially with the mammals and, among them, in the first place, with the anthropoid apes. Like other animals, he is begotten and born, and in due time, he dies. His life-span is longer than that of most animals and shorter than that of some. Similarly in stature he exceeds most animals but is exceeded by some. In this as in other respects, no striking privilege is granted him. With the majority of animals he is gregarious, and his societies bear a marked resemblance to some highly developed forms of insect society. Animal life is dominated by concern for food and shelter and for the perpetuation of the species. The same is true of human life, even in its civilized phases, exception granted for heroes and saints and those feeble and intermittent attempts which the rest of us have sometimes made to follow them. On the whole, the factual evidence for man's animality is overwhelming.

Biology singles out for study the living organism, both animal and human—a co-operative structure of cells, endowed with the tendency to maintain its dynamic equilibrium through processes of self-reproduction and self-repair. But biology is not content with focusing on the organic body. As ecology, it subjects the whole of the physical world to its peculiar scrutiny. Unlike other physical data, the organism is not simply an item within the texture of events. It is attuned to, and in interaction with, reality as its environment. The extension of an organism is not limited by cuticle or integument. It receives stimuli from a wider ambit, and it radiates its responses into this field of operation. The ecological sphere within which the human organism unfolds its energies reaches from the things we touch to the remotest of the visible stars.

Obviously the study of man cannot ignore the findings of biology. Yet the warning uttered first with reference to physics must here be reiterated. Man partakes of animal nature just as he partakes of material existence. But, strictly speaking, he *is* an animal as little as he is a lump of matter. Physics as well as biology proceeds by axiomatic abstraction, and both, deliberately and methodically, discard from their area of investigation that which characterizes man as human. This omission is the price they have to pay for their achievements. They thereby forego the right to function as arbiters in matters concerning human nature. Only as witnesses on a limited phase must they be heard.

This fact had been obscured by the success of Darwinism. It seemed as though biology, and especially biogenetics, was given the power to unsettle man's faith in his spiritual nature. But again not the facts but their fictitious interpretations disturbed men's minds. Whatever they themselves thought about the cause of their troubles, it was not the fact of our simian ancestry that upset our Victorian grandparents but their own belief in ancestry (a biological datum) as determining their nature. And this belief biology neither confirms nor disproves. Had they reflected that God, who is able "of these stones to raise up children unto Abraham," might well be credited with the power of raising up men of animal seed, they would have taken more kindly to these their low-brow forebears which, Darwin held, were preferable to savages.

On account of what has just been termed "the overwhelming evidence for man's animality," it is more important to point out the danger of biologism than that of physicalism. One is hardly claiming too much in describing as "tragic biologism" the natural conviction of man when he begins to reflect upon himself. In a grim or in a melancholy mood, he will ring the changes on the theme: we are born, we grow up, and in a little while we die. In order to break this deadlock of thought, mankind had to put forth the intellectual effort embodied in its spiritual religions and in philosophy. The modern spokesmen of that ancient disillusionment borrow their vocabulary but not their ideas from science. The outlook on life as expressed by T. H. Huxley or Bertrand Russell finds its closest parallels in the somber fantasies of the old Norse bards. They too celebrate animality glossed over with desperate heroism.

The study of matter and the study of life lead up to the question "What is man?" They prepare the material for an answer, but they do not answer it. Any answer to it deserving serious consideration must fulfill two conditions, and philosophers have been hard put to it to fulfill both rather than to sacrifice one to the other.

In the first place, the distinctive mark of humanity as over against materiality and animality must not be considered a power or faculty residing in man as merely an additional endowment. Man, it is true, is capable of achievements beyond the reach of animals. Language and rational thought are given him alone. But if we understand the ancient definition of man as *animal rationale* in that sense (not the sense intended by its originators), it defines a hybrid rather than man. Nothing more monstrous than an animal, living, feeding, mating, perishing as an animal, but endowed with intelligence. Only a dehumanized man may approach this condition. Rather than being engrafted upon animality, the distinctively human element must inform and transfigure animality. Man is human not only by virtue of his ratiocinative power. He calls his matings marriage, his begetters parents, his feeding taking meals, and, conscious of life, he foresees the oncoming death. For better or for worse, he is an altogether unique being, projecting, as it were, into a dimension foreign to animality.

All this is not said in confutation of the idea that rationality is the *differentia specifica* of our race. If only we fight shy of that emasculated idea of reason that infected post-Cartesian philosophy (reason cut loose from passion and debarred from vision), we may find the ancient concept still useful. Or rather it will prove indispensable. It alone meets a second requirement to be fulfilled by any definition of man. It assigns to him the place of a potential spectator. As rational, man does not live in an environment only, but in a world. He is able to discover things as they are by themselves, and he does so for the sake of discovery. Immersed as he is in the totality of things, he may yet rise above participation and face the world (including himself) as a spectacle. Cosmology, not ecology, describes his status.

Only for a philosophy which encompasses man in the role of a rational spectator do the elements of abstract knowledge acquired by the natural sciences coalesce into a concrete picture of reality. For natural science presupposes a fact which no natural science will ever make intelligible: the human observer. Only by virtue of understanding himself can man understand his sciences.

3. What Ought Man to Be?

Before the microscope was invented, people were ignorant of those smallest units of living matter which we now call cells. Prior to modern microphysics, physicists did not suspect the existence of sub-atomic structures such as electrons. These were discoveries in the fullest sense of the word. Philosophy does not boast discoveries of this sort, although it does claim the attainment of authentic knowledge. There is a cognitive achievement different from discovery. Let us call it "enlightenment." Things dimly or vaguely espied are made articulate through elucidation and so become truly known. In this type of concrete knowledge philosophy excels.

We know ourselves, our fellow-men and fellow-creatures, and the world in which we live, even before we begin to reflect and to ask questions. This common-sense awareness reveals to the student of the mind a definite structure and an astounding complexity, overlooked by traditional rationalism and traditional empiricism alike. To restore the concept of experience to its original integrity no mean intellectual effort was required. Modern phenomenology, initiated by Edmund Husserl, inculcated the urgency of the task and contributed more towards it than any other school of thought. A variety of moves in the field of modern thought pointed in the same direction: William James's psychology, A. N. Whitehead's critique of physicalist dogmatism, and the metaphysically enlightened empiricism of the late R. G. Collingwood.

The world as given in commonplace experience is more than the point of departure for the natural sciences. It is their object. Remote from the commonly known things though the conceptual system of mathematical physics seems, it is designed to explain these very things. To be sure, physics confines itself, through abstraction, to a rigorously limited region—to things as metrical. But this region is still a region within, or an aspect of, the familiar reality.

Philosophy too sets out from the common understanding of reality. But it is related to this understanding in a totally different way. It seeks to achieve clarity without surrendering concreteness. Common-sense experience shows a staggered arrangement: the clearly discerned foreground shades off into a receding background, and this background, dimly perceived and yet dominant, is afforded by a view of reality as a whole. Philosophy, instead of screening off this view, articulates and organizes it. Rather than abandoning commonplace awareness it renders it transparent; and commonplace awareness in turn, obscurely "totality-conscious" as it is, is potentially philosophical. Hence the relation between philosophy and common-sense experience is one of tension rather of distance. While mathematical physics and related abstract sciences appear recondite and almost unhuman (the public admiration granted them is actually addressed to technology), philosophy appears either abstruse or strangely familiar, even though unintelligible. In any case, it is a challenge, and it sets up a disturbance. This explains its peculiar attitude towards the great reservoir of concrete experiences, language. Unlike the abstract sciences, philosophy cannot dispense with the wisdom enshrined in words by supplanting them with terminological contrivances. It is natural for the philosopher to have his eyes on the lips of the people and his ears open to the strains of poetry. Not that he bows to language as to an unfailing oracle. But he thinks it reasonable to hold in respect the good sense put into language by generation after generation.

Only one application of these general observations may here be made. Talking about human situations and historical events as we frequently do (most human speech is about human affairs), we may say: "Rommel, defeated at El Alamein, retreated towards Tunisia." The German general, we imply, did one thing, but he might have chosen otherwise. Instead of extricating his army by skilful maneuvers, he might have elected to offer another battle. Then, slightly varying our terms, we might express the same fact as follows: "Rommel, defeated at El Alamein, was thrown back towards Tunisia." This second sentence seems to treat the general as though he were an object pushed rather than acting. However, accurately interpreted, the sentence does not treat him so. Much against his will, it suggests, the general had to give ground—a meaning never to be attributed to a mere weight, pulled or pushed, except metaphorically. So every report on human actions tacitly assumes freedom of choice. Every actual deed is, as it were, surrounded by a halo of excluded possibilities, and meaning accrues to the things done from their conjunction with things left undone. Even in actions performed under compulsion, choice is involved, though it is a choice reduced to impotence. Deprived of the choice between several courses of action, we still choose between modes of acceptance—between joyous acquiescence, for example, and dull resignation. Even a report that tries to convey the idea of ineluctable Fate must show man struggling against the overriding necessity, and to that extent fatalism defeats its own purpose. Only as free choosers do we suffer coercion.

The problem of the scope and relevance of choice is surrounded with formidable difficulties. But the onus of proof does not rest with the affirmer of free choice. It is the determinist who must show that human actions are describable in terms not implying choice. And this he will never achieve. His is not a distressing view of life. If he is consistent, he must overlook life, even while he endeavors to study it. He is in the situation of a man who hopes to understand a painting by measuring it. To be sure, a painting is measurable but not *as* a painting. Similarly, actions exhibit the same causal nexus that characterizes all events but not *as* actions.

There are two sciences which, by their very nature, are tempted to forget these basic truths about man: psychology and sociology, both developed in recent times through emancipation from philosophy. Like philosophy they are constrained by fidelity to their object to maintain the concrete, multidimensional vision of reality which is characteristic of common experience. But at the same time, allured by the ideal of mathematical exactness, they agree too readily to barter their logical integrity against would-be scientific formulas and pseudo-deterministic laws. Human nature is curtailed in order to make it amenable to methods borrowed from the natural sciences. Happily, a type of studies survives which, by its very existence, is a protest against this error. The historian, the philologist, the student of antiquity, the student of art—they all can acquiesce in a maimed picture of man only on pain of frustrating their own efforts.

4. Whose is Man?

Physics can neither confirm nor deny man's freedom because the aspect of reality which it studies does not encompass man as a person. For the same reason, biology has no theoretical jurisdiction over the humanity of man. There exists, however, an ordered totality of things, embracing all regions of study and all perspectives, things both human and subhuman—and the superhuman things as well. This totality does *ex hypothesi* encompass the human person, and since we conceive of totality as an orderly whole, the problem of freedom recurs and cannot again be discarded. On the plane of metaphysical and theological considerations, it becomes inescapable. How can man be exempt from determination in an orderly, i.e., law-determined, world?

This ultimate problem, it seems, does not admit of a solution save in analogical, i.e., logically imperfect, terms. The analogical argument takes us beyond an anonymous totality to the idea of God. We conceive two types of dependency or determination, one perfectly known, the other largely unknown. Into the opacity of the largely unknown relationship we probe by means of an analogy based upon the familiar relationship.

First we look at the mastery which the human maker has over his own handiwork. It is nearly complete. Whatever the artifact is or does, it owes everything to the artificer. But with all his technical skill, one talent he cannot bestow upon his creatures: spontaneity. They are all tools, slaves and, as it were, prolongations of his own will.

We then imagine the divine Maker, of infinite power, manifesting His omnipotence in works that surpass human works by a distance infinitely wider than that separating an engine from a living being, plant or animal. These unique creatures He endowed with the power to be His by their own free resolve. But if they should elect not to adhere to Him, they were still to be His, though in misery.

As an isolated argument, the suggested analogy hardly carries conviction. It falls an easy prey to the criteria of logical stringency rightly insisted upon in other fields of inquiry. But if placed where it belongs—in the focal point towards which all human aspirations converge—the wisdom of the ages and the truth of Revelation combine to give it strength. It then helps reveal to man a self-affirmation that is won through self-surrender, and a freedom that is perfect service. Man is not his own master. He is God's property.

To let the conception of man measure up to his true stature was our first concern. But his final exaltation to a likeness of God involves his utter humiliation: "What is man that Thou art mindful of him" (Psalms, 8:4). So philosophy, gathering up whatever is known about our race from other studies, combines all observable traits into a unified picture and, in a final effort, tries to express what man is. But to give reliable truth to this concluding affirmation it must be counterpoised by the negation which shows what man is not. In maintaining this balance—the grandeur of man poised against his misery—philosophy expresses the very life of the humanities, the humanity of man.

Chapter VI

LANGUAGE STUDY

Howard R. Huse

IT IS PROPOSED to restrict this consideration of language and the humanities to foreign language study alone. There are several reasons for this rather narrow limitation.

The vast and useful fields of comparative linguistics, phonology, morphology, phonetics, and so on, tend to become, as far as possible, scientific, and in that sense to escape from the usual concept of the humanities.

The psychology of language, or "semantics," as divorced from philosophical speculation, is a new field which has only begun to be cultivated in schools and colleges. Some day this subject matter may form the very core of our curricula, and teachers may teach not merely how to convert symbols into sound, but how to read critically. Students would learn how to interpret words in terms of motive, probability, laws of evidence, meanings or referents. Such knowledge would mark the end of the reign of many who dominate through commercial, political, and sometimes even religious propaganda. But that deliverance belongs to the future, not to the present.

When we consider courses in English, the emphasis is on application of language, on composition and literature, rather than on language itself. In the case of most students, whatever knowledge of grammar and of the mechanisms of speech they acquire comes through study of some foreign tongue. Thus, while English satisfies the "humanistic" side of the equation, it does not always satisfy the "language" side.

On the other hand, the relationship of foreign language study to both language and the humanities is quite clear. Originally humanism implied the study of Greek and Latin as preliminary to everything else, and wherever the humanities have been valued, foreign language study has been emphasized. Although some modern language teachers now stress practical and utilitarian aspects of their studies, originally the modern languages secured admittance to the curriculum as substitutes for Latin and Greek, and, in spite of much promoting and rationalization, the only solid claim the modern languages can have for a place in the required curriculum must be based on cultural or humanistic grounds.

When foreign language study is considered apart from literature, the problem of justification can be stated somewhat as follows: Is there any human or cultural or intellectual value in learning foreign words, mechanisms of speech, idioms (or idiocies, since all languages are largely irrational), declensions, irregular verbs, and so on; in short, in studying linguistic form apart from logical linguistic content? Here is something that has plagued millions of students for centuries, something that has caused rivers of tears, nervous disorders, sad failures, broken spirits, hatred of school, of teachers, and of study. Here also, unfortunately, is the happy hunting ground for mediocrity, a seed-bed for some of the most luxuriant growths of pedantry, a field where those who possess neither notable brains, nor emotions, nor imaginations can flourish and soothe their pride. To know the origin of the word "supercilious," to learn the name for a spade or a lily in a dozen languages (without having a single additional concept) requires memory and industry, but little else, and even if humanism is invoked, we must realize that crimes can be committed in that name as well as in the name of other gods, such as liberty.

The complaint that language learning requires work, hard work, and often, at present, unnecessary work, can hardly be denied. Certainly study is necessary in the case of most language learning by "studial" methods in school. That sweet and marvelous device of many educators, namely, "unconscious learning," here must be ruled out. This is not to say that "unconscious learning" is always impossible. A grasp of certain large matters, such as "romanticism," or "classicism," or "economic determinism," can never be insured by memorizing a formula. It comes through experience with many details. But you don't learn that "dog" is *chien* or *Hund* while your mind is wandering, or at least you don't learn it rapidly and with economy. Learning linguistic facts is often like learning the multiplication table. It means memorizing, and to memorize you must concentrate, and concentration is painful, like work. It is true that our native tongue comes almost painlessly, but the process requires a lifetime, and we never reach the end of the task. Most of a small child's waking hours are spent learning his language. He spends, say, six hours a day for ten years at that unconscious labor. That is equivalent to a class a day for about twenty years in school. But in school such slow and diluted learning would be largely canceled by other more intense linguistic influences, so that keeping even without making any gain would be difficult. And we are considering here only a ten year old's accomplishment. We study our own language, all of us, all our lives, and never know more than a part of it. The hope of making foreign language learning an unconscious, painless process will always prove a delusion for most students, as it always has in the past. If students must never have to work at all, but just play (as some would seem to imply), then language study should be abandoned entirely.

But it is a mistake to suppose that children or adults must hate work under all conditions. Work can be interesting, as every child who works to build things knows. To make work acceptable, the main requirement is that the worker should know exactly where he is going and why. In general, rapid and easy learning depends on finding means to insure brief moments of intense concentration. Those who have seen what can be accomplished in learning verbal material in time measured not by hours or by minutes but by seconds, will be in a position to understand this precept.

Such concentration could be made attractive to the student if the object were always clear, and the means to accomplish that object direct and efficient. Unfortunately, in much foreign language study at present that is not the case. A dozen ends confuse. The student is supposed to learn not merely to read or speak or write, but to do all of these at once. He is supposed, moreover, to study literature simultaneously with language, and there are still other aims, varying from mental discipline to sympathy for a foreign nation. Efficient work demands isolation of the task. An electrician who had to do plumbing, bricklaying, carpentering, and painting all together, would never gain any momentum and would be frustrated by the slowness of his progress. Unless each task is isolated, the goal is confused, and the student is disoriented. Probably nothing in school is taught so well as the multiplication table. That is because the task is isolated, not confused with applications to engineering and dynamics which must come later, and because the methods used to learn it are studial and direct.

To find their work acceptable students must also feel that the teacher or textbook writer is helping them to learn easily, to cut corners, instead of making the task more complicated and difficult. When moral factors loomed large, and emphasis was placed on mental discipline, this helpfulness did not always seem to be so important. The harder the job, the greater the discipline, the more admirable the moral triumph. In this respect, grammarians and language teachers have been among the worst offenders. Language textbooks not long ago looked like reference books, or works for finished scholars. To learn the meaning of a word or phrase, the student had first to *find* that meaning, which required thumbing a dictionary, or searching for a note in an appendix, or hunting for a grammatical rule under, say, Paragraph 395, C, 2. Sometimes in order to follow the sense of a passage a student would have to look up twenty or thirty words for each page of text. Such thumbing was not profitable work, and students knew it. Some of the words and expressions would turn out to be so rare or so technical as to be useless for a working vocabulary. All words were treated as of equal value, from "metempsychosis" to "is." In considering some Latin methods in use not long ago, it would seem that teachers had combined to make language learning as painful, time-consuming, and wasteful as possible. The situation has changed considerably, but much remains to be accomplished before the various aims for which language study is undertaken are isolated, and methods used to accomplish these ends efficiently. Progress is slow because the old methods eliminated from the language teaching profession many of those who were seriously offended by inefficiency and waste.

When each unit of work to be memorized is outlined as concretely and rigorously as the multiplication table—a definition that can be accomplished by means of frequency counts of words and locutions—then the task of method makers (or rather of textbook writers) will be to see how much economy of student effort they can insure in their presentation of the material. This economy of effort is a measurable quantity, and it may ultimately be possible to bring the subject of language methodology out of the azure of theorizing and make of it something rigorous and scientific.

If this were done, the student could hardly fail to perceive how the teacher was co-operating in his task. He would appreciate this co-operation, in the absence of which, study is often a test of docility or of lack of spirit. The progress, moreover, would be so rapid as to change entirely the character of the work. To illustrate: If a reading aim were proposed in a given course in French or German, students could stop trying to learn the gender of nouns. That burden on the memory is unnecessary for reading. This example of a saving is only one of many. In order to speak a language, cognates must be learned the same as other words, since in speaking you cannot be sure that there *is* a cognate, or if so, exactly what its form may be; but in reading, these words are immediately recognizable and do not enter into the learning problem. For any given purpose, our present methods waste probably about half of the students' time. And this waste affects the morale of the students and is thus compounded.

The purpose of this paper, however, is not to show the inadequacies and wastes of foreign language study, which have led to its abandonment in some places, but rather to show the value of such study from a humanistic viewpoint. The tendency of most people would be to concede the humanistic values in the case of the study of foreign literature, but to deny them in the case of the language itself. Language and literature, however, are two things which, instead of being inseparable, are often in conflict.

Literary interest in what is being read frequently distracts attention from the linguistic forms on which the student should concentrate if he is trying primarily to learn the language. Literary vocabulary often leads away from the central core of language to the periphery, to terms like "fardels" and other rare synonyms for common words. One piece of literature may contain a vast nautical vocabulary and another the vocabulary of an antiquarian's shop, or what not. All this confuses the linguistic task which should require starting with, and learning first, the central part of language common to almost all discourse. No two individuals ever speak with exactly the same words and phrases, but the language of literary stylists is often farthest from the common linguistic norms.

If interest lies principally in the logical content of reading material, apart from the language itself, learning a foreign tongue is not necessary at all. At best only one or two foreign languages can be learned sufficiently even to be read with pleasure and ease; in the case of other languages adequate knowledge is not possible. Thus is it not convincing to say that Greek or Latin or French or German or Italian or Spanish or Russian are all indispensable when the necessary limited choice shows that, considered separately, they are not. Most of the world's great literature has been translated into English, and, while there is a real loss in most translations, that loss can easily be exaggerated.

Only in the case of poetry, and especially lyric poetry, are translations completely or even seriously inadequate. In the case of historical, philosophical, religious, travel, and didactic literature, memoirs, most fiction, essays, etc., if the students lose something because of the inadequacies of translations, they are likely to lose still more by trying to read the original language because of their imperfect knowledge of it. The task of acquiring sufficient vocabulary to read literary works in any language with pleasure is so great that only specialists can do it. Professors of French, after years of experience, must still use dictionaries in reading new literary material. Out of the millions who have studied Latin, very few read a Latin author for pleasure or profit. The branches of literature which defy the skill of almost all translators are, for most people, minor forms. English lyric poetry, especially contemporary English poetry, for instance, can be understood by only a minute proportion even of native English speakers.

The practical value of foreign language study can also easily be exaggerated. At the present moment, after the Army experiment which many do not hesitate to interpret and acclaim, there is a tendency for the practical men, who think in terms of jobs and promotion, to prevail over those interested mainly in culture. The battle between these groups, like the war between the extroverts and the introverts, between Shaun and Shem, goes on continually, and for the moment, the practical men are on top. Whether particularly useful or not, foreign languages will be taught in school for speaking, and classes will be filled with the job-minded.

Learning to speak a foreign language, however, by any definition of "speaking" is a serious and difficult undertaking. No miracles are accomplished, in spite of the reports of promoters. We have only to look around at foreigners to see how, after thirty or forty years of practice in English, they still make errors both in pronunciation and in syntax. A five year old child can detect such a foreigner almost the moment he begins to speak. For an adult to duplicate the thousands of words and concepts in his mind, to parallel all his mental experience in another tongue, is a difficult task that demands, at best, grave sacrifices. In the opinion of most of the students of the problem, bilingualism is a hindrance to mental development, a misfortune of those peoples who, like the French Canadians, Welsh, and Bengali, are obliged to acquire it.

Although parents and outsiders can easily be impressed, the practical skill in using foreign languages acquired in school alone will always be, as now, imperfect for most students. Another difficulty is that a boy of fourteen or fifteen can hardly foresee which foreign language he may ultimately need. He may study Spanish but secure a job buying tobacco in Salonika or in Cavalla, where modern Greek would be more useful. Others forced by the curriculum to choose a foreign language may never work a day outside of the United States. As a money-making skill, moreover, an active knowledge of a foreign language can seldom compete with bookkeeping, accounting, welding, bricklaying, personnel direction, advertising, and other skills. There are always occasions when a practical knowledge of a foreign language is useful and even indispensable, but the wise course is to wait until the particular need is immediate or fairly certain. And, in that case, the best plan is to study in the foreign country.

Most of the *ad hoc* advantages of foreign language study, i.e., of language study as a preliminary for something else, can hardly stand a rigorous analysis. If the subject matter is useful, it must be useful in and of itself. Otherwise the choice of the particular language would be the prime consideration, since the practical contingencies involved are, for most students, unpredictable.

The first reason for making the study of some foreign language a required discipline is that language itself is important, and the only way a person can know about any language, his own or that of a foreign country, is through foreign language study.

The importance of language is always casually admitted, but seldom deeply felt. Language is the principal influence in our lives. We are constantly talking or constantly listening. When no one is around to hear our remarks, we talk to ourselves—we think or dream.

Words are the means by which our civilization is developed, maintained, and passed on. Our language determines largely the character of our intelligence, our loyalties and disloyalties. We live in words, we are surrounded by them, they line the streets, they fill the air. And the only means we have to get outside of our own language so that we can even look at it is through foreign language study.

No one can know the characteristics of his own language, its features, defects, qualities, without some knowledge of another tongue. Qualities exist only in relationship: nothing is high or low, good or bad, except by comparison with something else. A foreign language furnishes a necessary term of comparison.

Languages have diverse characteristics: they are as different as faces. German looks different, sounds different, feels different from French. The very exercise materials in French, in German, in Italian, and in Spanish vary in character. Some seem straight-forward, direct, clear; others have a sympathetic homeliness. Latin can suggest even to a small boy the order and weight of the legions. Only by being aware of the quality of another tongue can we have even an idea about the character of our own.

From the first day of a new language course the student is plunged suddenly into a new mental atmosphere. Almost at once he senses the quality of the language he is studying: the vocabulary, the sound and order of the words, their methods of composition and derivation, all that is a new world in which other minds—millions of them—have lived, and live.

Through foreign language study a person perceives how conventional all language is, and he becomes conscious of the mechanism of his own speech. The Englishman who considered the French a silly people because they call their mothers "mares" and their daughters "fillies" represents an extreme, but natural, linguistic ignorance. Without knowledge of a foreign language we are caught in our verbal subjectivism, like a squirrel in his cage. Labels and sounds appear to have a direct, immediate and logical relationship to what they symbolize. Things and symbols are confused in what may be, and often is, the worst of confusions.

The argument of mental discipline is no longer fashionable, to say the least. The tendency is to discount all claims on this score except in relation to exactly similar skills or activities. Yet, to give up these claims entirely would be to reject most of the traditional subjects of the curriculum. In daily life, few use skills similar to those involved in algebra, ancient history, chemistry, physics, and so on. Yet these disciplines apparently effect changes so noticeable that a few minutes of casual conversation usually suffice to identify a man who has undergone this training.

Language study enforces meticulous observation, careful attention to details. No bluff, no rationalizing will do. You are almost always either right or wrong without appeal. Required language study tends to eliminate those who are incapable of rigorous attention or understanding, but who can pass many courses in other subjects because of the vagueness and imprecision of the testing.

In the absence of courses aimed directly at increasing English vocabulary, much knowledge of English must be gained by studying Latin or one of the Romanic tongues. It is hardly necessary to point out that if a student knows *aqua*, "aquarium," "aquatic," "aqueduct," "aquatint," "aqueous," and even "aquacade" become understandable. Common observation shows that graduates of the classical curriculum of Arts colleges usually do better in formal English than veterinarians, agronomists, and others whose foreign language study has been neglected—a fact that selection alone does not wholly explain.

In spite of much abuse and some deserved ridicule, the exercises in translation from a foreign language into English offer about the only organized practice in the study of meaning that the curriculum offers. The one outstanding fact about translation is that you must really grasp and understand the meaning of what you are translating. There may be a few exceptions to this rule in the case of metaphysical and emotive cognates which are not understood in either tongue, but that is about all. In so far as *understanding* is important, the process of translation from the unfamiliar to the familiar should be extended to all branches of study and should constitute the fundamental and principal educational discipline.

Apart from the thought, history, literature, and culture of a foreign country, which can be presented sometimes advantageously in translation, there is something of the intimate spirit of a nation and of its civilization that can be grasped only through its language. Those who have studied just a little Latin, Greek, German, or French are aware of this, although they may never have progressed much beyond exercise material or read an entire book in the foreign tongue. There is something broadening, destructive of provincialism and of intolerance, in the sympathetic understanding that linguistic study makes possible.

To summarize: It is not on the practical value of foreign language study either for speaking or reading that the claims of this subject in a humanistic program must primarily be based. Those claims, like most practical, *ad hoc* values for formal school study are often spurious; and the practical ends involved are seldom adequately attained. But the knowledge of other peoples and other minds that comes through foreign language study is immediate and direct. There is "surrender value" for each unit of work, even if that work lasts only a few weeks. And it is only through foreign language study that we can understand the characteristics of any language, including our own. We live in a universe of things in which science has proved a helpful and comforting guide; but we live also just as intimately in a world of communication, and as a preliminary to any knowledge in this field, foreign language study is essential. Just as in the past foreign language study constituted the fundamental humanistic discipline, so now, in the new flood of written and spoken words, it remains a vital and basic discipline.

Chapter VII

MUSIC

Glen Haydon

THE ART OF MUSIC has always been a strand of some importance in the history of civilization. A representation of musical instruments on an inlaid vase from the Sumerian civilization of the fourth millennium B.C. shows that music had an important place in this ancient time. Singers and players are depicted on Egyptian reliefs and wall paintings. With the rise of Greek civilization, indications of musical activities multiply rapidly; and throughout the middle ages, the Renaissance, and modern times, the stream of musical development has widened and deepened.

At the present time, entirely aside from concerts, operas, and other specifically musical events, the average man, whether he will or not, hears music from cradle to grave: music at home, school, and church; on the radio, in the theatre, and at the movie; and on almost all public occasions including even football games. So it is not strange that we should stop from time to time and wonder why. Why, when we attend a funeral, a wedding, or almost any kind of ceremonial, do we demand music? We cannot go deeply into the matter here, but we may make one or two suggestive observations. Man is, in his fundamental nature, a feeling, thinking, and willing being; and music appeals most directly to the feeling, or aesthetic, aspect of his nature. Society and convention have crystallized man's deeply felt emotions at the common crises of his life into ceremonial rites. In them his aesthetic nature finds at least a partial expression through music. Of course, the other arts also contribute to a ceremonial occasion: architecture, painting, poetry, the dance, and drama. Our concern here, however, is music, with its direct appeal to the feelings.

Formal education has centered its attention on understanding and basic attendant skills. It has sought to educate man's rational nature. Moral or religious education has been the concern of the church. Aesthetic education, however, has been grossly neglected. In considering the reasons for this we shall refer chiefly to music, but what we have to say will apply, in principle at least, to all the arts.

Aesthetic education has been neglected because of the difficulty of teaching the arts. This difficulty arises largely from the fact that the development of sound aesthetic judgment and enjoyment in the arts depends upon a great deal of first-hand experience in them, some understanding of the principles of the arts, and an insight into their fundamental nature. It is not easy to bring a large measure of first-hand aesthetic experience into the lives of large numbers of students. In the sciences, one may easily teach the facts and the principles involved and check and evaluate what the student has learned. Even in the field of language and literature, one may determine the results of instruction by objective tests even if it is not so easy to know to what extent the student has developed an appreciation of good literature. And yet this is the crux in teaching literature, for what is the use of learning facts without gaining the feeling for the aesthetic experience that is the soul of literature?

Besides literature, which we try to teach everyone to appreciate, we require our students in the general college to have courses in the natural and social sciences, in mathematics, and in language. But where are our general requirements for discipline and experience in the other arts? True enough, some institutions are requiring courses in the arts, but the practice must be regarded at present as experimental rather than definitive. It is doubtful at the moment whether one should advocate the general introduction of such required courses into the curriculum, for to do so might defeat the very purpose of the requirement, namely to develop an appreciation of the arts. Perhaps we should not require a student to take a course in music when he has no interest in it and does not like it. And yet, if one is thinking of the elements of a liberal education, it is hard to conceive how an education can be liberal without some appreciation of the arts. We require students to take mathematics, but one wonders how many ever learn to like it.

Perhaps, after all, we should insist upon some work in the arts just as we require mathematics. Then we are faced with the task of helping students required to take work in the arts to come to some appreciation of them.

A liberal education can never be a purely intellectual matter. Understanding depends not merely on knowledge, reason, and reflection; it also involves an element of immediate awareness, of intuition or, more precisely, of perceptual intuition. This latter aspect of knowledge is essentially irrational; it is fundamentally non-intellectual. It is aesthetic in the original meaning of that term. Whatever its shortcomings in other respects, Greek education, from early Athenian times through the period of the broadest extension of Hellenic culture, recognized this fact. In the youthful or irrational, impulsive period, the emphasis was placed on gymnastics and musical performance such as singing and playing upon the flute and lyre. Only at puberty or in the rational period were mathematical subjects, dialectic, and sciences stressed. At the same time, it must be noted, the subjects of the earlier training were continued in more advanced studies. On this basis the Greeks produced intellectual and aesthetic ideas that have been the wonder of subsequent times. Here were laid the foundations of the liberal arts that were to endure, though not without vicissitudes, through the ages.

Practical music was an integral part of Roman culture in the early years of its history, but, after the first Punic War, as Rome began to adopt Greek ideas of education, theoretical music received more attention. Thus Varro (116-27 B.C.) included in his work *Disciplinarum Libri Novem* a treatise on music which became one of the chief sources for subsequent theorists. From Boethius on, the music taught as part of the quadrivium was entirely theoretical, a division of mathematics to be studied after arithmetic. Boethius himself is reputed to have known nothing of music as an art. For centuries, the mere singer or performer on an instrument was not regarded as a musician in the learned sense of the word. Nevertheless, it is true that through the middle ages those schools that excelled in the teaching of music as a branch of the quadrivium generally were held in high esteem for their instruction in practical music in the elementary grades. The schools of Metz, St. Gall, Soissons, Fulda, Mainz, Reichenau, and St. Amand were famous for their practice of music.

During the Renaissance a similar state of affairs seems to have obtained in the universities. The requirements for the master's degree always included the theory of music in the tradition of Boethius. Practical music, of which there was an abundance during the period, was taught elsewhere. Since then, however, leaders in educational thinking have generally recognized in practice or precept the significance of practical musical training with the attendant implications of the development of man's aesthetic nature. Luther, Castiglione, Montaigne, Thomas Morley, and Comenius bear testimony of this in the sixteenth and early seventeenth centuries. Even John Locke, though he placed music at the very end of the list of "accomplishments necessary for a gentleman," acknowledges some value in practical music. His opposition to music and painting was apparently based primarily on the belief that "to accomplish a tolerable skill" in them "would require too much of a man's time." In the reforms of Rousseau, Pestalozzi, Herbart, Froebel, Spencer, and Huxley are to be found, though with varying emphasis, arguments for the development of man's aesthetic capacities. And in the twentieth century, with educational theory and practice in a state of flux, there is ample evidence of the growing recognition of the importance of an enriched aesthetic experience as an integral part of a liberal education.

In the early American colleges music was not included in the formal curriculum. College authorities and parents, although they did not regard participation in musical activities as bad in itself, were, like John Locke, fearful of wasted time. In 1803 one of the laws of Brown University read, "No student shall play on any musical instrument in the hours allotted for study, on the penalty of eight cents for every offence." On the other hand, religious services and public ceremonies required music, and there is considerable evidence that music was taught and practiced informally from the beginning. This was true at Harvard College in the seventeenth century, and has been true in principle throughout subsequent times. College musical societies and choirs were established; student orchestras, bands, and glee clubs flourished; and other miscellaneous musical activities, such as musical composition and literary discourses on music, were common. As early as 1757 students at the College of Philadelphia, now the University of Pennsylvania, presented a masque, "Alfred the Great," with music by Arne and some new music composed by one of the students, possibly Francis Hopkinson. During the first part of the nineteenth century several colleges provided instructors in music. In 1841, Oberlin College even appointed as professor of sacred music one George Allen, a pupil of Lowell Mason. Instruction in vocal and instrumental music was provided, and vocal and instrumental music was available for both religious and secular activities.

Many voices were raised in favor of the arts. For example, in 1849, the Reverend J. A. Thome, formerly professor of rhetoric and belles-lettres at Oberlin College, expressed the belief that the colleges neglected the sensibilities, for it was the notion that only subjects to develop the intellect were proper; but he emphasized the importance of taking the feelings into consideration in the process of educating college students. And Thomas Hill declared that "if a love of beauty and an ear for harmony were cultivated proportionately to studies in other departments, they would add depth and character to the emotions." Further, he believed that "since the feelings are more powerful than intellectual convictions in directing action, they should be of vital concern in systems of education." These ideas merit our serious consideration.

By the last quarter of the nineteenth century courses in music became firmly established in the curricula of many colleges, and in the twentieth century music instruction has grown more and more rapidly. This development, however, has encountered many difficulties because of the inherent complexities of the total situation and the absence of a comprehensive, generally accepted philosophy of the place of music in education. During the period of the great expansion of music instruction in American colleges, most of the leading teachers had received their musical training abroad. They had gone abroad to study performance and composition. They thus came under the influence especially of the German conservatory system, and it was only natural that in many instances music instruction should be set up in American colleges on the conservatory plan. The aim was to produce composers and performers at the artists' level. The general college student was neglected.

Another peculiarly difficult problem has been that of determining the amount of credit toward the Bachelor of Arts degree that may be allowed for music. Credit for theoretical and historical courses was generally allowed as for corresponding courses in other departments, but applied music presented the problems of evaluating a skill rather than an intellectual attainment. It has generally been acknowledged that training in applied music is essential to a vital music program, and figuring on the intangible but nevertheless significant basis of what such training means in terms of the ideal of a liberal education, a modest amount of credit is allowed for practical music. In terms of this philosophy it is thought, for example, that a student singing in the glee club under the guidance of an experienced member of the faculty would earn in four years roughly the equivalent of credit for one course in any literature. Similarly, the study of piano is accredited, not on the basis of the hours of daily practice, but in terms of the musical literature covered. Thus musical performance is recognized in the liberal arts course not as an end in itself but as a means to an end. In conjunction with the courses in musical theory and history it lays the foundation on which an understanding of the art may be built.

Supplementing the courses in musical performance are the survey courses in musical literature, music appreciation courses, in which the lectures, discussions, and reading are combined with listening to musical examples provided on phonograph recordings, radio broadcasts, formal concerts, or informal performances in class. Such procedures are in accord with the ideal of the unity of knowledge and experience which affords the basis for insight, understanding, and a sense of values, not only in the humanities, but even in the sciences.

In addition to the formal courses in music, most American colleges today provide many informal opportunities for the enrichment of aesthetic experience in music. Concerts by student musical organizations, faculty and student recitals, performances by guest artists and visiting musical organizations in concert series, and programs of recorded music are common on most campuses. Collections of recordings for playing in especially provided audition rooms, musical scores, books and periodicals are available for the general college student during regular library hours. Furthermore many courses in literature, drama, history, folklore, art, sociology, education, philosophy, and even psychology make use of the music department's facilities in the ordinary routine of their instruction. Music is an element of civilization, and in many instances musical illustrations help to vivify the understanding of a phase of culture in a manner scarcely to be achieved by any other means. The importance of music, among other arts, is now generally recognized; in 1920 President Butler of Columbia declared that no adequate comprehension of the history of civilization could be reached without a knowledge and appreciation of the aesthetic aspects of civilization along with a knowledge of the scientific, literary, institutional, and religious sides. Evidence in support of the significance of the enriched aesthetic experience in the realization of the individual's highest personal capacities could be extended indefinitely, but perhaps enough has been said to suggest the main lines of this thesis.

So far, our thinking has been chiefly in terms of the needs of the general college student. We have now to consider briefly the situation from the viewpoint of the student especially interested and talented in the arts and more specifically in music. As the problem has many ramifications, we restrict our discussion to the relatively large group of students moderately or exceptionally gifted in music. Here, as in the other fields of artistic and scientific specialization, the question of professional training looms large.

In the fields of religion, medicine, law, engineering, and the like, we find highly developed, standardized curricula extending from one to four years beyond the undergraduate level. To a greater or less extent all these programs are superimposed upon, or worked out in conjunction with, a certain modicum of basic training in the liberal arts. In music, for reasons that scarcely require enumeration, there has been a pronounced tendency to emphasize intensive special training at the beginning of the college program and at the expense of general college courses. Witness the many flourishing conservatories and schools of music, privately endowed or commercial, frequently affiliated with liberal arts colleges.

The problems involved are complicated and serious, and a detailed analysis and discussion of them would far exceed the scope of the present paper; but certain aspects of the situation are pertinent to our general theme and need to be mentioned briefly. The demand of the properly qualified college student for professional training in music is, we believe, a perfectly legitimate one. The question is not only how can, but also how ought, this demand be met in the light of the many, and often conflicting although apparently justifiable, requirements of the total situation. Whatever the ultimate solution of the problems may be, we can only suggest here our deep conviction that the professionally trained musician of college calibre needs the broadening influence of the general college program in order best to fulfill his functions in a society rapidly becoming conscious of the significance of the arts in our culture. His is a difficult program; but the rewards are rich and deeply and abidingly commensurate with the devoted efforts and, in some sense, with the sacrifices which the program requires. And the results will lead to the amplification and fuller realization of the ideal of a liberal education.

Although this is not the place for an extended discussion of the problems of music in the graduate school of a university, our discussion of music in the humanities would not be complete without some reference to the topic. From Greek and Roman times, through the Middle Ages and the Renaissance, and on down to the present, the persistent quantity if not always the quality of learned, systematic, historical, philosophical, and critical writings concerning music has been truly remarkable. A mere list of the names of writers on music would read like a roll call of the illustrious thinkers of all times. This fact alone bears eloquent testimony to the suitability of the scholarly approach to music to the graduate curriculum. During and since the last half of the nineteenth century the application of the techniques of modern scientific methods to the subject materials of music has produced a volume of scholarly musical literature that has been recognized by the great universities of the world through the establishment of appropriate curricula and professorships. In the last few decades American universities have followed the lead of older European universities; and musicology, the scientific study of music in its systematic and historical aspects, is rapidly being established in the graduate curriculum on a basis comparable to advanced studies in other traditional fields of learning. On the graduate level applied music has no accredited place, and musical composition is recognized for credit only to the extent that it may be justified as being compatible with normal graduate aims. Advanced studies and excellence in applied music and composition may be recognized by appropriate professional degrees.

In the beginning we suggested that man is a feeling, thinking, and willing being. In planning his education we provide for his practical needs through his professional training leading to the economically secure and socially useful life; we look after his intellectual needs through his scientific studies leading to his perception of the truth. Let us not neglect his aesthetic needs by failing to develop his sense of values concerned with the beautiful. In this way only may we hope to offer him a chance to reach that most cherished of goals, the truly abundant life. But such categorical thinking is sure to be misleading if it implies undue segregation of the several aspects of man's nature; for man is not merely a willful being whose life is a matter of desires, wishes, urges, and volitions; he is not merely a rational animal whose life is a life of cold rationalization; and he is certainly not merely a sentient, feelingful, emotional creature whose life is a matter of affective experience.

The normal, ideal man is an integrated personality in whom these qualities are indissolubly fused so as to produce a certain equilibrium of moral, intellectual, and aesthetic elements. And this we conceive to be the high purpose of the humanistic ideal: the discovery and exploitation of the supreme values in all the arts and sciences for the fullest realization of the human personality and destiny.

Chapter VIII

THE FINE ARTS

Clemens Sommer

THAT THE FINE ARTS have taken their rightful place among the humanities is a fact. Whether that place is legitimate is a question of the past. More important is the question of the future, how they will maintain their proper and definite place in higher education. That can be decided only when our world becomes a world of order once more. We cannot tell how many changes our educational system will undergo in the meantime.

But there is another question which can and should be answered immediately: In what way can the fine arts contribute to the program of the humanities? If you scan all that has been written lately on the subject, you are forced to admit that the definition of this flexible term is more or less a matter of personal opinion. Too much of the old has been broken down, too much of the young is still in the process of growing, to allow us to form any absolute definition. In my opinion, the main purpose of the humanities is the establishment and interpretation of human values. These values should be integrated into a common whole, but the function of each field of the humanities should be to establish its specific and proper values as derived from its own and from other pertinent material.

In order to find the values which are relevant to the fine arts we must analyze the very nature of a work of art. A work of art is the result of a meeting between the objective world and the individual. The static and established order of the existing world is approached by the transitory and changeable mind of the individual. In this approach there are two definite possibilities. The individual can accept the existing order as a fact, or he can subject this order to his personal interpretation. In the first case, all the facts about objects and their relationships are taken over in their natural order. In the second case, the individual tries to change this order according to his own desires. In each of these two procedures there will be again two different approaches. The individual might be interested only in the single object and might in his work of art express only the essential qualities of this object. We will call this "realism" as it is concerned only with the object (*res*). On the other hand the interest might be focused on the relationship of a number of objects, that is, on their entity, which we will call "naturalism" since the entity of objects is the universe (*natura*). In these two approaches the individual accepts the existence of a given order. At the moment in which the individual gives any interpretation of this order, he no longer accepts the universe as an established entity. He may still keep the wholeness of the relationships, but their place in this whole is no longer given by the natural order but by the individual's interpretation. He will begin to stress certain parts which seem to him of greater importance and will de-emphasize the less desirable ones. This process will almost by necessity lead to the elimination of minor parts and to the selection of those parts which are to be the carriers of specific interpretations. So, as the last consequence, the individual may select one single object and make it the expression of his own intention. The second approach may be called "decorativism" (from *decorare*, to beautify), so long as it is concerned only with a rearrangement of the whole. As soon as it begins to break the order of the whole it might be properly named "selectivism."

The sequence of these four approaches forms a definite cycle. The process moves from the single to the multiple, building up to a definite and complex whole and dissolving this whole again into single units. We might call it a process of integration and disintegration, a process which seems to follow the evolution of all life.

The four qualities which we derive by this analysis have their counterparts in the sphere of human values. So long as we are interested in the existence of the single object, we are trying to gain evidence for its existence. We regard the object as a fact and see the nature of it as a statement. The value in this case would be a *documentary* value. As soon as we search for the relationships of the objects to one another we are no longer asking for a factual statement but for a history. We are looking for *historical* values: historical is to be understood in the broadest sense, as the ultimate relationship of the existing world.

As soon as we begin to subject the existing order to our interpretation, even with the best of intentions, we change the order of the world to make it fit our personal satisfaction. We rearrange the world to make it in some way more pleasant, more understandable. We are looking for *aesthetic* values. Even though we try to avoid any distortion, once we have allowed ourselves to become involved in our own interpretation, our emotions will carry us on until finally we disregard any given order and see the world as the embodiment of our emotions. The *emotional* values are singled out and connected with isolated and distorted facts.

Just as the four qualities of realism, naturalism, decorativism, and selectivism form a continuous cycle, so also the four corresponding values form a natural sequence. Only by adding fact to fact and knowing their interrelations, can we understand the story of the whole, and only by breaking down this whole and selecting the proper elements can we make it serve our individual purpose. Art is the purest and most sincere expression of this process which is the source of our life. If, with this new understanding, we look at the fine arts of the past as well as of our time, at the work of a single artist or of any group of artists, be it defined by nation or by race, by civilization or by culture, it will always follow this pattern.

Let us glance very quickly through the evolution of Western art as a whole. The art of Egypt (and not alone its art) is concerned mainly with the single fact. It is realistic, and accepts the existence of an unchangeable order, in which each individual has his eternal place. Are there any other documents more eternal and indestructible than the Pyramids, the tombs of the Pharaohs, or the basalt figures of gods and kings? Egyptian art, even though itself subjected to the changing values of the cycle, remains in its basic character, realistic, static, and documentary.

When the Greeks take over the heritage of the Egyptians and build up their incomparable organism of culture, their interest is from the beginning directed to the whole. Not the single fact, but the entity of all life is their aim. In spite of the changes of values noticeable in passing from the *kouroi* and *korai* of the archaic period to the classic example of organic relation in the Parthenon, and, in turn, to the *genre* scenes and portraits of Hellenistic and Roman times, the basic character of classic civilization remains static, naturalistic, and historical. Even the gods of Olympus are subjected to fate, and to an intrinsic order.

But when the Christian idea penetrates the Western world, there is no longer an unchangeable and absolute center from which the world is activated. God can rule according to his own intentions. Christian art is not striving for the expression of an existing and perfect order, but is trying to express the desirable and the satisfactory. It arranges all things in a relationship which is not of this world. In the great sculptural cycles of the medieval cathedrals, we find an arrangement which is not based on the order of nature but on the imposed order of the Church. And, natural as the paintings of the Renaissance masters seem to be, they are all striving for satisfaction, be it of groups or individuals. Again we see, from the realistic, documentary stage of the Romanesque period, the naturalistic, historical tendency growing throughout the Gothic and the early Renaissance, and we see the stress of the decorative aesthetic values of the baroque dissolving into the selective emotional character of modern art. But in spite of all these changes there remains in Christian art an indestructible desire for something better, something more satisfactory, a longing for a subjective beauty which was foreign to the Egyptians as well as to the Greeks.

So the art of our Western civilization developed through three phases of the cycle. As for the coming age, it might be tempting and frightening to draw conclusions.

In the same way that we have followed our cycle through

the sweep of Western civilization, we can follow it through any specific phase. The realistic documentary values are certainly predominant in the frescoes of Giotto, whereas Masaccio's Brancacci chapel could hardly be surpassed in naturalistic values. The decorative aesthetic qualities of Raphael's Stanze are still as outstanding as ever, and Tintoretto's cycle of the Scuola di San Rocco may serve as an everlasting example of the selective use of emotional values. But, different as those artists of the Italian Renaissance appear in their personal expression, they are united by one basic tendency which is the common tendency of Christian art; their chief aim is the creation of aesthetic values. Let us take as a final example the figure of a single artist familiar to all of us, Michelangelo Buonarroti. Does not his work proceed from isolated statues, such as the David or the Pietà in St. Peter's, to the intrinsic unity seen in the Julius tomb or the Medici chapel, and, in turn, to the broken and distorted exclamations of grief in his latest Pietàs at Palestrina and in the Palazzo Rondanini?

So in the art of the individual as well as of the greatest periods, we see a repetition of that ultimate sequence of changing values. We can be sure that this same law which has ruled the past is ruling the present and will rule the future. We can draw our conclusions and can look at art under this aspect as a manifestation of life, and we can try with this understanding to integrate art in our lives. We will, then, no longer look at art as something which is a pleasant entertainment for leisure hours, or a business which can be done during office hours, but as an integral part of our culture. There can be no longer any doubt about the pertinence of art to the humanities.

It seems to me that the proper place of art in our educational system should be determined by these values and by the understanding that these values are not derived by the application of an intellectual system to the material but by an understanding of the organic growth of all works of art from a common source. That will keep us from interpreting art history as a mere accumulation of knowledge on the one hand, and on the other, from a distortion of creative art into a mere activity, be it for commercial purposes or for entertainment.

The student who looks at the humanities as a source for the building of his personality will find it possible to integrate art with other educational fields, or will be able by developing his artistic faculty to gain an understanding of his own creative potentialities. He might later on develop his critical interpretative ability as a student of art history or he might as an artist bring his creative faculty to the point where he could express his ideas in visible form. But he will never forget that whatever he achieves in his field will come from the same source, which is the understanding of the human mind, that is, from the integration of all human thoughts and activities into one whole, the humanities.

Chapter IX

THE SOCIAL SCIENCES

Howard W. Odum

THE PROBLEM of interpreting the social sciences in relation to the humanities is twofold. One is a problem of definition and the other is a problem of the relationships. That is, we need to sense the meaning of both the humanities and the social sciences as determined by present-day usage and also the role which each is likely to play in the education and culture of the future. This assumes an understanding of the cultural backgrounds of humanistic education.

One way of approaching our appraisal is to define the several disciplines of learning in terms of their classification in the total scheme of scholarship and education and to note certain interrelationships between and among them. We approach a general definition of the humanities as they actually exist at present when we note that in recent years it has been customary, in college and university circles, to set up three main categories of subjects, namely the natural sciences, the social sciences, and the humanities.

In the natural sciences are catalogued what are usually termed the biological sciences and the physical sciences, or together, the five "basic sciences," astronomy, mathematics, physics, chemistry, biology, with their several subdivisional special sciences. Added to these in the later ramifications of science, research, and technology are the many applied sciences that have grown up to comprehend specialized research, invention, and technology in numerous fields of modern endeavor.

In the social sciences the catalogue of subjects usually allows for some overlapping with the natural sciences and the humanities, as well as with the professions. The range of the social sciences includes history, economics, political science, sociology, anthropology, social psychology, statistics, social ethics, human biology, human geography, human ecology, jurisprudence, and often philosophy, education, and religion.

In the humanities, the catalogue again is often a widening one going somewhat beyond the older traditional humanities of classics, literature, and the arts. Included in the total current range of subjects are history, education, philosophy, religion, the fine arts, the English language and literature, foreign languages and literatures, and the ancient languages and literatures.

Indicative of the range and complexity of the current problems of education and culture and of the prevailing discussions of liberal education and of the humanities is the degree to which there are increasing overlappings in the several groups and the extent to which subjects fall into more than one category. Psychology, biology, geography, anthropology, ecology, and statistics are both natural and social sciences. Anthropology and ethnology, especially in the study of folk culture, also belong to the humanities, as does psychology when it studies at length such subjects as the phonophotography of folk music, the measure of aesthetic activity, or the nature of emotional expression in the fine arts or in Freudian literature. Education, appraised as both an art and a science, is commonly listed in both the social sciences and the humanities, as are philosophy and ethics and less specialized aspects of religion. However, both education and religion are also classified among the professional subjects, which really constitute a fourth division.

Outside college and university circles, in the upper brackets of learned societies and activities representing higher education and scientific research, these three larger divisions of natural science, social science, and the humanities are represented by three main national learned councils, respectively, The National Research Council, The Social Science Research Council, and The American Council of Learned Societies. There are three other overall agencies, which indicate the further interrelationship between individual disciplines and levels of learning, research and activities. The American Association for the Advancement of Science includes the social sciences and some of the humanities in its membership and programs. The oldest of all American learned societies, The

American Philosophical Society, tends toward a preponderance of scientists over philosophers in its roll of honored fellows. The American Council on Education tends toward a unifying of all subjects in its studies and policy-making groups which may be composed of representatives of any or all of the major groupings.

Of great importance in the modern world and adding complications to both the problem of education and definition is a fourth group, the applied skills, which, considered on the professional and vocational level, may be said to grow out of the application of the basic disciplines of learning. Professional writers and journalists come pretty close to the humanities. Social work, public welfare, public administration, public law, commerce, criminology, and psychiatry come pretty close to the field of the social sciences. Public health, medicine, engineering and agriculture come pretty close to the field of the natural sciences. Many levels of occupational training and vocational guidance fall within the field of education.

It thus happens that in so comprehensive a framework of modern culture and education, appraisal of the relation of the social sciences to the humanities will probably be best sought through a process the reverse of that which has been customary in times past. That is, our first inquiry must be that of ascertaining the place of the humanities in the total framework of current education, culture, and civilization. Then we must appraise the role of the social sciences in determining the place of the humanities, similarly the place of the social sciences themselves in the total framework of education and culture.

This is a complex situation and a difficult assignment. In the first place, the social sciences would accept the definitions of the humanities as formulated by the majority of educators in this field. That is, they would agree that the humanities constitute a key to liberal education; that they train for intellectual leadership; that they conserve and transmit to each new generation the best that mankind has produced, and that the quality of teaching in all the subjects in the humanities should be preserved and raised to the highest possible degree.

What the social sciences would insist upon, however, would be that the humanities are a part only and not the whole of any education, and above all not of the general education of modern folk in the contemporary world. The social sciences would reject the claims of exclusive values made by extremists among the advocates of the humanities. Moreover, the social sciences themselves would claim some contribution to humanistic education on its newer and higher levels.

On the premises of the social sciences, the fundamentalist nature and the undemocratic assumptions of traditional humanism are untenable in the modern world. Illustrations are available in two notable instances. An eminent defender of the humanities once demanded that the University of North Carolina should stand firm as the one final state university in America to preserve a liberal arts curriculum by refusing to admit women. This stand, we believe, reflected no definitive value of the humanities but a reactionary opposition to change. In the first place, there was no inherent relationship between women and the liberal arts and, in the second place, it has been through women's colleges and the increase in women students in the war years that the liberal arts enrollment has been increased. The same professor was more accurate in his protest against the inclusion of sociology, economics, and education in the curriculum, for this conformed to an earlier accepted concept of the humanities. From the viewpoint of the social sciences, however, nothing would contribute more to the humanistic education of youth than an understanding of human culture through the cultural-historical approach which makes the people and their human relationship the chief factor in civilization's problem.

The second example which reflects profound contradictions from the viewpoint of the social sciences is the dictum of President Hutchins recommending an "education" based upon understanding the world's hundred greatest books. When it was argued that many people would not agree with his selection of the hundred books, even if they might constitute an adequate basis for liberal education, he replied that not more than five per cent of the people were competent to know what was a good book. This would seem to assume that education was at least controlled by not more than five per cent of the people, and that only a small proportion of the people would be capable of that education.

Perhaps the relation of the social sciences to the humanities, in both their role and their viewpoints, may be reflected best through the experiences of the American university. This history has epitomized the evolution of American education from its original classical base to a wider range and emphasis upon the broad field which includes social life as well. First we recall the earlier religious bases of our American universities in those days when Harvard was founded to give deeper learning and understanding to the religious leaders of the new world; then the founding of King's College, Princeton, and Yale; thence down the long road of chartering state universities, most of them directed by scholars from the great Eastern universities. There was always the thread of religion, piety, and humility running through the fabric of their scholarship and learning. This was what the people wanted and what the leaders of those days, in conformity with the early American pattern, desired and voted.

Then came the powerful influence of European culture and the example of European universities that stressed the classics, science, and philosophy, molding and conditioning the ideals and patterns of America's growing college and university life. This was in line with the earlier European influence on American culture in the East and in the South.

From this development the universities tended to become, like European universities, more and more aristocratic in their assumptions that education and culture were something that could be obtained only by a relatively small number of the people, and that it must be founded on the learning of the past and on the laboratory which studied science for science's sake.

No matter how realistic and true that level of university education and culture may have been, it was contrary to the basic assumptions of the "American Dream," the open sesame to good citizenship and equality of opportunity for all men. Consequently, there developed another level of university education, symbolized in the rise and rapid development of state universities, starting in the Middle West, spreading southeastward and then farther to the other Wests of expanding America. This was a movement in the direction of democratizing university education. As Frederick Jackson Turner has pointed out,

> through the state, the university offers to every class the means of education, and even engages in propaganda to induce students to continue. It sinks deep shafts through the social strata to find the gold of real ability in the underlying rock of the masses. It fosters that due degree of individualism which is implied in the right of every human being to have opportunity to rise in whatever directions his peculiar abilities entitle him to go, subordinate to the welfare of the state. It keeps the avenues of promotion to the highest offices open to the humblest and most obscure lad who has the natural gifts, at the same time that it aids in the improvement of the masses.

Nothing in our educational history is more striking than the steady pressure of democracy upon its universities to adapt them to the requirements of all the people. From the state universities of the Middle West, shaped under pioneer ideals, has come a greater emphasis on scientific studies, and especially on those of applied science devoted to the conquest of nature; also have come the breaking down of the traditional required curriculum, the union of vocational and college work in the same institution, the development of agricultural and engineering colleges and business courses, the training of lawyers, administrators, public men, and journalists—all under the ideal of service to democracy rather than of individual advancement alone.

However, the subsequent development of these great American state universities, founded on the basis of democratic service to the people, in many ways followed a trend of university education similar to that of the earlier endowed universities of the East and of later Western universities such as the University of Chicago and Stanford University. They tended to become "aristocratic" in the sense that their enrollment and their curricula followed the patterns of those in America's leading classical universities. So much was this true that when the second level of democratic state university education was set in the land-grant colleges of agriculture, engineering, and mechanics, it was customary to seek legislative funds for these institutions on the ground that the older state universities had become institutions for rich men's sons and for classical education. And in those states where the land-grant college was merged with the state university, the new college took on the name of "cow college" and the standards of university education were considered greatly lowered. Then followed the further extension of democratic educational policies in the establishment of special teacher-training institutions, normal schools and colleges, and special technical institutions. In later days many of these were to seek full recognition as standard colleges and universities, thus multiplying the units of state higher education and complicating the problem of university education.

It was therefore logical, if not inevitable, that the next trends in university development should have been set on the quantitative level, seeking to give university instruction in all the multiple fields demanded in the modern world by both the people in general and by special interests of varying sorts. This quantitative level of university education tended to make increasingly heavy demands upon the financial support of the people, thus bringing the university system nearer to the procedures of economy and efficiency in the use of public funds. At this point there developed a very realistic conflict between an education centered in the humanities and that education which came to be called vocational or practical. This trend continues to be the basis for conflicting concepts of education. The assumptions of the social sciences are as positive in opposition to solely quantitative values as are the humanities, but the social scientist's assumptions of a wrong trend do not lead him to recommend the remedy of merely reverting to the traditional liberal education of the past.

The state universities of the late nineteenth century had moved naturally into what might be called a popular level in two ways. First, they sought to provide ways and means for every high school graduate to attain that university education which the people had come to consider an open sesame to success; and secondly, they undertook in competitive processes to appeal for popular support and to develop alumni loyalties through adult education, extension work, and public athletics.

Now manifestly, these several levels of university trends were not necessarily exclusive one of the other nor was there always a clear line of demarcation. Rather, they represent the university's effort to adapt itself to a modern world of change and technology which also reshaped all our other institutions. In the midst of these levels and interwoven among them in the fabric of American college and university education, were still the hundreds of private colleges and universities seeking nobly to maintain standards and yet to adapt themselves to the qualitative needs of the people and particularly of their religious constituencies.

So, the cumulative heritage of these great university epochs reflects a major part of the biography of the United States of America in the rise and development of its great prosperity as measured by the crest of the 1920's. The biography of American colleges and universities is in many ways the biography of America. The education of the 1940's could no more be the education of Colonial America than could the nation turn back its clock of civilization.

The cumulative heritage of these university levels of achievement reflected an extraordinary body of learning in the humanities, the sciences, and the social sciences and a qualitative and quantitative contribution to knowledge and to method, never before approached in the history of learning and education. Notable in this heritage was the extraordinary personnel of the faculties and research staffs of the universities and colleges of the nation. Great professors and scholars they were, devoted and fearless, self-sacrificing and indefatigable, beloved of a vast body of students, symbolic of the people that America could produce.

And yet perhaps the most distinguished characteristic, the greatest merit of these scholars, was their specialized scholarship, their emphasis on individual intellectual superiority and humanistic attainments. They saw in their own intellectual lives the goals for all education, and tried to make the way clear and the facilities available for others to achieve these levels. Yet their premises again were based upon the assumption that only a small part of the people would be capable of or would want such an education. It was not only in the undergraduate liberal arts work that this intellectual isolationism was the mode, but in the major fields of research in the classics and other humanistic fields, as was represented by the high standards set at Johns Hopkins and later at Harvard, Yale, and Chicago.

In view of the early enthusiastic support of the humanities, during a later period when complex changes swept down upon the universities, as also upon industry and public affairs, it was natural for scholars to assume a defensive attitude, claiming that education which was not humanistic was therefore inferior. It is at this point that the social sciences offer a different viewpoint. Even as the modern world of democracy stresses the worth of the individual at the same time that it makes his task more complex, so the social sciences, recognizing the vast range of individual differences, seek to provide education for the largest possible number of needs. The social sciences continue to esteem the highest type of humanistic education as *an integral part* of all education, acquiescing in the validity of its work for those who want, and are conditioned to, this type of education. What it insists upon is that education shall conform also to the realities of other types of student.

The social sciences protest the contradiction which, assuming the essence of folk art and folk life and the folk as the basic resources for reinforcing scholarship, nevertheless negates this assumption by applying education in such a manner that humanistic scholarship can neither reproduce itself nor can its leaders replenish the scholarly population.

The education sponsored by the social sciences is based on an understanding and direction of society which in turn is founded on nature and natural resources, nurtured through universal cultural elements of the folk as they mature into advanced civilizations. It seeks balance and equilibrium between the people and resources and between culture and civilization where there is conflict between the people and their culture, with technology, power, industrialism, intellectualism, and statecraft tending toward totalitarianism. This is the balanced type of education which seeks not only quality in teaching and research, but also continuous evolution of the people toward higher standards and a wider reach of human achievement. In the conflict between culture and technological civilization, the social sciences have a major opportunity to bridge the distance between the exclusive humanities of earlier cultures and the realities of human society trying hard to recapture the elemental balance between the individual and the group.

Chapter X

EDUCATION AND PSYCHOLOGY

John F. Dashiell

LIMITED AND SPECIFIC though the term has come to be, interest in the humanities certainly stems from interest in things human. The literatures and the other arts are the flowerings and expressions of human productive imagination; the languages are the necessary media of such expression; while history in part of its role is a narrator of how these expressions come to be. However, much that is human is not humane in this academic sense; and it may well have puzzled many a thoughtful person just why two terms of such apparently different connotation continue to be used with no more difference of spelling than a terminal *e*. How the second, the narrower meaning, has sprung from the first, the broader meaning, may be better realized if put into certain perspectives. One is the study of man as he is by nature, his potentialities and liabilities; the other is the study of man as he has undergone changes under the control of this society and that. In short, we may well ask: how are the humanities viewed from the standpoint of psychology, and again how are they viewed from the standpoint of education? Now, the latter is much the older discipline, for societies have sought to direct the learning and maturing of the young for centuries before they became concerned to learn much about the nature of the young on its own account. Let us then essay first the historical perspective of education.

It is to be the suggestion of the present paper that an overview of the history of educational systems of all centuries and countries leads to the discovery of an enlightening dialectical principle.

Let us contrast the educational ideologies of three ancient peoples. First, Sparta. The martial character of that city-state, the concentration of collective effort upon warlike aims, had its counterpart in that conception of the individual virtues which is epitomized in the very word "Spartan." The ideal was the definite and practical one of becoming a good soldier, marked by hardihood, courage, self-discipline; and the means set up to develop this were equally definite, direct, and practical. When only a baby, the Spartan learned to depend upon himself with a minimum of adult ministrations; when a youth he was housed in military barracks, inured to many kinds of physical hardships, toughened by exposure and strengthened by heavy tasks, and for intellectual fare was given only the laws of the state and the chanting of some military music; as a young man the toughening process was extended to scourgings; and after the thirtieth year, although married and now a full citizen, he was allowed little of the gentleness and the sentimentalisms of family life. Could any system of training have been better devised to mould the plastic human individual into just the thing wanted, a soldier? What is to be stressed here is this: the Spartans had set up a perfectly definite training ideal, and they knew precisely what to do to attain it. And this ideal was a practical one, a useful one, the one on which the state was founded and on which it thrived. What was the consequence? The individuals were trained for definite, immediately useful duties and nothing else—and the education did that and nothing else.

Now, for contrast let us look to another Greek city-state, Athens. Here, where the free inquiries of intelligence and the nuances of feelings and perceptions were recognized as valuable in themselves, where spontaneous expressions of individuality in thoughtful discoursing and artistic creating were highly prized—here was to be found a radically different educational program. The young child heard his stories of the gods and the heroes. In school, later, his physical training was for adroitness and skill, grace and ease; while on the emotional-intellectual level he was given a rich and varied fare. Epic and lyric poems, dramas, stories, these he learned and loved, not with any single purpose to apply to them but to gratify interests in rhythm and harmony, in peoples and far places, in beauty and mythology. Then, too, upon his becoming a citizen the political and social life that opened up to him was permeated by ethical and poetic and aesthetic values; and the many sides of his humanness were quickened. These interests were fostered not for some useful application, not to insure food or shelter or to protect from beast or man, but for their own sake, or better, for his own sake. Humanism as the gratifying of the many sides of man and the cultivating of his highest sensibilities was fostered. Freedom was given in satisfying the more elaborate and more refined wants, and encouragement was offered for their nourishment and growth.

One more ancient civilization. When we note the manners of life among the Chinese of early centuries the contrast is again revealing. "Of all the methods for the good ordering of men there is none more urgent than the use of ceremonies." With this adage went a striking emphasis upon book learning of the most literal sort: the ancient Chinese classics and the books of texts that had to be committed to memory verbatim, with the most meticulous attention to form rather than to content and meaning—these written in a conventionalized polite language. So also with training in writing. It was intended to develop as close imitation as possible of the detailed manner and matter of the great classics. Scholars then were trained to transmit not their own work, nor even their commentaries on the classics, but the unvarying repetitions of what had already been done. At the same time, we should note the great reverence the Chinese people had for the man of learning. As the soldier was assigned to their lowest social stratum, the scholar was recognized as of the highest. In time, educational practice in ancient China had become so traditional as to be stagnant: it encouraged no drinking at Pierian springs. This was education at its most formal stage.

Surely the contemplation of these three so different types of education, the *practical* Spartan, the *liberal* Athenian, the *formal* Chinese, furnishes a suggestion as to the role of education in the life of man and his culture. The three examples set forth were contemporaneous with each other; but we will find them easier to understand if we consider them as the three stages in a historical dialectic, as cross sections of cultural spirals.

1. In the living of any folk the primary interests are of course the immediate and pressing biological and social demands. Where man is still close to nature and perforce is preoccupied with the shaping of techniques for controlling nature so that he may live, then the course of training of the young is necessarily set by practical demands. Practical life though not necessarily warlike, as was Sparta's, includes hunting and fishing, agriculture and herding, the building of huts, and the weaving of cloth. But let the folk develop these skills to such a point that the providing of life's necessities demands but a small portion of time and effort, and other interests of men, formerly shoved aside as useless indulgences (the carving of figurines or drawing of designs or toying with sounds of drum or pipe), now emerge. The purely bread-and-butter training becomes enriched.

2. The primitive's love for sounds and colors and folklore and dancing grows into a desire for the true, the beautiful, the good. Liberal values then come into their own as an objective of education. With this come new centers of enthusiasm, a new breadth of mental vision. Things and the patterns of things are studied by youth not for their ulterior comfort value, but because in their own right they are interesting, and because their refashioning into new and more complex and more delicate combinations gives a lift to the human spirit. They make life richer and the more worth living. It is at these stages of human evolution that truly liberal studies prosper. Such are the high epochs in the cultures of mankind: the T'ang and the Twelfth Dynasties in China and Egypt, the Periclean and the Augustan ages, the Renaissance and Elizabethan eras.

Meanwhile, practical needs are not overlooked: there must be training for foresters and agricultural experts, skilled mechanics, efficient clerks, certified accountants; for the economic demands (in the broadest sense) must continue to be met. They are the base of the pyramid.

3. The liberal values of life are created by the spirit of adventure and by the satisfaction experienced when one has done a novel and creative thing. But all must not be left to adventuring and individualistic self-expression. The result then

would be chaos. There must be conservation of the values discovered. In a culture where any advance is to come, the culture must have continuity, the exciting or revealing or satisfying moments of yesterday should be recorded in word or physical form, so that upon their records still further adventuring may be planned. The danger of course is that in the schools where there was once the encouragement of experimentation in new insights and tastes there is now fixation in form and ritual. The achievements of the Golden Age become fixed and standard. For some cultures, like the Chinese, this formalistic education persists for centuries; but in most it crumbles before the impatience of practical life and the urgency of daily needs. The hiatus widens between the values set up by the common man's original desires and these same values formalized and esoteric. It is then that the characteristic part of the culture of a people seems started upon another turn of the spiral.

Practical interests reassert themselves at first; a liberal enlargement and refinement of the interests then follows; and then a more rigid standardization narrowing the interests to specific channels.

The history of education affords many an example of this dialectic procession. There was the education of earlier Rome with its emphasis on personal duty to society and the state, which upon the infiltration of Hellenic influences and the expansion of the geographical horizon unfolded into the Augustan Age, finally to solidify into the imitative caste culture of late Imperial Rome, and then all to be pushed aside by the urgencies of a political calamity.

These three ways of viewing education, the practical, the liberal, and the formal, are all expressed in the American state university. The state expects its university to contribute knowledge that will lead to greater comfort and greater prosperity of the citizens: within its walls colleges of commerce, of engineering, of medicine, of agriculture are created. The state also expects its university to cultivate the interests which make for avocational and leisure-time sweetness and light: the departments of the college of arts are maintained and in the graduate school the roving spirit of inquiry is encouraged and even subsidized. The state expects its university at the same time to carry on established traditions and to help maintain the culture-pattern of the existent order: departments of history, literature, law, government, sociology, and the like, make the students aware of their heritage as something not to be lightly cast aside.

In this enterprise of educating the citizens of a state the humanities clearly emphasize the second and third motives. To be sure, there are the practical results to be gotten from the knowledge of contemporary languages, and from the knowledge of what happened when and how, and hence might happen again with the same when and how. Yet surely the study of languages should lead the citizen to an interest in literatures, and the study of history to an acquaintance with the motives of men; and the fine arts should furnish nothing if not encouragement and techniques in the refinement of human emotions and expression on their own account. The humanities are the conserving force in education, too. Particularly today as the exigencies and excitements of world events dictate many changes in the practical techniques, it is the peculiar duty of the disciplines that are farthest from the scenes of turbulence to hold steadfast to the very forms of the best that has been thought and felt in the world.

The humanities, let it be said, are in an enviable position. Less involved in current confusions of a practical world, theirs it is to keep alive in the citizens the interest in liberal and free-minded creative enjoyment, and to do this in part by maintaining some continuity through the formal records of the past. But it is also a function of the social and natural sciences to contribute to this end. For an example, let us examine the role of psychology in recognizing the citizen's interest in liberal and free-minded creative enjoyment.

Now, modern psychology looks to scientific methods for its view of the facts, but it recognizes the happiness of men as the ultimate ideal. In spirit and procedure it may well be called a natural science, in which the genus *Homo sapiens* is investigated by the observational and experimental techniques employed in zoology, physiology, and physics. In ultimate perspectives and objectives it may properly be named a social science, for man's part in social movements and organizations is as enticing a field for factual examination as is his place in nature. But whether we regard human nature from one or the other of these scientific angles, the attitude of mind, the ideal of the psychologist's methodology is the same. It is that of a factual science.

There are other factual disciplines, of course. How then are the sciences to be characterized, that they may be distinguished from other disciplines? A clear mark may be found in the type of evidence employed. The historian seeks to get at his facts by uncovering and collecting documentary evidence. The quest of the legal mind is for facts obtainable through testamentary evidence. The scientist, on the other hand, is insistent upon observing the facts himself and preferably under conditions controllable by himself. Let us examine this emphasis in perspective as we note man's interest in man.

Knowledge and understanding of human nature may be accumulated and organized in three different ways. The first—and perhaps the ultimate test, too—is the way of everyday *practical experience*. As a baby or a child is set upon the road of life, he meets other babies, other children; and as he receives contacts from them that are friendly and unfriendly so he must learn to make appropriate returns. And who or where is the man or woman who does not claim for himself special shrewdness and wisdom in sizing up other people about him? For them the story of life has been and is one of constant daily adjustment to these other agents, knowing better and better whom to approach, whom to avoid, when to approach, and when to avoid. We dare not despise the knowledge of human motivation thus derived; for any intelligent person owes his happiness to this ability to chart his own course among the hazards of intra-personal contacts. Native shrewdness is not to be despised.

A different approach to the understanding of human beings is the indirect one that works through the humanities, through *history and biography*, as the written records of men's conduct, and through *literature and the fine arts*, as the finest products of men's feeling and thinking. To obtain knowledge of man's nature is not the only objective in these humanistic studies, of course, nor indeed their primary one: for the aesthetic and intellectual satisfactions to be had from practicing and appreciating the arts will remain powerful incentives always. For our purpose, however, they assume importance as sources of revelation of the human creative spirit and the personal motivations that lie behind. The revelations and interpretations are to be found in an astonishing variety of materials, from the meticulously detailed dissection of other persons by a Dostoievski or a Conrad or a Henry James to the revealing of one's own inner urges and one's nuances of emotion by a Wordsworth or a Poe or a Willa Cather. This indirect avenue to a knowledge of man is celebrated to excess in Pope's lines:

> When first young Maro in his boundless mind
> A work t'outlast immortal Rome designed,
> Perhaps he seemed above the critic's law,
> And but from Nature's fountains scorned to draw.
> But...
> Nature and Homer were, he found, the same.
>
> . . . .
>
> Learn hence for ancient rules a just esteem;
> To copy nature is to copy them.

However rich and however penetrating the insights into man's nature afforded by humanistic studies, they are perforce subject to much variable interpretation and are sporadic to a degree that defeats the aim of constructing an organized and systematized discipline. The most definite and direct avenue to the facts of human nature is that furnished by the methods of the *sciences,* namely, observation and, whenever possible, experimentation, with analysis by statistical techniques. Unbiased and impersonal study of man began, it is true, with the Greeks. But neither they nor the medieval nor the early modern writers were able to advance much beyond points of view, theories, ways of looking at him. Before psychology could come of age it had need to wean itself from that intellectual mother of all the disciplines, philosophy. It had to learn to apply the rigors and the checks employed in the thinking of those most fact-minded of men, the modern natural scientists, whose one value is existential truth.

Was there no science in ancient days, it may be asked? Yes, and no. The Arabs and Egyptians and especially the Greeks did much descriptive work. They mapped the heavens and charted the courses of planets; they made great collections of natural objects, such as plants and animals, from all lands. But they did little experimenting: and it is experimenting that has made modern natural science. They did little counting or measuring: and it is statistical labor that has made modern social science.

It is well for us to pause a moment and—applying psychological insight—note the motives behind the interest in fact. "Fact for fact's sake!" is the shibboleth often heard. But is this all? On the contrary, the intellectual history of the matter is the history of a growing realization since the days of Roger Bacon and of Francis Bacon that knowledge is power, that if you can know the facts the facts can make you free. To be sure, intellectual interests have a *raison d'être* of their own, whether seen in a child's fun with a puzzle or in a research investigator's exciting adventures and risks in hunting out a truth; but it was precisely because this intellectualist passion could be exploited and made to work for other ends that modern science attained its position of eminence. The interest in fact for fact's sake, and the drive behind it, is never the *summum bonum* of any scientist: it is a working attitude that he puts on and takes off with his laboratory apron. When a physicist attends raptly to an orchestral crescendo he most certainly is not calculating the lengths, amplitudes, and compositions of the sound waves impinging upon his ear from (to use James's phrase) the scraping of horses' tails across cats' bowels. When the anatomist regales himself with a beefsteak he is not addressing himself to the fasciculae of striped muscle fibers bound in their sarcolemma sheaths in rigor mortis. And the astronomer gazing upon a sunset is surely not preoccupied with the differential refractions of ether vibrations or corpuscles. To turn the contrast the other way around, the surgeon while actually operating must not consider the personal character of his patient; and indeed in many states he is forbidden to practice on near of kin.

An unhappy misconception of major concern is the ready assumption that since the psychologist adopts the factual viewpoint and employs the hard-boiled methods of the experimentalist, the clinician, and the statistician, he is then inimical to humanistic ideals. Quite to the contrary! Describing and analyzing man in terms of observable and controllable processes and mechanisms does not at all imply any lessening of man's dignity from other angles. It is merely another way of looking at man. The salesman sees a man as a prospective buyer of wares. The teacher views him as something that can learn, and he is properly anxious to know how to accelerate that learning. The religionist thinks of man as a soul to be saved. To the chemist he is an enormously complex combination of carbon, hydrogen, oxygen, nitrogen, sodium, and other elements. To the politician he is a ballot-marker. The human being, then, may stand in any number of contrasting systems of relations; and while we treat him as a member of one system we do not necessarily make any implication regarding his membership in others. To think of man *only* as he is treated in a laboratory is as incomplete an appraisal as that of Jack London's character to whom all life is nothing nobler than "the crawling of the yeast."

Psychology does not dictate to other fields of values. Psychology only furnishes *techniques* by which other values may be *enhanced*, practical means by which man may have life and have it more abundantly, by gaining control over those factors that produce values. The methods of science are non-moral and non-normative; and to psychology as such the terms "good" and "bad" are irrelevant. But for ethics and aesthetics and for human welfare psychologists are busy erecting a solid foundation. As they acquire more and more adequate data as to why this decidivist or that neurotic, this failing student or that unsuccessful business man, behaves just as he does, then the means are put at our disposal for avoiding just such human events and for getting human nature under control. "Man may yet become master of his fate" is a phrase now freed of mysticism, and has become a practical program. And thus the psychologist may properly claim for himself a share in humanistic ideals.

In summary, now, we have noted the origins of the more strictly humanistic interests out of more general human interests. We have observed in the historical panorama of educational practices the frequent re-emergence of the intellectual and aesthetic values whenever man has found security and stability. We have seen also in the psychologist's studies of man a laying of scientific factual foundations for the securing of such values. While it is true that education and psychology are disciplines which are academically distinct in aim and subject-matter from the humanities, the close co-ordination of the three is possible and highly desirable.

Chapter XI

THE BIOLOGICAL SCIENCES
THE SCIENCES IN THE HUMANITIES

Robert E. Coker

1. What are the Humanities?

To write about the importance of humanities for students specializing in science might seem to imply acceptance of the long-prevalent distinction between the sciences and the humanities. On the contrary, I think that the distinction can be based only upon misconception of purposes and practices in good teaching of science. It is my strong personal conviction that sciences take high rank *among* the humanities. Furthermore, assuming that all who try to think on the problems of life need proper perspective, I see no essential difference between the value of education in *other* humanities for chemist or biologist and the need for training in the sciences for lawyer or poet.

A difficulty inevitably encountered in any attempt to discuss the part the humanities should play in a general education is that of definition. What are the humanities? What is a general education? Resort to the dictionary brings less help than would be desired and expected. In *Webster's International Dictionary* the word *humanity* is defined in several senses. Most appropriate for pedagogical use is definition three, reading in part as follows: "... usually in *pl.*, with *the:* The branches of polite learning regarded as conducive to culture." Naturally it depends upon who does the "regarding." We want to know also what is actually "polite" and what may be "conducive to culture." We turn, then, to the pertinent definition of *polite:* "Of, pertaining to, or characteristic of highly civilized or cultivated persons; belonging to an advanced culture—as *polite language or arts.*" The definition is clear enough only if we beg the question by assuming that the sciences are not *polite* learning or that acquaintance with modern science is not characteristic of highly civilized or cultivated persons. *De gustibus non est disputandum.*

Presumably each individual must entertain his own conception of what are the "humanities.'" At least, however, one need make no apology for assuming that the natural sciences are aptly described as "belonging to an advanced culture." Perhaps they are even "conducive to culture." I do not know what could constitute the "humanities," if there must be excluded any of those disciplines that have to do with the relation of man to his fellows of the past, the present and the future; any of those that have contributed in time gone by, and vigorously contribute even now, to the liberation of the human mind from ignorance, prejudice, and abject slavery to tradition; any of those that drive men toward independence of thought with full recognition of the limitations of the mind of the individual in its grasp of the whole; any of those that prompt and partially equip the mind of man to reach toward its highest possibilities of intellectual attainment. If, on the other hand, such disciplines as contribute toward these great ends do form a proper part of the humanities, then the natural sciences must take high rank in that benign category. Neither the ancient nor the modern languages nor the fine arts, invaluable as they are, have contributed more directly than have the natural sciences to the liberation of the mind, to its stimulation, and to the framing of perspective.

It has sometimes been said that science is concerned with facts, the humanities with values. The validity of such a distinction could rest only upon the assumption that, among the values, we are not to count understanding of the world in which we live, promotion of human adjustment to that world, and appreciation of the beauty of growing generalizations concerning protoplasm, development, speciation, electrons, and star galaxies; that we are not to recognize among the values, the development of the imagination or the freedom of the mind and spirit. If all of these have no place in the category of values which pertain to the humanities, the treasures of the latter group would seem to be substantially impoverished. Here is the dilemma: either the natural sciences are among the humanities or a leading part in the liberation of mind and spirit is left to non-humanistic disciplines.

2. Arts and Sciences

The question naturally arises as to why there should persist such a widespread and seemingly fixed habit of distinguishing certain *fields*, rather than *modes* of study, as humanities, arrayed against the social sciences (which, at least, ought to be *humane*) and the natural sciences. Why should we speak of a "college of arts *and* sciences"? Are history and philosophy, to say nothing of sociology, to be handled as art or as science? Mathematics, I should think, is distinctly more of an art than a science; or is it neither?

And what of the natural sciences? Can they be put to one side, as arrayed against the liberal arts? Can the natural sciences be surpassed for liberalism, in any sense in which that word may be employed? The very origin of science, or its rebirth in modern times, represented a liberation of the human mind from the bonds of "established" authority. Science has acquired whatever position and dignity it now has only through insistent effort to maintain freedom of inquiry and of judgment. It is as fully international as any other branch of learning, and it is at least as devoted to the freedom of the spirit as any other discipline. Science has helped to make a better world—not just a more comfortable and a more hectic world, but one in which there is a fairer distribution of leisure and beauty and responsibility, more opportunity for realization of the dignity of every individual, more real justice and more sanity in thought and action. It is appropriate here to quote from a recent paper by Dr. Henry E. Sigerist, *History of Science in Postwar Education,* which will probably be of particular interest to every humanist. Dr. Sigerist, let it be emphasized, was pleading not only for more attention to the history of science but also for better education of scientists in the humanities.

> History is not a luxury. The knowledge and views we have of our past are the most powerful driving forces in our life....

Science has not only revolutionized our economic life but has also profoundly influenced our views of life, our religion, philosophy, literature and art. . . .

If the teaching of history is to be more than an intellectual recreation, if it is meant to help young people to understand the world in which they live and to play their part in it intelligently, it must by necessity include the history of science, which must become an integral part of all phases of historical instruction.

If the distinction between liberal arts and sciences is without adequate logical basis, yet persistent, the fault clearly lies on both sides. Most probably the distinction arose in part from a certain prejudice against modern intellectual developments on the part of those who looked backward rather than forward. Even now there seem to be educational "philosophers" (not the real humanists) who assume that education is best derived from reading the works of those who lived so long ago as to escape contamination by any recently discovered facts about the universe and man. Such philosophers in education ought not to overlook a possibility that Greek civilization was great, in part, because it was highly modern for the time, and, possibly in part also, because leaders in Greek life and thinking were too wise to pay high regard to any Cassandras, who, even then, may have urged that education could be obtained only, or primarily, by reading "the ancients."

As a matter of historical fact, language, literature, art, philosophy, theology, and law long had the dignity and assurance that grew from antiquity. In modern times, the natural sciences entered the circle of education as invaders, if not upstarts. Necessarily, they broke from tradition. It is the very essence of science not to accept statements of facts or principles supported only by age and authority, not to follow outmoded procedures, and not to assume that an existing status is inviolable. Innovators naturally invite disparagement and even persecution. It is a fact that at the beginning the source of stimulus for the scientists was not found within academic enclosures but only in themselves and in their fellows grouped in volunteer organizations, which in some cases were better clothed in secrecy. The newer social sciences have arrived at a better time, but they still have to win full recognition as being "humane" and "polite."

Let us look at the other side, as the professing scientist may do with better grace. Undoubtedly, the distinction arose and has persisted in part from the overconfidence of some scientists who have proclaimed a self-sufficiency for science. It derives also from the narrowly restricted vision of those who would teach the sciences as if they were useful only to equip individuals for earning a livelihood or to enable mankind to have more gadgets and physical comforts. There do seem now to be those who conceive of science as a competent and sufficient source of religion, ethics, philosophy, and all human betterment. Certainly there have been some who were willing to send out from the university, adorned with a degree indicative of education, graduates who had had twenty-five or thirty courses in a particular science and a few courses in other fields of study prescribed only because of their value as service courses. It is the fault of teachers of science, as much as of anyone else, that many have come to think of the sciences in terms of *vocational training* rather than of education in the broadest sense, and a few even think of science as a destroyer of real values!

A critical attitude is not in itself helpful or to be lightly assumed; yet, if we accept the fallacy of a distinction between arts (in the pedagogical sense) and sciences, and seek its explanation, it is only fair to say that the difficulty has not been solely in the illiberality of professed proponents of the liberal arts, but equally in the illiberality of professing scientists. Have not some teachers of science failed to see their own particular field of interest in relation to the whole body of knowledge? Have we all grasped the possibility of teaching a science as a liberal art, of making our own subject a necessary element in a truly liberal education? Are we ourselves educated with sufficient liberality?

When we try to consider the place of the humanities, whether narrowly or broadly regarded, in college curricula, we face the familiar difficulty of prescribing for a general education. Let us assume a man whose educational career is quite unknown to us while we have intimate acquaintance with his intellectual and moral qualities. He displays high reaches of thought, imagination, and feeling. He appreciates beauty in human expression with pen, brush, or tool. He enjoys the lavish beauty in nature and shows real capacity to read its language. He dreams constructively toward some good end. He tries to play an effective part in making a better future out of the past. I should say that such a person, whether college-bred or not, would have the equivalent of a general education; yet could we even conceive of a person of such qualities who had no knowledge of the natural sciences? Without some grasp of the fields of science, much of the world of thought and imagination, a great part of the beauty of human expression, much of the creative work of past and present and a considerable share of the glory of nature would be entirely closed to him. Certainly, truth, beauty, and nobility are not the exclusive property of those who learn only from books.

One could hardly overrate the value of knowledge of a foreign language which enables the possessor to read in the original the thoughts that not only found expression in the language, but actually helped to create the language. The most neglected language, the one most foreign to so many, is the language of nature, in which, after all, are to be found the sublimest expressions of thought and of order. This language, universally present, is the most difficult to read; it is never mastered. Some great poets and prosewriters have read it sufficiently to derive inspiration and understanding. Needless to say, it is not adequately read in the easy act of admiring a beautiful sunset, the brilliance of autumn colors, or the shapely contours of mountains and valleys. On the other hand, one does not have to be a Bernard, a Humboldt, or an Einstein to read nature's script with some profit. Here is a very elementary illustration. America's first great oceanographer, Lieutenant Maury, enlisted the aid of every shipmaster in systematic observation of winds and currents and temperatures. "Never before," he said, "has such a corps of observers been enlisted in the cause of any department of physical science—never before have men felt such an interest with regard to this knowledge." And this is what one seacaptain wrote him:

> For myself, I am free to confess that for many years I commanded a ship, and, although never insensible to the beauties of nature upon sea or land, I yet feel that, until I took up your work, I had been traversing the ocean blindfolded. I did not think; I did not know the amazing and beautiful combination of all the works of Him whom you so beautifully term "the Great First Thought."
>
> I feel that, aside from any pecuniary profit to myself from your labors, you have done me good as a man.

To "do one good as a man," by inducing him to decipher painstakingly a little of the actual language of nature, is not entirely foreign to the purpose of education.

Another man might be saturated with facts from a field of natural science but ignorant of history and of literature, blind to the creative expressions in the fine arts, and innocent even of the humane implications of the factual knowledge he does possess. Regardless of the adornments of earned and honorary degrees, he would be an uneducated person. In molding the future of a nation, or of an institution, we should not want to be too strongly guided by leaders ignorant of science or by those knowing only the facts and principles of a particular science. Perspective is of vital importance, and that, I should say, is a primary objective of general education.

It is our plea that we should not distinguish liberal and scientific fields of study; but rather that any subject may be liberal or it may be merely factual and grammatical in approach. On the other hand, it is not argued, and definitely not believed, that the teacher of chemistry or biology should be didactic in method. For students in general there must be some better reason for studying organic chemistry and comparative anatomy than merely to gain entrance to a medical school. The humane aspects of science are inevitably revealed in the historical approach, which is so often the best pedagogical technique in introductory courses. The sciences have, indeed, played a strong part in the vanquishing of ignorance, prejudice, superstition, and cruelties as features of everyday life. If that fundamental fact should be discovered by the unwary student, surely no great harm would be done. The ivory tower has its place; but is it any more beautiful and fitting as a home for the scientist than it is for the most aristocratic humanist?

3. Education in the Past and the Present

We used to be reminded by commencement speakers that the word education came ultimately from the Latin *educere,* meaning "to lead out." In the process of education one is led out into a wider world of literature, ideas, imagination, and feeling. I sometimes think that certain orators on such occasions really meant, not that we were led *out,* but rather that we were led *into* a secret retreat—the sanctum of the seven mysteries. There we could have the intellectual and emotional thrills reserved for the chosen few who were to be the priests of the race. At any rate, the function of the universities was to train "leaders."

The idea of being led out by education to a wider intellectual and spiritual world seems unimpeachable if it be properly interpreted. The educated person is really led out to a vantage point that permits a view of a larger part of the whole scheme of things, a vantage point that gives perspective. Now there does not seem to be the slightest reason why only those gifted with a capacity for leadership, even if they could be selected in advance, should enjoy this privilege. If our social order is to make the greatest possible progress, the greater the number of people who can see the various aspects of life in proper perspective, the more rapid may be our progress; indeed the stronger is the likelihood that proper potential leaders will occupy positions of leadership. This is said with all recognition of the fact that a great number of people may be wanting in capacity for perspective or may lack an interest in much that lies outside of a very narrow field of specialization or of service. Such persons may be highly useful, even if their interests lie almost exclusively in the systematics of mosses or of insects, in a particular group of carbon compounds, in the construction of dams, the marketing of bonds, or the laying of brick. In the final analysis, such a person may in his own way make invaluable and enduring contribution to the progress of man.

It has been said often enough that the old-time colleges, in which classical education predominated, were actually professional schools, training men for law, politics, and the ministry. Whether or not the products were well trained from the point of view of a liberal education is, I am sure, questionable. Many of the most successful of these graduates used theology, the classics, and philosophy as tools of trade to much the same extent as the surveyor used his mathematics and the chemist his retorts.

In certain ways those who completed a narrowly "classical" curriculum some centuries ago were well educated. They knew a good deal of history, which is the basis for perspective in human affairs. They were educated in the sense that they had been taught something with thoroughness, had been forced into partial mastery of some fields of thought. They were introduced to the literature in which were stored the thoughts and ideals of the great of all times, and they must have absorbed something of the genuine values that have given to such literature its durability, its power to interest and inspire readers of all subsequent times. At the least, they learned that others, long, long before, had thought and felt, reasoned and puzzled, about the eternal problems of how men may live with each other—and how a man may live with himself.

As educators trying to form plans, we should, however, as I think, look for the evidence that the recipients of college diplomas a century ago actually did more to improve our civilization than is being done now by the products of modern colleges and universities—that they were more effective in maintaining within human society and within themselves those immutable humanistic values that constitute the very heart of life. To me it is not clear that the answer to this question can be in the affirmative. At any rate, I am unable to see that the products of the system of education in the early and middle 1800's were much more competent in solving the problems of human life than are the products of the best universities of the early 1900's. How either group may compare in such capacity with the graduates of the best institutions of the twenty-first century, not even a guess may be ventured: we may only hope and strive.

4. Planning for Education

Meantime, in planning for education, we face the practical problems of what to do about the sciences, the literatures, the fine arts, the social studies, mathematics, and philosophy. We may theorize about it indefinitely; but every year we face literally hundreds of practical situations. A student has come to us or been sent to us. What are we going to do about him? Maybe we should first ask: What is he? Much depends upon the answer to that question. In a slight way we are like a mechanician who is given material and is expected to make something out of it. He may think that this or that is a beautiful or a useful thing to make; but he will not get far in his task until he knows what the material is upon which he works. Of course the analogy is quite inadequate—for the simple reason that the material, the student, is not inanimate nor overly plastic, but alive and virile. Regardless of our plans, purposes, and procedures, he is going to make something of himself; we can only help—when we do. The material in this case is a person, and a person is important and very dynamic.

Indeed, if there is one thing the biologist should be clear about it is that neither the student in question, nor any man, is compartmentalized. He is not just the sum of so many organs or cells or chemicals; he is not a mere combination of identifiable qualities. Each student is a single organized whole, a person with innumerable facets and with unfathomable potentialities—infinitely greater in himself than the sum of his parts. His capacities for development are not capable of precise measurement or pre-appraisal, and this is said with a reasonable respect for the value of psychological tests. We can help him, but we cannot make him; he himself is the best master of his fate. But we should open vistas for him, and not just one vista. This is one reason for a general education.

On the one hand, the person is an individual; on the other

hand, he does not stand alone in the population, in space or in time. Sociologically, ecologically, and historically, he is an integral part of a closely interrelated whole. It is fashionable just now to exalt the individuality of man. The "sanctity of the individual" has a measure of truth, but only a measure. The individual is never independent. Theorize as much as one pleases, no man lives but by grace of his fellows and indeed of the rest of the animal world—of the plant world, too, we may well say. We might go further, of course, to recognize that no man lives but as he is permitted to do so by the elements, by the revolution of the earth, and by the movements of celestial bodies. This is only a crude way of arriving at the inevitable conclusion that the individual, with all his dignity, is only a part of a whole to which he has inescapable responsibilities. He cannot live to himself and be in all fullness a man. The importance of man to himself is not questioned—yet it can be overemphasized. His importance to the whole should have equal emphasis. Should the individual not have some scientific knowledge about the rest of the organically interconnected whole of which he is so small a part—let us say, again, a highly significant part, but, equally, a highly responsible part?

Our problem is how best to open vistas for our students. Personally I am not one of those who think it will be done by merely talking *about* things: *about* the sciences in "survey" courses, or *about* literature and languages—for which "lecture and demonstration courses" have yet to be proposed. We need to *experience* things. Let the student get into the several fields of study by serious work that tests his mettle, for his own information about himself, his capacities and his interests.

If I attempted to outline an ideal curriculum for a general education, I should say that it ought to include some biology, in order that a student may at least sense something of the conditions that inevitably underlie his health, his feelings, and his behavior, that he might have some personal experiences of the methods and ideas of a science that has profoundly influenced modern thought, and, in addition, that he might better enjoy and appreciate the marvelous world of plants and animals. In this world he lives, and upon it he is inescapably dependent. He will not know much biology if he has no knowledge of chemistry, physics, and mathematics. What is more to the point just now—he lives in a chemical and physical world, and the recent revelation of it signally affects the whole thought and life of man. He ought to know something of the principles governing the inter-relations of individuals and of peoples, something about social, economic, and governmental organization. He is a member of a human world; the very etymology of *morals* (acceptable human *mores*) and *humanism* attests man's responsibility to man. He ought to have some grasp of the history of his own people and of peoples of the past, from whom we have derived so much and should derive more. He ought to know something of how other people think or have thought and be able to read some of the finest expressions of great thoughts in the language in which the thoughts were expressed; for language and thought are not incidentally connected. His world is idealistic too; the impact of man upon man is effected at least as much through written ideas as through formal organization; in very truth, the individual today, if properly equipped, can associate more intimately with Aristotle, Cervantes, Shakespeare, and other great writers than with the current heads of government or leaders in industry. He ought to have a chance at the fine arts—at least to see or hear them, and not just read, or be told, about them. He is surrounded by a world of light and shadow, form and color, rhythm, harmony, and beauty. Knowledge of all this, and more, is desirable for all, although it may be too much for a college program. Nevertheless everyone should have the opportunity to get some such introduction to his physical and cultural environment.

As the student's definite interests develop, the individual, according to common practice, goes on to specialize in moderate degree and to pursue supporting studies and some that are assumed to be merely broadening. Now we come to the crux of the original question. What studies actually offer support for any given special interest? For the specialist in medieval history, is biological science or chemistry or astronomy a sound supporting subject? I must leave that question to others.

Those who specialize in science know, of course, that they need German and French. For the biologist, let us ask, are Greek and Latin language and literature, Renaissance literature, or ancient and medieval history supporting studies? The answer depends, I think, on whether the particular individual wishes merely to master elemental facts in a narrow field or wants to know something of the significance of biological science, of its impact upon recent thought. Is he interested in its relation to all human knowledge? As an intellectual, ethical, and idealistic, or practical, individual he may wish to have a little understanding of the broader significance of biological discoveries and theories. What have they done and what may they do to mankind? He may want to see his own science in perspective. For this he requires background. If he has pat answers to the fundamental questions, he probably has not the background. The more background he has, the truer is his perspective and the better he grasps the limitations of present vision—at least, the more he is likely to avoid seeing what is not there.

We have already quoted from Dr. Sigerist. Let us quote once more, without concern as to whether his distinction between humanities and science is conventional or based on difference of viewpoint.

We all know that it is very difficult today to find young people who are equally well trained in the humanities and in science. It was different in the past when the humanities were the gateway to university studies. This is why in the nineteenth century great scientists, and physicians, men like Berthelot, Du Bois-Reymond, Virchow and many others were able to make important contributions to the history of science. When they became interested in the history of their field, they had a background from which they could draw.

5. Academic "Failure"

It is easy enough to point the admonitory finger at American educational endeavor of the past half-century and to say: "You claim to teach men to think and to be humane, and you have put the natural sciences and modern social studies in your curricula; yet you have not made rising generations keep out of wars; you have not even led them to see the obvious necessity of timely preparation to save civilization. Your product was not prepared to preserve the national and international conditions under which enduring values can be kept from submergence by false philosophies and under which a humanistic idealism can thrive." It is easy to make these charges against contemporary educational institutions—because they are true. We ought to admit this and engage in some soul-searching. One might, of course, ask if the humanistic education of the Greeks enabled them to preserve their own way of life, if Roman education properly prepared Roman people to survive the onslaught of our barbarian ancestors. Did the most ideal humanistic educational practice in any subsequent period of history actually turn people effectively against offensive wars and revolution? After all, was it not those who profited by the best education afforded in those times who generally played the leading parts in national behavior that was no better than, and not even as humane as, recent American behavior?

Perhaps it is not the function of the college to teach men how to keep a place for idealism. Possibly a liberal education has no concern with the preservation of the basic conditions under which it can continue to exist. If this is true, then ought we not to bestir ourselves immediately and earnestly to create some other public agency with the function just mentioned? After all, if we are to practice humanism, we have to keep a place for it. Academicians may be logical in maintaining that a liberal education has no concern with the physical, but only with the intellectual defense of liberalism; but we are not very sensible when, in frantic defensive reaction, like dogs recently mauled by a bear, we begin to snarl at each other. One says that as a people we are in a mess, and that it is because we have neglected the humanities or philosophy and favored the natural and social sciences; another says that the humanities have ceased to humanize in a practical way and are overly idealistic; still another complains that religion is losing its vitality.

The trouble about all this is that each group has so ready a rejoinder. The scientist claims that it is science which is saving us, that we found we had not near enough of it, and that no discipline is more internationally-minded and so fully committed to co-operative effort as is science. Just as readily the sociologist asks how we are to maintain conditions of peace without effective social reorganizations and how youth is to be prepared for changes except through social studies. The professional humanist may rise to ask if, after all, it is not the internal and humanistic qualities of courage, idealism, a sense of values, and the spiritual gallantry of individual men at the front that actually bring victory. Nor will the teacher of religion be out of place if he reminds us that a consciousness of relationship to something greater than weapons of war, something stronger than man or nation, along with a capacity to pray, contribute effectively to victory in battle and to success in peace; at least he will not be called out of order by those who have gone through the battles of Europe and the Pacific.

The fact is that, for triumph in battle *and in peace,* there is a place for the humanities, for the social sciences, for the natural sciences, for philosophy, and for religion. Perhaps all of these are humanities in a broad sense. The point is that, if we are to solve the seemingly insoluble problem of developing a liberal education that both liberates the mind and *also* preserves conditions of social, intellectual, and spiritual liberty, it will probably not be done by brick-throwing between academic buildings. Self-analysis might be more helpful: for one thing, we might ask to what extent the several "disciplines" are now really *disciplines* in more than a metaphorical sense. The difficulty may be less with subjects and curricula than with teachers. We, as well as the students, have too little "general education." We have our own ivory towers and the students naturally build their own. Occasionally we find, and generally in a rather painful way, that there is a tremendous world outside of academic walls—and it is not a world of sciences and humanities but a seething and sometimes dangerous world of actual folks, who need more education than we can now give.

Chapter XII

MATHEMATICS AND THE PHYSICAL SCIENCES

Archibald Henderson

I

THE PRESENT PLIGHT of the humanities, coupled with the accelerated declension of the classics in recent years, has evoked an impressive ebullition of enthusiastic praise from countless votaries. These clamant voices have eloquently described the incomparable cultural contributions of the humanities to civilization. This quest for the golden treasures of the past, the Holy Grail of the race's aspiration, in literature, language, and art, has revealed many of the richest attributes and noblest potentialities of humanity. The contemporary battle of the cultures, however, indicates that the scope and perspective of "humanism," so-called, because of its steadily declining appeal as academic program and cultural discipline, stand in need of enlargement and clarification. One arresting end-product clearly emerges—the need for a redefinition, on broad philosophic principles, of humanism, a discovery of the true role of the classics in a liberal education, and a reorientation of attitude and approach toward the broader type of humanism indispensable for the new generation destined to face immitigable crises and disquieting destinies.

In any approach to a new humanism, it is desirable to arrive at a clearer and fuller understanding of the tremendous impact of mathematics and the natural sciences upon contemporary life. We are living in a period of the most creative and sustained thought-taking about the cosmos since the days of Sir Isaac Newton. At no period in history has there occurred such comprehensive and at the same time such minute study of the microcosm and the macrocosm—of time and space, matter and energy, gravitation and electromagnetism, the structure of the universe, the origin of life, and the ultimate destiny of humanity. The world is intoxicated and exhilarated with a sense of the magnitude and the might, the magic and the mystery, of overwhelming and irresistible power bequeathed to mankind by mathematics, science, and invention. The present war has heightened our consciousness of the vast increase in number and efficiency of death-dealing instruments of destruction, and the consequent menace to humanity's future. It is not surprising that a nerve tension, a psychotic dread, is epidemic, especially among proponents of liberal education and humanistic culture who fear lest the returning young "veterans" of a global warfare and the new generations coming to the fore demand a type of education dominated by mathematics, the physical sciences, engineering, and technology.

Momentarily, humanism has arrived at an impasse. A backward glance may disclose the cause of this regrettable situation and suggest the outlines for amelioration. The original division of the seven liberal arts into the trivium and quadrivium has led to consequences now recognized as unhappy. Accentuation of divergence, certain intrinsic dissimilarities between the two disciplines, at first gave rise to friendly rivalry and noble emulation; but in the final event this fissure, which has steadily widened through the centuries, has assumed the proportions of a crevasse. Had humanism first flowered during the period 1650-1750, it might well have been decorated with the names of Newton, Leibniz, and Hooke, rather than with the less eminent names of Vergerio, Aretino, and Castiglione. In order to bring about a real *rapprochement* between the sciences and the humanities, the most promising avenue leads to recognition of their interdependence and mutual needs. The hard and fast philosophic contrast and distinction between science and art as noumenon and phenomenon is the fundamental cause of the present dilemma in education.

II

The widening gap between the humanist and the mathematician, between the artist and the scientist, arises less from intrinsic differences than from temperamental qualities, a somewhat supercilious attitude of each toward the other, resulting in surprisingly superficial estimates. The humanist, seeing in mathematical analysis a purely intellectual process entirely devoid of emotion, looks down upon the mathematician as a creature without heart, liver, bowels (of compassion), or other bodily parts, a bloodless machine which might have been created by some super-Vannevar Bush for the sole purpose of making intricate calculations. For his part, the mathematician is inclined to look with a measure of contempt upon the humanist because, being endowed with the artist's nature, he is so readily swayed by his emotions, affected chiefly by subjective influences, and unable to arrive at indisputable and final truth by reason of the vast number of unknowns and imponderables to be found in the human equation. It is this habitual duplex defect in understanding, a sort of temperamental myopia, which, as F. O. Koenig amusingly puts it, "makes scientists unable to see that artists have brains and artists unable to see that scientists have souls."

A philosopher with a deep insight into mathematics and the process of scientific and philosophic thinking, John Dewey, in his *Art and Experience* has beautifully clarified and illuminated that twilight zone of creativeness where both artists and scientists function. The fault lies in a literal, unperceptive psychology which cannot or does not distinguish modalities in imagination, or nuances in intuition. In both artists and scientists, Dewey rightly maintains, "there is emotionalized thinking, and there are feelings whose substance consists of appreciated meanings or ideas." He gives a masterly comparison of the two modes of approach:

> The thinker has his esthetic moment when his ideas cease to be mere ideas and become the corporate meaning of objects. The artist has his problems and thinks as he works. But his thought is more immediately embodied in the object. Because of the comparative remoteness of his end, the scientific worker operates with symbols, words, and mathematical signs. The artist does his thinking in the very qualitative media he works in, and the terms lie so close to the object that he is producing that they merge directly into it.

In the process of discovery of truth, the mathematician and the scientist experience an aesthetic satisfaction which, if more intellectual and austere, is comparable to that experienced by the artist in disclosing beauty in nature or in the human form. For many there is yet to seek the deeper implications of Keats:

> Beauty is truth, truth beauty—that is all
> Ye know on earth, and all ye need to know.

The most satisfying expression of the aesthetic qualities of mathematics is that of Bertrand Russell, both mathematician and philosopher:

> Mathematics, rightly viewed, possesses not only truth but supreme beauty—a beauty cold and austere, like that of sculpture, without appeal to any part of our weaker nature, without the gorgeous trappings of painting or music, yet sublimely pure, and capable of a stern perfection such as only the greatest art can show.

A profound study of Greek life, civilization, and culture, which yet remains to be made from the angle of mathematics and science as cultural influences, will, it is believed, disclose that the Greeks were scientists—a discovery that thinkers culturally so far apart as Arnold and Huxley announced, perhaps without quite knowing why. The historians who have written of the "glory that was Greece," knowing little of science and understanding mathematics even less, have given paramount place in Greek culture to art, especially sculpture and architecture; literature, in particular, drama; philosophy; and history. The Greeks were pure scientists, and not natural scientists in the modern sense, in that laboratories, experiment stations, and distinctly modern disciplines such as physics, chemistry, geology, archaeology, paleontology, and numerous others, did not exist or had not then been developed. Yet, by observation of the heavens and by geometrical analysis, the Greeks succeeded in developing remarkably ingenious mathematical concepts—chains of circles, cycloids, epicycloids and hypocyloids—for explaining the dynamics of the heavenly bodies, their separate movements and intricate interrelationships. When the fully qualified historian of Greece arrives, equally at home in mathematics, astronomy, literature, and art, we shall discover, in the very texture of Hellenic life and civilization, the deep interpenetration of art with science, of music, sculpture, architecture, the vase and the frieze with mathematics, perspective, anatomy, and design.

III

Until comparatively recent times mathematics has been almost universally denominated the pure science which deals with quantity, measurement, and computation. These, it cannot be too urgently stressed, are the pedestrian, accountant aspects of mathematics which are purely mechanical, and by their very monotony and deadening repetition, are wearying even to the mathematician. The lay mind is seldom brought into contact with any parts of mathematics which are not primarily concerned with enumeration and computation. Many, if not most people, unacquainted with the intricacies, marvels, and subtleties of the higher mathematics, regard it, in the spirit of Sir William Hamilton, as a dry and soulless subject, fatal to the development of the sensibilities and the imagination. Abstract logic, pure ratiocination, are indispensable attributes of mathematics, wherein they are displayed in the most perfect and most recondite forms. Yet reason is not the sole characteristic of mathematics, nor the faculty which particularly characterizes the highest exemplars of the strange composite of scientist and artist. America's greatest mathematical logician, Benjamin Peirce, named conception, imagination, and generalization as the essential features of the born geometrician.

The history of mathematics and natural science is filled with illustrations of the spectacular display of imagination and intuition. The results lie open on the surface; the means by which they are arrived at are often obscure. One illustration continuing through the ages is the work of the image maker. The poet is always the image maker; and the astronomer and the astrophysicist are image makers on the cosmic scale. One need but mention the mighty line between Pythagoras and Einstein: Ptolemy, Copernicus, Galileo, Kepler, Tycho Brahe, Newton, Descartes, Laplace, Newcomb. Not all were makers of new universes; some tinkered with current conceptions and attempted to repair the universe as it was then understood. But all displayed a virtuosity in conception, an intuitive power in projecting fresh images and new mental constructs for the cosmos, which places them among the great imaginative thinkers and poetic creators of all time.

Imagination, fantasy, intuition, discovery by mental lightning flashes, constitute the supreme creative faculty or faculties of the scientist. The great scientist shares this godlike quality on equal terms with the poet, the dramatist, the painter, the sculptor, the philosopher. The sensitive Santayana, who thinks of science as an "efficacious dream," does not hesitate to affirm that it is "in its essence no less essentially fictitious and imaginative than poetry and religion." The most epochal discoveries of science, with few exceptions, are the offspring of the happy conjunction of intuition and experience. In the large, the whole history of science is the record of the successful struggle of intuition, fortified by reason, to penetrate the obscure secrets, and read aright the inscrutable riddles, of nature.

IV

The creative contributions of great modern mathematicians, physicists, and astronomers—Gauss, Lobachewsky, Klein, Poincaré, Gibbs, Peirce, Clerk-Maxwell, Mach, Riemann, Newcomb, Eddington, Jeans, Michelson, Millikan, Minkowski, Compton, Hubble, Einstein, Birkhoff—accentuate the conclusion that science, and in an exceptional degree the one pure science, mathematics, is aesthetic in character and partakes of many of the qualities of art. The interrelationship of the liberal arts, as Mark Van Doren has suggested, has never been ideally perfect, even at some now undiscoverable point in the history of Greek civilization. We should strive for the establishment of a harmonious symbiosis, along the broadest lines, of the two disciplines of the trivium and quadrivium. Perhaps the happiest illustration of such a state is found today in the profession of stage management, where the co-operative fusion of the seven liberal and lively arts is sometimes realized in a form approaching perfection.

All art, as Plato long ago suggested, has a certain mathematical element; for, as he expresses it, "measure and proportion always pass into beauty and excellence." No artist can function successfully, for example, without some adequate knowledge of perspective—the Matisses, Picassos, and Van Goghs to the contrary notwithstanding. Architecture, which represents in its higher forms the successful interpenetration of art and science, is basically mathematical, yet malleable, fluid in shapes of beauty. In his *Metaphysics*, Aristotle expresses a view not unlike that of Plato, quoted above: "The main elements of beauty are order, symmetry, definite limitation, and these are the chief properties that the mathematical sciences call attention to." Measurement, magnitude, and quantity, which in earlier times were accepted as the defining properties and attributes of "the mathematical sciences," have more and more, during the past two centuries, yielded place in appreciative recognition to qualitative values: order, projectivity, perspectivity, elegance, richness, variety, beauty.

The mathematician delights in the "elegance" of a demonstration, an expression implying certain aesthetic qualities in the conduct of the mathematical operation. Conspicuous among these qualities of elegance are brevity, conciseness, originality, economy of materials, imaginative power, intuitive penetration, perfect adaptation of means to end. In commenting upon Locke's description of geometry with its "long trains of consequences," Scott Buchanan in his *Poetry and Mathematics* luminously observes:

> The structures with which mathematics deals are more like lace, the leaves of trees, and the play of light and shadow on a human face, than they are like buildings and machines, the least of their representatives. The best proofs in mathematics are short and crisp like epigrams, and the longest have swings and rhythms that are like music. The structures of mathematics and the propositions about them are ways for the imagination to travel and the wings, or legs, or vehicles to take you where you want to go.

V

In his original and stimulating work, *Aesthetic Measure*, the late George D. Birkhoff has traced the emergence of the mathematical element in art and its growing recognition, not only by critics and historians of art and music, but also by scientists and philosophers, mathematicians and aestheticians. Art and science constantly interpenetrate one another, and at times appear to coalesce and to become indistinguishable from each other. The critic is often tempted to employ the terminology of one discipline to explain another. In describing architecture as "frozen music," for example, Goethe employs the suggestive analogy of the poet rather than the clear-cut dictum of the critic. Ever since the betrothal of music and mathematics was solemnized under the aegis of Pythagoras, they have come more and more into general recognition as united through the underlying principles of ratio, proportion, scales, patterns, harmony, and design. Although falling far short of the whole truth, there is chilling plausibility in the famous saying of Leibniz: "Music is the pleasure the human soul experiences from counting without being aware that it is counting." Dewey describes as the very "canons of science" the formulas into which the innumerable rhythms of the cosmos are caught—of molecule, atom, and electron; of planet, star, and island universe; the very "swing of the Pleiades." As he phrases it,

Mathematics are the most generalized statements conceivable corresponding to the most universally obtaining rhythms. The one, two, three, four of counting, the construction of lines and angles into geometrical patterns, the highest flights of vector analysis, are means of recording or of imposing rhythm.... Today the rhythms which physical science celebrates are obvious only to thought, not to perception in immediate experience. They are presented in symbols which signify nothing in sense-perception. They make natural rhythms manifest only to those who have undergone long and severe discipline. Yet a common interest in rhythm is still the tie which holds science and art in kinship.

VI

It is by no means only the scientists who avow the existence of distinguishable relationships between science and art. Artists, poets, philosophers, historians of art testify to the same effect. Poe's famous essay, *The Philosophy of Composition*, is an analysis of the art of versifying from the scientific standpoint. In his *Rationale of Verse* he conjectures that aesthetic elements of order have a definite weight, and that our aesthetic pleasure is progressively enhanced with increase in richness and complication of design.

Let us examine a crystal. We are at once interested by an equality between the sides and between the angles of one of its faces: the equality of the sides pleases us; that of the angles doubles the pleasure. On bringing to view a second face in all respects similar to the first, this pleasure seems to be squared; on bringing to view a third, it appears to be cubed, and so on. I have no doubt indeed, that the delight experienced, if measurable, would be found to have exactly mathematical relations such as I suggest; that is to say, as far as a certain point, beyond which there would be a decrease in similar relations.

The philosopher Hemsterhuis clearly anticipated Poe and succintly expressed Birkhoff's basic thesis in the profound comment in his *Lettre sur la sculpture* (1769): "The beautiful is that which gives the greatest number of ideas in the shortest space of time." In his original and provocative studies in what he called *Dynamic Symmetry*, the late Jay Hambridge, in an even more precisely numerical fashion, presented the ideal mathematical proportions underlying Egyptian and Greek art, as exhibited in architecture, the frieze, and the vase. A poet sufficiently gifted as a scientist to command respect for his views on art and science, Goethe has pithily voiced the profound truth: "The mathematician is complete only in so far as he feels within himself the Beauty of the True."

One of the most original of modern geometers, W. K. Clifford, has broadly defined science, whether pure or applied, as everything that is, or has been, or may be related to man. The salient objective, both direct and remote, of the scientist is truth; and there are few more exciting adventures than its pursuit. "Disinterested scientific curiosity," asserts the brilliant mathematician-philosopher, Alfred North Whitehead, "is a passion for an ordered intellectual vision of the connection of events." The scientist is always fortified by the consciousness that truth's pursuit is fully worthy (*dignus*) of man's highest effort; and so he fully meets that requirement of which the humanist makes so much: dignity. If we venture to judge the mathematician and the natural scientist from the cultural and humanitarian standpoint, in terms of the value of their contributions to civilization, it cannot be doubted that they are worthy of the high praise popularly accorded them, yet denied them by the peculiar cult of the Neo-Humanists. The philosophers have waxed dithyrambic over the delights of thinking things through; and one of the artist-philosophers of our day, Bernard Shaw, has presented a huge panorama of human life, *Back to Methuselah*, five plays in one, to celebrate the ecstasies of thought. Indeed, he conceives of the pleasure of thought attaining to orgasmic intensity; and thereby vividly reminds us of Thomas Aquinas, who believed that a future of creative thought may be definitely more blissful than the past of merely procreative animal reflexes. Shaw's nymph, just passing into maturity, outlives somnolence and finds nocturnal pleasure in meditating on the properties of numbers.

About science to the scientist, as about art to the artist, there is a prevailing color, allure, and glamour, analogous to romance. For the scientist there is a dramatic quality, dynamic and exciting, in the pursuit of truth. Success in that pursuit procures consolation and reward: a deep sense of security and intellectual dominion. "Scientific thinking,". says Santayana, "involves no less inward excitement than dramatic fiction does." A chief reason for this is that the conclusions of science are seldom if ever final; there always remain veils behind veils, well-springs beneath well-springs, to lure on the seeker, the would-be discoverer. The conclusions of science are provisional; and hence the exciting quest must continue. The pursuit of the ever elusive and evanescent ultimate carries its own thrill. "The old beauty is no longer beautiful," to employ Ibsen's phrase, "the new truth is no longer true." There are always new beauties to find, larger truths to discover and disclose—for the scientist no less than for the artist, for the natural philosopher and the mathematician no less than for the painter, the sculptor, the novelist, the dramatist, the poet.

The common heritage of the artist and the scientist, the consanguinity of the meanings and objectives of their quest, find verification in their not infrequent exemplification in one and the same person. Another argument for a more intimate *rapprochement* between the humanities and the sciences is found in the mere mention of salient representatives of the unexpected, apparently inexplicable, composite of artist and scientist: Goethe, Poe, Echegaray, Schnitzler, Lewis Carroll, Wells, Oliver Wendell Holmes, Osler, S. F. B. Morse, Marston Morse, Shaler, W. B. Smith, Einstein, Eddington, Jeans. America's supreme examples from the golden age of the struggle for independence are Jefferson and Franklin, citizens of the world, classic embodiments of scientific and artistic culture in harmonious conjunction. What more convincing arguments for a broadening culture embracing mathematics and the natural sciences does the humanist need than the supreme embodiments of the harmonious union of artistic and scientific genius: Michelangelo and Leonardo da Vinci? Michelangelo stands forth as a profound scientific student of anatomy and the human form, and triumphant executant in their pictorial and sculptural representation. In support of the affirmation that science is of the nature of art, Havelock Ellis speaks with shattering plausibility: "In the vast orbit in which Leonardo moved, the distinction [between the artist and the scientist] had little or no existence.... The medium in which the artist worked was Nature, in which the scientist works; every problem was to Leonardo a problem in science, every problem in physics to be approached in the spirit of the artist."

VII

In his higher cultural manifestations, man always strives to realize the cosmos, whether material, intellectual, or spiritual, through some *tour de force* of transubstantiation, some fresh communal miracle of the bread and wine. In a memorable address, Einstein has magnificently described man's effort to achieve the supreme goal of realization and reconciliation:

Man seeks to form a clear and simplified image of the universe, in harmony with his own nature, and to conquer the world of reality by replacing it to a certain extent by this image. This is what the painter does, the poet, the speculative philosopher and the research scientist, each in his own way. Into this picture he projects the center of gravity of his emotional life, in order to find there a peaceful sanctuary, free from the dissonances of turbulent personal experience.

One may also naturally inquire why it is that this noble exercise of man's highest and subtlest form of intellect does not achieve more general recognition for its emotive and aesthetic qualities. Surely it is because so few are sufficiently gifted with both intellectual and aesthetic endowment to look into the blinding face of truth. If science itself be but provisional, erecting with infinite care structures which are predestined to furnish merely the foundation for more stately mansions, so too man himself is provisional, incapable of grasping fully the strange, baffling shape of things to come.

If the humanist is ever to understand the scientist and to sense the beauty and poetry and drama of science, he must learn to grasp the inner meanings of science and put himself understandingly, perceptively, in the scientist's place. It is for this reason that the humanist should accept the "gospel according to St. John's"; for in prescribing the reading of the world's great books—in mathematics no less than in art, in science no less than in literature, Newton and Einstein as well as Milton and Dante—the educational pioneers at Annapolis have indicated the general direction, if not the precise paths, the new humanist is predestined to follow.

It is to the poets—Giordano Bruno, Dante, Shakespeare, Milton, Shelley, Tennyson, Noyes—that the scientist must look for sympathetic appraisal and sensitive appreciation. The poet, as critic in the Crocean sense of sympathetic understanding, may yet interpret to the humanist the inner meanings, subtle overtones, and higher harmonies of mathematics and science. A gallant beginning has been made by a poetic genius of our own day, Edna St. Vincent Millay, whose classic sonnet, "Euclid," might apply with equal historical fitness to Newton:

> Euclid alone has looked on Beauty bare.
> Let all who prate of Beauty hold their peace,
> And lay them prone upon the earth and cease
> To ponder on themselves, the while they stare
> At nothing, intricately drawn nowhere
> In shapes of shifting lineage; let geese
> Gabble and hiss, but heroes seek release
> From dusty bondage into luminous air.
> O blinding hour, O holy, terrible day
> When first the shaft into his vision shone
> Of light anatomized! Euclid alone
> Has looked on Beauty bare. Fortunate they
> Who, though once only and then but far away,
> Have heard her massive sandal set on stone.

VIII

One of the most conspicuous consequences of the amazing contributions to civilization and knowledge of the world and man, especially the contributions of the mathematician, the astrophysicist, and the astronomer, during the contemporary era, is the vast enhancement, in philosophic recognition, of the dignity of man. The colossal magnitudes of the giant stars, the illimitable depths of interstellar space, the incredible speeds of the fleeing nebulae, the runaway gaits of the island universes, the apparently accidental emergence of life itself, the concept of an eternally expanding universe, the insignificant position and role of the earth, as the presumably sole home of man, in the cosmos—all tend, under a superficial scrutiny, to accentuate the staggering immensity of the universe and the consequent shrinkage of man and his place therein. Profounder reflection induces the conviction that although, from the purely material standpoint, the earth appears dwarfed to infinitesimal proportions beside the immensities of the cosmos, man himself, viewed *sub specie aeternitatis*, gains immeasurably in dignity, significance, and greatness. He is the discoverer and interpreter; the thinker and the analyst. His is the mighty brain which grasps and estimates the cosmos.

The new teleology tends to elevate the mathematician to a position of lofty eminence in the hierarchy of humanity. The discoveries of the last and the present generations of scientists attribute to the mathematician almost godlike qualities; and give new meaning to the Biblical aphorism that "man is made in the image of God." Paley's conception of the creator as a sort of supreme watchmaker, set forth in his *Evidences of Christianity*, widely influential in its day, is as ruthlessly discarded by the philosophically minded scientist of today as is the concept of phlogiston or spontaneous generation.

In essence, the new ontology is a rediscovery that nature does not act in this mechanical way. In his search for a new interpretation of the meaning of "reality," the contemporary astrophysicist is driven by a wealth of new discoveries to a resumption of the faith of Bishop Berkeley that the cosmos is a thought in the mind of God. In measured phrases of ringing sonority, the good bishop says:

All the choir of heaven and furniture of earth, in a word all those bodies which compose the mighty frame of the world, have not any substance without the mind. ... So long as they are not actually perceived by me, or do not exist in my mind, or that of any other created spirit, they must either have no existence at all, or else subsist in the mind of some Eternal Spirit.

Many centuries ago, one of the mighty Greek philosophers, seeing in the heavens the handiwork of God and in the operations of natural law the workings of the Divine Mind, aphoristically stated: "God geometrizes continually." Today Hermann Weyl sees the mathematical lawfulness of nature as a "revelation of Divine reason," and surmises that the Pythagoreans regarded the universe not as a chaos, but as a "cosmos harmoniously ordered by invariable mathematical laws." Galileo thought of nature as a great book "written [by the Creator] in mathematical language." Kepler, and Newton after him, regarded the universe as irrefutable "evidence of a marvellous mathematical uniformity and perfection in God's work." So today, in the light of abundant and accumulating evidence, physicists suggest the unlikelihood that the universe was planned by a biologist or an engineer.

The discoveries of natural science, the divinations of literature, the theories of philosophy, tend anew to establish an inescapable *rapprochement* between art and science, and to recognize in the Creator both artist and scientist. In a familiar poem, Kipling denominates God the supreme artist, and describes the universe as an artistic masterpiece still in process of execution. In his *Dance of Life,* Havelock Ellis envisions all existence as aesthetic rhythm, a terpsichorean fantasy. Bergson identifies God with a mysterious *élan vital,* the activating impulse of creative evolution. Bernard Shaw images God as an imperfect, aspiring Life Force, striving evolutionally forward and upward toward Godhead, an indissoluble Trinity, three in one and one in three, of Beauty, Goodness, and Truth. This new mystical interpretation of the world and man, God and the Cosmos, this neo-Berkeleyan philosophy of time, space, life, matter, and energy, is beautifully expressed by Jeans in these memorable words from *The Mysterious Universe:*

> To my mind, the laws which nature obeys are less suggestive of those which a machine obeys in its motion than of those which a musician obeys in writing a fugue, or a poet in composing a sonnet. The motions of electrons and atoms do not resemble those of the parts of a locomotive so much as those of the dancers in a cotillion. ... The Universe can best be pictured, although still very imperfectly and inadequately, as consisting of pure thought, the thought of what, for want of a wider word, we must describe as a mathematical thinker.... The universe begins to look more like a great thought than like a great machine.

IX

The wide gap between science and the humanities can be bridged only through sympathetic understanding and an evolving liberalism. Such *rapprochement* cannot be successfully effected until the scientist recognizes the validity as well as the value of conclusions reached through subjective process and until the humanist acknowledges the existence of the aesthetic impulses of the scientist. The scientist who recognizes no humanism which is not humanitarian requires of this curator of the race's welfare, guidance and counsel in handling the great discoveries and inventions which may prove alternatively to be either a boon or a curse to mankind. The humanist must approach the study of humanity in the spirit of scientific research, disinterested passion for truth's discovery, regardless of immediate repercussions or remote consequences. Each must stand in reverence and humility before nature and humanity, deeply aware of man's imperfections and nature's mysteries, conscious of the never completely fulfilled need for sympathy, fraternity, and labor in scholarship, enterprise, and achievement.

Part III

THE HUMANITIES AND THE HUMANISTIC IDEAL AS VIEWED BY PROFESSIONAL MEN

Chapter XIII

MEDICINE

George L. Carrington, M.D.

"Life is short and the art is long; the occasion fleeting; experience fallacious and judgment difficult."—First aphorism of Hippocrates.

FOR THE TERM "MEDICINE" if we substitute in our thinking the ancient Aesculapian concept of "The Healing Art," we have at once a change in perspective and a much better approach to our subject. The broad sweep of its inclusiveness and contacts with other fields of thought and action become evident. Man does not conceive of himself as being a mere series of mathematical formulae, physical waves, electrical charges, or beautifully arranged molecules. He does not like to think of himself as just a structure of cells, however well arranged into organs and correlated systems. He believes that a temple is more than the brick and mortar, the carved wood and stained glass that go into its making. He believes that he is more than the sum of his material self.

The biologist, the embryologist, the comparative anatomist, and the geologist have pretty well convinced him that he came up from the primordial slime. Their chain of evidence is not complete, but it is too great to be denied. Man, so far from being abashed by his lowly ancestry, however, raises his head proudly, sticks out his chest and says, "Yes, but see where I've gotten to." He is certain that there is something in him that has enabled him to ascend in the scale; that there is something that constantly urges him upward. But he has found that one man cannot travel this upward path very far alone. If he tries alone he defeats himself. He has to take some of his fellow men with him or not go himself. The factors concerned with this interrelationship between men on the upward course are studied in the social sciences. The humanities are concerned with man's individual spiritual, intellectual, and aesthetic progress.

Pasteur, after upsetting the religious conception of disease as being a visitation from God, died with a crucifix in his hand. W. W. Keen, in the midst of the controversy that raged after Darwin's *The Origin of Species* was published, found it advisable to write "I Believe in God and in Evolution." Both were holding to something beyond themselves.

Yet consider where the world would be if there had been no Pasteurs, Kochs, and Walter Reids, and no Listers, Keens, Halsteads, and Mayos. Remember, too, the Oslers, Holts, Bantings, and Flemings. "He who has health has hope; and he who has hope has everything," wrote Aristotle. Without them for millions there would have been no health or hope—nay, not even life.

The carefree student in the humanistic subjects reveling in the lofty thoughts of the ages is apt to pity the poor medical student grinding away learning and memorizing fact after fact and detail after detail. The student in medicine reciprocates with a certain contempt for the liberal arts student and his fine generalizations but lack of concrete knowledge and specific skills. He remembers that the physical characteristic that distinguishes man from other animals is the opposable thumb with the resultant ability to do manual work. But breadth of vision with its sweep of thought and specific knowledge with the complete mastery of thousands of minute details are both needed in medicine. So on a percentage basis, if you want good doctors who are not mere prescribers of pills, injectors of ampoules, ablators of tonsils, and removers of appendices, you will find them graduating from medical schools that have high academic requirements for admission. If the proof of the pudding is in the eating, this alone would be justification for thorough grounding in such subjects.

The main objections to such extensive premedical studies have been the time and expense required of the student. Yet in the long run, for the community, the lack of such grounding may be more expensive, and, for the doctor, less satisfying.

There are exceptions, of course. A few people without any formal education to speak of are broadly humanistic in spirit. There are some who no matter how heavily vaccinated with cultural subjects never obtain a take. But by and large the rule holds.

Attempts at healing are older than the race. Organisms have unconsciously developed many biological defense mechanisms. Some of the lower animals have consciously developed others. Man's heritage of organized knowledge of the art of healing dates essentially from the temples of Aesculapius on the islands of the Aegean Sea twenty-three hundred years ago. The priest healers there combined psychic therapy with baths in the hot natural springs, simple mechanical procedures, and keen observation to form a nebula of medical knowledge that Hippocrates was able to solidify. He also set the lofty scientific and spiritual standards that for twenty-three centuries have in the main held the profession on a high plane.

The psychic or spiritual element in treatment had a prominent part until fifty years ago. The tremendous increase in factual and scientific knowledge that then began to accumulate about things medical, as about most other things in the work-a-day world, caused a decided swing to mechanical, physical, chemical, and biological treatment of disease. The age of great scientific discoveries and medical progress had arrived. New things were constantly being learned and a whole host of infectious, metabolic, degenerative, and mechanical diseases and defects for the first time could be cured. Many of the great scourges of the world no longer held terror. Man was learning truth, and truth was setting him free. Too much cannot be said for these contributions to man's physical welfare.

The priest healer was now rapidly becoming just a physical healer despite the fact that man had proclaimed himself something more than a mere chemical formula and group of correlated cells. The doctor, however, found many patients who did not improve under this new regime of medication. There was something lacking in his *armamentarium*.

This weakness was seized upon by outsiders who set up cults that sometimes obtained marvelous cures of persons who had psychic and psychosomatic disturbances, and often hastened the deaths of others who had easily curable diphtheria, syphilis, cancer, tuberculosis, or appendicitis. It was a field day for the

Christian Scientists, chiropractors, naturopaths, layers-on of hands, and faith healers in general.

Sensing the need for missionary work in this wide realm, Dr. Richard Cabot set out to write a little book for laymen about preventive medicine and how to stay well. He wound up with a philosophical treatise on *What Men Live By: Work, Play, Love, Worship*. He stated that functional nervous disease practically never develops in people who have those elements—all of them—balanced in their lives. The Mayo Clinic adopted his idea. Freud and others found that irregularities in sex life and mental conflicts are the bases of many functional illnesses. The psychoanalyst began to come into prominence. Oliver indicated that functional nervous disease does not develop in a person who has a feeling of personal relationship with God.

So the healer is again back on the threshold of an enlarged temple. This new hospital-temple has many new gadgets and altars, with X-ray machines and chemical laboratories, with diathermy and physical therapy, with electro-cardiographs and light waves, with antitoxins and vaccines, with sulfa drugs and penicillin. But he is back at the temple again dusting off the altar cloths and recognizing man's claim that he is something more than himself.

To understand and treat man adequately, the practitioner is beginning to find again that he needs to draw upon all the spiritual heritages of the ages. He must know the thoughts and aspirations, the sadnesses, disappointments, loves, hopes, fears, joys, and faiths of man through the ages. These things he finds in the paintings and sculpture, the music and poetry, the philosophy and drama through which man has expressed his thoughts and his feelings. Most of all, perhaps, he needs to understand religion. In the study of these things the student acquires an understanding of others, and himself takes on added stature. So, thus re-armed, the priest healer is ready to re-enter the newly equipped temple.

On the steps of the temple, however, the healer finds himself face to face with the problem of the integration of himself and his cult with the rest of the social order. It is a threefold problem involving private practice, socialized medicine, and state medicine. Often state medicine is sponsored under the cloak of socialized medicine because it is more attractive under that coat. ("The voice is Jacob's voice, but the hands are the hands of Esau.")

To obtain a perspective of the problems presented in these three forms of practice it is necessary to examine carefully both the forces that have been active in man's progress and the present pattern of living.

It seems evident that man's progress upward has been governed by the principle of the greatest good for the greatest number. Any other controlling rule must have negated progress. This rule is full of paradoxes and seeming contradictions. It is a long, long rule. Experience in the short term is often fallacious. Often what looks at the time like a good idea turns out later to be either a literal or figurative headache. Parents have learned this kind of thing in rearing children. They have learned, many times too late, the terrible handicaps that they have placed on their children while trying to give them advantages that the parents had lacked. It turns out that in such things handicaps are often advantages and advantages are often handicaps.

The indigent are a problem. How much should be done for them? How much can be done for them? Why are they indigent, anyhow? That is the important question. How much should compassion overrule reason, and when should reason overrule compassion? How much can we afford to tamper with the old law of the survival of the fit? When is it a matter of the survival of the favored rather than of the fit?

Suppose that under the present setup our infant mortality rate continues to decrease as a result of the care of the unfit or less fit by the more fit. Eventually in such a democracy as ours the governmental control may be expected to pass to a low-intelligence group. How then will such a nation survive in a competitive world? Will there not have to be evolved some control of the propagation of the hereditarily unfit and some check on his power in government? Should there not be some requirement for earning suffrage, or gradations in suffrage?

Initiative and incentive are necessary. Without them a profession, an institution, or a society stagnates then dies or is subjugated and is replaced by another.

In the last fifty years, however, the pattern of society has changed as a result of the progress made in medicine, sanitation, farming, manufacturing, and transportation. Many more people are living on this earth than ever lived here before. Big businesses and large cities have developed. Many capable people have become dependent upon continued work in large enterprise for sustenance. They are trained workers in highly technical crafts. But employment is variable. They live in crowded cities in close contact with many other people who may harbor disease and spread it. Their water supply must come from a distance and must be free from disease. Their food must be brought from many hundreds of miles. This food must be safe. Some method of protecting the food and water is necessary. Some method of providing medical care for all the deserving is desirable.

Our founding fathers made a mistake when they said that all men are created equal. Such things may happen on the assembly lines of automobile factories where each similar piece is stamped out by an identical die, but it is not true of the human assembly line. Men are not born equal, and if they were, they would not long remain so. Equality before the law is a different matter. Men are not equal physically, mentally, or spiritually. They are not equal in their abilities to provide for themselves food, clothing, education, and the necessities of life. Neither are they equal in their abilities to provide for medical care.

The question thus arises as to the proper place in the social order for the various forms of medical care. To what extent is private practice best? To what extent should medicine be socialized through insurance forms and endowed clinics? To what extent should the state engage in medical practice? If some fundamental fixed principle, some absolute truth, were available, the answer would be easy. In the presence of absolute truth in any field I presume there could be no problem. But truth is always seen as a relative thing.

It is interesting to speculate on why Christ did not answer Pilate's question "What is truth?" Bacon says that Pilate was jesting and did not wait for an answer. There is nothing in the text, however, to indicate that Christ did not have ample opportunity to answer. He answered other questions readily enough. Render unto Caesar the things that are Caesar's and unto God the things that are God's. Sell all and give to the poor. Do not sell the alabaster jar of ointment even for the poor, because there will always be plenty of them, and some things are more important even than charity. Truth appears to be a relative thing whether we deal with religion, ethics, economy, government, medical care, or even mathematics. Einstein settled that last stronghold of dogmatism.

Where truth is relative, good judgment is the priceless ingredient of decisions. For the long course of time it needs to be well balanced. A knowledge of history is a tremendous help in forming such judgments. It is a great pity that more history is not taught by men who understand it and are energetic enough to correlate it: the movements that have occurred and why they have occurred; the causes and effects; the underlying bases in geography, climate, human necessities, and psychology.

Thoughtful men in other fields have left certain observations that are helpful in this connection. Two came from Chapel Hill. Horace Williams, professor of philosophy, was fond of saying that if a thing worked it was true. The catch, of course, is in the time element. It must work for a long, long time; not like prosperity on borrowed money until the time for repayment comes. Parson Moss, of the Presbyterian Church, also had a pertinent comment. He used to say that everybody was in a hurry except God. The mills of God grind slowly, yet they grind exceeding small.

Confucius was going to reform everybody through the state. The state was going into the business of religion. His plan did not work any better than the combination of Catholicism and the state worked. Christ had more wisdom. He knew that the individual is not made good by the state, but that society and the state progress as the individuals that compose them progress. The basis of His approach was the individual. Rewards and punishments were individual affairs, dependent upon the individual's desire and effort to improve himself. Salvation was never forced upon him, though he was urged to seek it.

It would appear, then, that as in other problems which confront human beings, so in medicine the best solution is one that leaves the largest measure of freedom and initiative to the individual. On that basis co-operative (insurance) associations for medical care should be considered just as necessary to the individual as are similar associations for protection against fire and death. Some health problems that because of their scope cannot be handled in either of these ways should be handled by the government. The governmental unit involved should be the smallest possible one capable of dealing efficiently with the problem.

Let us now return to the relationship of these matters to our central thesis. Medicine, whether the healing art of the ancients or the medical practice of our day, is not a thing apart from our actual living, but is integrated into the rest of the workaday world. The health of the individual, the prevention of epidemics, production in industry, the digging of a Panama Canal, the care of troops, transportation in the tropics, and traveling in the stratosphere are all closely dependent upon it. Government, medicine, religion, and education are all interrelated. They are part of our social order, just as the specialties in medicine are part of general medicine. In medicine no specialist can be a safe specialist unless he has had a thorough grounding in general medicine and then has learned his specialty's place in the whole. Otherwise, he is liable to treat a secondary ill and miss the main problem. The same holds true for the medical profession's part in the larger field of living. It must be integrated with the rest of the social order. Here it is that one sees the reason for the student's grounding in the knowledge of human society and of the humanities before entering upon the study of medicine itself.

From either point of view, that of the individual practitioner understanding his patient and himself, or that of the profession adjusting itself to society, studies in the social sciences and the humanities are desirable.

Even after acquiring all the general and special learning that is available, the follower of the healing art will find that the first aphorism of the father of medicine still holds true:

"Life is short and the art is long; the occasion fleeting; experience fallacious and judgment difficult."

Chapter XIV

LAW

A. A. F. Seawell

THE EDUCATION OF A LAWYER never ends. It is on from the time he opens his Blackstone until he closes his office door, or steps down from the bench, for the last time. Indeed, if he has been fortunate, it was begun long before he took up his special training in law. It began in the studies which gave him a cultural background, inculcated in him those humanistic ideals so necessary to the successful prosecution of his profession, and to the contribution which, as a lawyer, he may make to a saner jurisprudence, a more predictable justice under law.

When the college gate has closed and the courthouse door has opened—from then on he will have plenty of incident and opportunity to test and prove those ideals, however acquired. Many years of active practice, and additional years in official legal positions having to do with law and lawyers, have strongly impressed me with the humanistic spirit of the profession and the fact that in its thoughtful and conscientious members this spirit is greatly strengthened by the daily contacts and experiences of the practice. However, a newcomer in the profession will have found little in the study of mere legal rules, or in the history of their adoption, to aid him in the problem of personal orientation. Even the great constitutional guaranties—the Bill of rights, Magna Charta, trial by jury, so humane in their significance—will not appear to him as visible parts of a great submerged pattern of human liberty, the rest of which will come to light in due time. They seem to him, as indeed they are, sporadic uprisings against the tyranny of contemporary power, occasional in their nature, without coordination or continuity of purpose; and some of them already imperiled by the courts.

The forward and upward surges in the law have been born in burning and idealistic humanism, have matured in an atmosphere of curbs and restraints, and, all too often, have been buried in the arid syllogisms of a lifeless and mechanistic formalism. No sooner has the idealist brought to the law the vision of the better way than practical men have begun to crystallize and define and codify the vision; in this process the vision suffers and is sometimes lost under a veil of pragmatism. This is the law as the student finds it—an art which men are forever striving to reduce to a science and which stubbornly reasserts its empiric formulas. Immediately he sets himself the task of mastering this great body of wisdom and lore of a highly technical profession. He finds himself occupied with a study of mechanics, his professors zealously and persistently urging him to learn to operate deftly the levers and gadgets of the law. He finds that not only does the law constantly tend to become an end in itself, but that almost his entire time and attention is devoted to the mastery of techniques terminating in this short-sighted end. Thus, to the extent that he advances in professional fitness and efficiency, he tends to become an astute and expert technician, a mechanic rarely looking beyond the result of his labors to the ultimate effects of those labors. In other words, he develops a technique but not a philosophy. It was this devitalizing tendency of the study of law which Dr. Oliver Wendell Holmes had in mind when he assured the future justice that no man could become really great in the law.

Granting this strong undertow of formalism in the law, if there is brought to the study of law and its practice a strong sense of individual justice and a broad sympathy for the humanities, men can still live nobly and grow greatly in the law, which lets no day pass without bringing to their attention rights to be defended and wrongs to be righted. Just as Jefferson insisted that the tree of liberty must be constantly watered with the blood of tyrants, so this sense of humane values is constantly watered from daily life with examples of wrong and suffering and helplessness. Given a deep appreciation of the humanities, the study and practice of law may well sharpen the humanistic spirit. But barring those rare instances in which a spark is touched off in the mind of some genius of a philosophical turn, the inspiration, and certainly the enlightenment, must come from without.

For this reason I have always regarded a liberal education in the humanities as indispensable to the great professions which intimately serve the public in relations of trust, particularly the practice of law. We know that in such an education there is an enlargement of the personality, stimulation of the imaginative faculties, power, poise, discipline, and useful analogy. But in the study of philosophy, dialectic discussion, literature, art—the culture which marks man's greatest creative achievement in all ages—there is an inspiration toward faith in the ultimate purposes of humanity as essentially noble, an altruism which will make the needed sacrifices to attain them, the spirit which has given a new significance to the expression "*liberté, égalité, fraternité.*" In this atmosphere are created attitudes and loyalties which make for the highest standards of professional service.

Sometimes we become confused as to what is real and what is ideal when no actual antithesis is involved. Humanistic ideals are not an evasive, illusory product of sentiment, impractical in a hard-thinking, hard-hitting, modern age. That would be true if man had nothing to speak of beyond his biological reflexes and genetic behavior; but he has a moral and spiritual endowment too richly inclusive of incident and attainment for description here. Indeed, humanity is not yet ready for the lexicographer because it has not finished defining itself. Into that definition must go all the books in the world, all the philosophy, literature, and art; all of the mines, factories, farms, and battle fields; all of the schools and churches, prisons and palaces, and an undefined catalog of struggle, of failure, and of success; and last of all, all the courthouses, in which men, armed with authority, have, sometimes in sympathy and sometimes with austerity, sought to deal with a humanity big enough to hold all that, yet small enough to be epitomized in its humblest individual. Just in the simple fact that the story is not yet finished rests the case for the humanist: What can man expect of the law and of those who are its professional exponents in his expanding life? Drawing from my own experience and observation of the profession, I believe that the practicing lawyer of today is answering that question, not in the musty clichés of legalistic doctrine but in the newer language of his disciplined humanism. His vocabulary is beginning to include words that are not iconoclastic but are nevertheless unfettering.

Within the range of its assumed control over human conduct, the law touches humanity in almost every phase of its aspiration, motivation, and achievement. It traces with authority the intricate lines which define human relations, determines within them the ambit of the individual and of society. It may, and it does, fix the minimum of social duty and the maximum of social adventure. Humanity, *pro tempore*—that is, until it arises and breaks its bonds, which, periodically, it does—is subject to the law. Yet the manner in which the law has been forged and fitted to this enormous but delicate task is thus described by the future Justice Holmes in one of his lectures on Common Law:

> The life of the law has not been logic: it has been experience. The felt necessities of the time, the prevalent moral and political theories, intuitions of public policy, avowed or unconscious, even the prejudices which judges share with their fellowmen, have had a good deal more to do than the syllogism in determining the rules by which men should be governed.

Society has developed greatly since this description of the law was written. Its demands upon the courts have become more insistent as its problems have become more complex and readjustments more necessary. The pragmatism of the courts, a natural outgrowth of the empirical formulas in which they have traditionally dealt, has in many critical stages of social development put a ceiling on progress which the best current thought has considered too low; has denied social aspirations which might have found room within the frame of existing law; and has approved ideologies, operating in derogation of individual right, which might have been constitutionally condemned. On the whole, society in its forward movement has not been able to lead the courts far from their positions of conventional fixity—their traditional attitude of protecting the *status quo*. They have not appreciably narrowed the gap between law and progress. There is still room there for an ambassador of good will between the estranged camps.

I think this is what Judge Cardozo had in mind when, in 1926, he recommended the creation of a Ministry of Justice to advise the lawmakers and to inform the courts of defects in law and law-administration which fail to promote justice, and assigned the initiative in that movement to the legal profession. However, there is no question that the members of the profession have been vocal in presenting to the courts the humanitarian view of the "social lag" in the law and its relation to individual and social justice, if, indeed, we could conceive of a high judicial officer as indifferent to the obligation of self-enlightenment—just minding the mill while its wheel is still turned by the muddy current of antiquity—overextending precedent drawn from the mechanics rather than the philosophy of the law or from concepts of law and society which were better forgotten.

Popularly, the ineptitude and ineffectiveness of the law as an instrument of justice, where they become apparent, are considered a reflection on the profession. And where, indeed, outside of the legal profession, may we look more reasonably for responsibility in the care and guidance of the law?

We are accustomed to judge a lawyer as we see him in the courthouse and office where his human qualities are more in evidence, rather forgetting his influence as a member of the profession in the formation of public opinion and his direct participation in molding the law. Although the frames of the law were forged in the shops of antiquity and were mainly designed for the convenience of the governing power rather than the distribution of justice to the governed, the law has been greatly reformed in modern times largely by the lawyers themselves, either through their membership in legislative bodies or their creation of public demand by writings, addresses, and the action of local and national associations. One is bound to be impressed with the fact that the guiding spirit of these reforms is plainly humanistic, made in an honest endeavor to adjust legal devices to a nicer appraisal of human values; in short, to make the law a living force in securing human justice and aiding human progress. The statement of the purpose may be multifarious, the result is unitary. There is indeed but one end in view: to find inspiration for the law in the nature and purposes of humanity, which is subject to the law's control; to bring the administration of the law into closer functional relation with the efforts of society toward a better way of living, so that it may not appear merely as an appanage of power.

We are beginning to understand that there is no essential difference between "social justice" and justice to the individual. When society is injured, the individual suffers, and there is a vast amount of misery for both of them when warring groups lose sight of the common interest in the equal administration of justice and succeed, through temporary political advantage, in turning the cutting edge of the law against society's weaker members.

The experimental approach to the major social and economic problems in this country is still typically innocent of the syllogism. How many of the disturbing factors listed by Mr. Holmes may have been present in the creation of the laws and agencies recently devised for their solution is not for me to say. Nevertheless, the situation with which we are now dealing with respect to the insistent demands of modern pressure groups within our social structure is as practical as Runnymede; and, because it is practical, the humanist will look with suspicion on cloister-bred theories, conceived in splendid abstraction, which would achieve a benevolent uplift of humanity *en masse*—the social plasma—and forget the importance, the dignity, the everlasting sacredness of individual man. In any blueprint of democracy, a man is an event, not an incident. He is an end-product of those influences, moral and cultural, through which humanity hopes to reach a higher level, toward which its institutions are wishfully framed. Democracy sees society as a multiplication of the individual. The individual does not lose his flesh-and-blood identity, and should not lose his meed of justice, by being funneled through the dictionary of the law as a collective abstraction.

Our rapidly expanding economic and social legislation, and the multiplication of commissions and administrative boards to administer these laws, have provided new forums of distinctly human interest. Some of these boards are sharply challenged because, contrary to the classic concept made imperative in many constitutions, they commingle the legislative, judicial, and executive powers, and severely restrict appeals. However convenient these powers may be to boards which are essentially regulatory in character, the plain fact remains that in others the more realistic approach to speedy settlement of controversies involving fundamental rights and freedoms smacks of an attempt to dispense justice by rule of thumb; and there is an insistent demand that the jurisdiction be restored to the courts. But while they stand, it must be remembered that to these new jurisdictions have been transferred some of the most intimate human problems which formerly engaged the attention of the courts, and much of the fight for a more humane attitude—often for the most exigent rights of the individual and of society—is in these forums.

It is, however, to the more familiar atmosphere of the courthouse and the office of a country lawyer that I should go to find the humanism of the lawyer at its best.

I think the lawyer who enters the practice with a highly idealized conception of its purposes and possibilities for human betterment goes through at least three psychological stages which bear strongly upon his development. In the first he has a sense of exhilaration, of satisfaction that he has at last reached his first objective and finds himself safely inducted into what he regards as the greatest of all professions. This is a period of intense observation and burning desire. He is anxious for the opportunity to get into the fight for human justice; and presently the battle is on, and his enthusiasms have their day. Then comes a period of disillusionment. Face to face with the realities of the practice through his repeated bouts in court, he comes to realize that the law itself is not as perfect an instrument of justice as he had supposed; also, that respect for law and love of humanity are not the order of the day with many who "serve about the altar," but rather the immediate personal advantage or profit, the desire for a doubtful prestige. All the diverting evils in the philosophy of the opportunist corrode the picture. Next is the period of decision, of confirmation. That lawyer is not merely lucky, he is just honest in his purpose and strong in character, whose reaction is a resurgence of the fighting spirit. After all, his mission is not to ladle out justice to humanity with a golden dipper from an unobstructed and inexhaustible source; it is a fight calling for skill, discipline, courage. There is a tightening of the muscles of the soul when the gage is thrown down, the *gaudium certaminis,* which the lawyer feels in the battle with his peers. If, in retrospect, we find that man at the top of his profession and assured in the esteem of his fellow men, we may know that at these critical stages in his career he was true to his ideals.

All of us who have been some time out of the practice feel now and then a poignant nostalgia for the courthouse atmosphere, the tense moments of great trials we have known, or in which we have been privileged to participate. The thrill of the eloquence of some of the great members of our bar as they made their impassioned pleas to the jury is still with us. Sometimes it has seemed that Justice herself had laid the flat of her sword on the shoulder of the advocate and conferred upon him the accolade of knighthood. Not infrequently, under the spell of such a man we have witnessed a miracle of re-creation, when counsel has exhausted his challenges and finds himself still confronted with an obviously adverse jury. Every man has a dual personality: the person he is, and the person he knows he ought to be and in his subconscious feeling would like to be. It is the task of the advocate to raise the jury to the level of his own ideals, to lift them out of their passions and prejudices into reasoning men who love justice and seek the truth.

In the endless repetition of the same courthouse scenes, one begins to wonder: What is the meaning of all this, what is it all about? At times, when addressing the jury, the present scene, like a dissolving picture, fades into those which are to come, and the feeling comes home that the judge sitting on the bench, the lawyer who is addressing the jury, the jury itself, are fleeting as figures in a kaleidoscope—just men giving expression to their ideals for a brief moment and passing on that office to those who succeed them. They themselves are the temporary, impermanent factors. The real things that abide are the principles with which they are dealing, the frames within which they express themselves, the system, the ideals and purposes with which and toward which they work; we are impressed with the reality of the unseen. These indeed are the permanent, important things. We see at the end of it all a more perfect system for the attainment of human justice, to which the instructions of the judge, the advocacy of the lawyer, the verdict of the jury are but the day's contribution. In a similar way, there are few lawyers who, in arguing important matters of first impression before a court too obviously unimpressed, have not sometimes suddenly been made to feel that the real client is the law, that they are defending the law, and that its downfall through the weakness of their advocacy might have disastrous consequences in the lives of men and women whom they have never known.

A man's loyalties are intensely personal. If they are misplaced, he is almost as badly off as if he had none. The lawyer must make up his mind where those loyalties lie, as an obligation to his profession. The practice of the law has two aspects; in one, which we have been considering, it is a public service; in the other, it is a means of earning a livelihood. There was a time when public sentiment was so strongly suspicious of corrupting justice that no fee was permitted to be charged for legal representation. Even today the lawyer is an officer of the court, and his official conduct is subject to scrutiny. The aspect of his practice as a public service still looms large in the public mind. In that are to be found the humanistic ideals and the loyalties which would discipline his conduct, as well as put his service to mankind on that high plane which insures his personal success in its truest sense. The lawyer who has no higher conception of his profession than a means of earning a livelihood may, in a small way, accomplish that result, and even acquire a questionable local prestige; but the standards he has set for himself will destroy his larger usefulness and imperil the interests entrusted to his care.

Unquestionably, the first duty of a lawyer is to the law. Whatever its shortcomings, it is still an instrument of justice, and next to humanity itself, the most sacred thing with which he deals. Often his offices can only be extended to explaining the law to his client, never to devising means to defeat it. To prostitute the law for any ulterior purpose is to destroy its human value and degrade the standards of the profession. If there are apparent conflicts between the law and the interests of a client, the manner in which they are resolved is often a measure of the stature of the practitioner, both as a man and as a lawyer. No man is more arrogant in his attitude or more ruthless in his methods than that person who has robbed the people of some rights and is goose-stepping toward those which remain. The alignment of the lawyer will be determined by his own conscience and the respect he has for the profession.

Of course, there is shysterism in law, just as there is charlatanry in medicine, and through it the bar has come in for much criticism which, in its want of discrimination, is undeserved. Unfortunately, the wisdom of the law is of an esoteric type, and none can invoke its aid or challenge its penalties without calling upon a lawyer. The fact that the law has a language of its own and that the courts have achieved a cabalistic form of expression and a legalistic way of thinking objectionable to the laity is hardly the fault of the lawyer, although it has caused him to be misunderstood since the institution of this, one of the oldest professions. There are, however, practices as objectionable to the enlightened and conscientious bar as they are to the public, of such long standing as to be almost one of the traditions of the profession, and which have subjected lawyers to jibe and jest, irony and ridicule, from Chaucer to Rodell. The remedy is a better educated bar and less tolerance by the profession of practices which sometimes enter at unexpected levels.

Ethical canons promulgated by associations or established by law will not adequately control professional conduct, or remove the menace to society. Observance of these rules often merely serves to streamline a practice dangerous to the public and unacceptable to the profession. There must be within the lawyer the principle of self-discipline which will give him a high regard for the profession, and the things for which it stands, in the performance of an inviolable trust and a privileged and sacred service, both to humanity and to the law.

A strong humanistic spirit in the profession, which is the outcome of practical experience with the needs of humanity, is attested by the fact that the bar itself has instigated, and its associations have sponsored, many reforms which put service to humanity above considerations of private income. Amongst them are legal aid clinics, the suggested abolition of private prosecution in criminal cases, and the creation of the office of public defender. If the lawyer is jealous of the unauthorized practice of law by corporations, it is because he justly feels that it should be kept to the traditions of a personal service, with all such service implies.

I think there is no finer tribute which the lawyer can pay to his profession or the cause of humanity than his defense of an indigent man to whom he has been assigned as counsel in a criminal case. The protective cloak of innocence which the law throws around a man charged with crime and facing the jury is no more significant in its high regard for truth and justice than the zeal and courage which the lawyer brings to the defense of such a man. In all my experience I have never known the assignment to be declined or the duty performed casually or perfunctorily. The service has been full, unstinted, and conscientious; and such is the feeling of the average lawyer for human justice that he often follows the case to the highest court, regardless of precious time and personal expense.

I am no perfectionist. I do not believe that the teleological purpose in human affairs contemplates any condition or state of humanity beyond which there can be no improvement; the end is not *finis*. The goals toward which we travel are alluring shapes limned on ever-retreating horizons. The road only comes out of the fog as we tread it. As for the law, the end is in the support which it gives humanity in its forward struggle, and in the justice and mercy of its discipline.

Law is the footpath beat by countless hosts of men across the wilderness in their never-ending struggle to reach God.... It is the age-old search for the Philosopher's Stone which, in due season, will answer not only the baffled minds of men, but the longing of hungry hearts as well. (Dillard S. Gardner in *The Law*.)

To meet the pressing needs of humanity today, the law must be revitalized, must shake off the dust of ancient cloisters, re-clothe itself and achieve the common touch; it must march with progress. As Justice Brandeis puts it, it must be a living law. To be included among those who have seen that vision and fought for its fruition is, I believe, the highest privilege of a profession which has contributed so much to the human adventure.

Mankind has trekked a long way since the Renaissance. Only yesterday we were seriously wondering whether the world was not to be plunged into another dark age. Recent events in the battle to preserve civilization have encouraged the hope that man will not again be forced to wander without a light amidst the destruction wrought by his own devices— a renaissance befitting the times. The world left to us for reconstruction will indeed be a new world, with new and varied problems. Surely human values should, in this tragic period, emerge as things of prime importance. In the solution of these new problems, we shall doubtless be found reconsecrating ourselves to old ideals. We shall miss, in this reconstruction, the steady brains and willing hands of many young men who have gone out of this University and similar institutions, splendidly prepared for such tasks, trained in the humanities, full of the humanistic spirit, and inspired by the enthusiasm of youth. They were destined to make the supreme sacrifice in a more heroic service to humanity. *In absentia* they rededicate us to a task now become doubly ours, so that through the resurgent years the traditions of this institution, which they also loved, may live and relive in work and faith.

Chapter XV

BUSINESS

Thomas C. Boushall

THERE IS A STORY about Columbus ending on the note that when he set out on his now famous voyage he did not know where he was going. When he touched the shores of a new continent, he did not know where he was. When he returned to Lisbon, he did not know where he had been.

Despite the probable truth of these statements, he had made contact with a new world. He had set the course for all the wonders that would arise out of this new land and the peoples who would seek refuge, who would here find great expression of their visions and capacities. In this far country the dreams of men would come true beyond belief.

Men in the current business world are somewhat analogous to Columbus in their yearnings to sail westward in search of new routes to commercial achievement. They are not all sure where they are going. Some have touched new continents of industrial development and industrial relationships. They are not all sure where they are. Some whose life span is running out in their days of retirement are not sure where they have been.

Yet it is apparent today in the middle part of the twentieth century that there is a new world with which they have made contact. This new world in commerce is as full of glittering promise as was the new world Columbus brought into the orbit of man's knowledge in the last part of the fifteenth century.

The purpose here is to point out that in the bustling area of commerce and industry, finance and public services, there looms before us a high plateau on which are being implemented the several philosophies contained at once in the connotative ideas, first, of democracy taken in its broadest material sense; second, of the Christian-Humanist principle of the recognition of the ultimate dignity of the individual in its deepest spiritual meaning; and third, of the fuller expansion of our economy as a means of advancing the well-being of mankind.

The discovery Columbus made was not repudiated as a fact or as an advantage because he had merely touched upon the fringe of his new world. The potential significance of North and South America was not discounted when discovery marked out their far reaches merely because the full use of these two great continents had not been totally developed simultaneously with their discovery.

The significance of the discovery being here discussed, wherein through evolutionary economic action we are touching upon the potentially great advancement of the material and spiritual well-being of man, should likewise not be discounted because these great continents of promise have not been totally developed simultaneously with their recognition.

Here is the basic discovery in economics that is rapidly emerging from a concept in men's minds to implementation in actual practice: Future economic expansion is directly tied into the rising capacity of the whole people to consume. Stated in its simplest terms this means that greater production in this and other countries can only be profitably carried on if the consuming power of all the people is elevated by all the people having more money with which to purchase the things they need and want. To that extent, the standard of living of the whole people can be raised; to that extent there is a greater call upon production facilities.

To many this may seem an obvious corollary. But the basic point is that we have already learned how to produce more than the people can normally consume *at their present rates of income in peacetime.* Therefore production is at its peak. It becomes static or falls away unless the people as a whole can earn more, be paid more, and hence can consume more. Only then can we increase production on a profitable basis.

The businessmen of America are setting out to find ways and means of increasing the earning capacity of the total people, of putting more money into the consumers' hands, so that they can buy better things and more of them. This means that business is being oriented to the proposition that it can only hope to grow and expand if it develops and maintains an ever-rising standard of living for an ever-increasing proportion of the people.

While this proposition for practical purposes is immediately contemplated as a part of the American scene, it must in time overflow into the area of all people throughout the world.

Is there black magic here? Is there a sinister motive? Will the people finally become victims of such a program? Is it a practical one to implement, develop, and extend?

It comes to this: Industrialists have seen the rise of American wealth through the installation of steam and water power to enlarge our supply of mechanical horsepower. With the aid of our inventive geniuses they have developed complicated machinery to do quickly and automatically things previously done laboriously and tediously by man power, the power of limb and muscle, of human endurance in back-breaking, heart-wearying processes. As these mechanical devices have multiplied and production has been cheapened, an upgrading of skills has been required to operate them.

People who can tend a machine that will do the work of twenty men can be paid more for doing so than each one of the twenty replaced men formerly earned. This upgraded worker earned more, and therefore could buy and consume more. The nineteen replaced men eventually got jobs running additional machines or went to other work.

Skilled labor needed in this advanced mechanical age has naturally earned more than common labor. This skilled group offers a far greater market for goods than does the group of common laborers or unskilled workers. Hence the simple proposition: To what extent can we put everyone to work, not only as skilled workers, abolishing as nearly as possible common or unskilled labor but how can we keep on upgrading these workers to tend machines of constantly increasing complexity? These men can contribute more and more to values in the conversion of raw resources to a finished, usable state. They can share more and more of the earnings thus created. As they share more, they can consume more.

This process went on for the first thirty years of the twentieth century. The record is interesting. Our national income in 1900 was 16 billion dollars. Our national wealth was 80 billion dollars. But by 1930 the national income had risen by five times and stood at 80 billion dollars—an annual income equal to our total national wealth thirty years before. The national wealth had risen five times and stood at 412 billion dollars.

It is this record that gives promise now to the orientation of our economy upon this developed thesis. It was not developed by intention. It is merely a demonstration that holds promise for the future. But today it has been recognized as the basis upon which a vast expansion of our economy can occur.

It is a pleasant phenomenon to behold. Business faces the task of providing the means to elevate the people to constantly increasing levels of well-being in order that business may find its larger expression! The realization of business in its greater terms can in business' own concept of itself be fulfilled, if the people are to be served, if the needs of the people are to be recognized, if the needs of the people are to be met in greater measure.

It is a happy prospect to view because it is an evolution of the processes of business. This concept does not stem from a religious idea drawn from without the realm of economics and superimposed upon it. It does not derive from a political formula or a system of government or of bureaucratic control. It wells up from within the burgeoning processes of economics. It heads in the direction of a central theme toward which religion and government in their sublimated ideologies also have set their compasses.

As this concept of expanding business depends for its success exactly upon the degree to which it carries before it the rising well-being of all the people, so the Christian-Humanist ideal is the revelation and recognition of the ultimate dignity of the last and least individual. Democracy in its modern fuller meaning of material satisfactions for all and the freedom to express the totality of one's inherent capacities, finds complementary expression in the Christian-Humanist principle and in the success of the new economics.

No one of these three factors in human fulfillment has really forced evolutionary progress upon the other. Each has wended its own way through the long maze of man's history. As these three currents flow toward a center where they may all one day merge to effect man's liberation and fullest expression, they each become more and more similar in purpose, in operation, and in effect.

This fact is made very clear if we take the new economic concept apart at this point to see that there is a quick ceiling to the limited idea of upgrading the skills of most of the people.

When men and women are able to earn enough money to satisfy their normal wants of food, shelter, recreation, and relaxation, and some degree of indulgent luxury, they have a tendency voluntarily to limit their working hours. Their desire to improve their earning capacity wanes. Satisfaction of wants sates also the desire for acquiring added skill and greater earnings through sustained effort.

The enlightened businessman has seen that material well-being, achieved through the simple process of a greater use of horsepower, labor-saving devices, and upgraded mechanical skill to operate complicated machinery, is not enough. He sees that there is an equal need to educate the cultural appetites of all the people, that they may want not only better homes and environment, better food, and nicer clothes, but they must want higher educational levels, broader horizons of travel, more books to read, a higher quality of moving pictures, as well as more frequent opportunities to hear good music and see better renditions of all forms of art.

Businessmen know that the elevation of cultural appetites brings on more desire for recreation and leisure, more inclination to question the backdrop of the cosmos. Culture and leisure stimulate the desire to pause and contemplate the aspects and attributes of the universe.

And so there stems out of the material a positive stimulus to the spiritual elevation of man. Fanatics and crusaders, zealots and devotees, often seem not to realize that it is hard to preach a spiritual gospel successfully to a hungry animal. Ethics and aesthetics are of but small concern to men, women, and children who are cold, forlorn, drab, tired, and worn with the effort to sustain life with no reward beyond the questionable boon of actual existence. If we are to bring the whole of mankind into a contemplative, appreciative concept of the spiritual nature of the individual human being, we must first ease his urgent and insistent effort to earn a living. We must afford him leisure and stimulus to develop his curiosity as to his origin, his reason for current existence, and his possible posthumous destination. If we are to do this for one, we must do it for all. If, in our Christian and humanistic concepts, we glorify the full dignity and magnificence of the individual, we must face the fact that we cannot choose among men which one or which group is to be selected. We must seek to bring fulfillment to the last and least of mankind.

Here we see the economic process seeking its own salvation, its own rising importance through the approach toward the cultural and spiritual evolution of mankind. It thus approaches in its successful implementation the basic principles of Christian humanism. In its realization it overruns the concept of the fuller expression of the democratic ideal.

It has been heretofore hard to see how Christian humanism could be practically carried out in a cold, commercial atmosphere of hard and successful economics. It appeared that the church and school must conquer the counting house, the executive manager's office, the power company's board of directors, and unbelievably put the spirit of human brotherhood in the circulation of commerce's very blood. Too, it was difficult to find a way to implement the best of the democratic ideal unless we surrendered to some form of communal ownership of all our productive facilities and shared its output through governmental procedures.

But business or economic processes are themselves opening the paths by which the Christian-Humanist principle and the democratic ideal can penetrate its area, not as an impractical imposition upon it that might alter, hamper, or defeat it, but as a further expansion of the function of all three human endeavors on the material and spiritual levels of economics, political concepts, and spiritual ideals.

These are prospects and not realizations. We have merely touched upon the fringes of these vast new continents of promise, just as Columbus only landed on the islands off the mainland of the Americas. There are yet charlatan doctors, shyster lawyers, corrupt politicians and teachers, hypocritical priests, crooked businessmen, and exploiters of the people. They represent the lower or infrared edges of our social organization.

There are the devoted men of good will who in each calling and profession, each trade and industry, seek to fulfill and find ways of implementing the fuller economic life of all the people, who seek to put spiritual doctrines into practice and try sincerely to find political formulas that make for world-wide union of all men striving for universal well-being. These are the souls who represent the ultraviolet or upper edges of our social organization.

There exists, in between, the great body of people who must evolve through time into the upper reaches of a sublimated society. We are in no sense touching upon a millennium. We are not approaching any form of Utopia. The Kingdom of Heaven isn't just around the corner here on our rather messy earth.

But perhaps with greater clarity than at any time in man's history there is a more universal understanding of the idea that working for the well-being of the whole of mankind is the most profitable way possible for the economic function to express itself at the greatest profit to itself and to everyone encompassed within its area of action. Perhaps we can see more clearly today a growing relationship or identity among the ideals contained in each of man's basic concepts of politics, economics, education, and religion.

Of this much we can perhaps be surest—there has appeared in the economic world a rainbow comparable to the one Noah saw when he came out of the Ark on the summit of Mount Ararat. He heard a voice as recorded in Genesis: "And God spoke unto Noah, saying... 'the waters shall no more become a flood to destroy all flesh.'" Perhaps we, too, can stand under the great reaches of a rainbow in our modern sky and hear a voice: "The forces of this earth shall no more become a yoke upon the shoulders of mankind to enslave all flesh."

For one end of this rainbow rests upon the concept of social gains for all people, while the other rests on the basic principle that every effort of man shall have a sound economic base. The conflict we have with us today stems from the extreme leftists who advocate social gains, no matter what their economic unsoundness and our inability to support them, and from the extreme rightists who insist upon a sound basis for our economy, no matter that all social gains are denied. Both groups are equally dangerous to the permanent well-being of our society and our economy. For if either should prevail, we shall in time wreck our total social and economic organization.

But we have seen that our rainbow of promise rests at one end upon realistic social gains of mankind. The other rests upon a successful economic principle. Definite forward movement in the progress of man seems assured when the leaders of industry express their faith in an economy that looks for the measure of its fullest expression in terms of the social gains it provides.

The humanistic spirit and business have found a larger measure of common expression in the first four decades of the twentieth century than in any other far longer era of man's efforts here on this earth. The interruptions of a first and a second world war and a prolonged depression running throughout the decade of 1930 to 1940 have retarded the development of business as an instrument in the evolution of man's progress. But these interruptions have in no sense dampened the desire of enlightened business leadership to express through our economy this belief in rising levels of material and spiritual well-being for our people.

Chapter XVI

JOURNALISM
THE HUMANITIES AND
THE COMMON MAN

Gerald W. Johnson

IF THE HUMANITIES are defined in the old manner as those mental disciplines included in the trivium and quadrivium and if the common man is understood as meaning the sort of man most frequently encountered—as in the phrase "common or garden variety" of flowers or vegetables—then the answer to the question, "What are the humanities to the common man?" is short and simple. It is, "Nothing whatever."

The common man in the United States is not an illiterate, but neither is he a college graduate, nor even a high school graduate. The statistical evidence is not conclusive, but in all probability the largest single group in the population stands educationally at about the eighth-grade level. Yet even if this were established beyond debate it would not be quite definite for the purposes of the present discussion. We dislike to admit it in a democracy, but the bald fact is that there are people who simply do not count, socially or politically. They do not vote, they do not enter into discussions of public affairs, they do not generate ideas of their own nor furnish support to the ideas generated by others. That part of the populace below a certain educational and intellectual level is inert. As producers and consumers they have some economic importance, but their influence upon the development of civilization in the republic is imperceptible.

If these ciphers are disregarded, it may be that the educational level of the common man is somewhat higher—say somewhere between the first and second year of high school. This is a liberal estimate, but if it is accepted, at least for the purpose of argument, the answer to the question remains the same. The common man has never heard of the trivium and quadrivium, and while he may know the names of some of the seven disciplines and may even have attended classes in geometry, logic, and Latin, they usually represent to him merely ordeals, incomprehensible in purpose and inconsiderable in effect. To him the humanities, as such, simply do not exist.

But the matter assumes another aspect if the question is understood as relating to the indirect effect upon the life of the common man of the possession of the humanities by others. As a rule he is not intellectually arrogant. He is willing to accept opinions from those whom he has reason to respect; and if these leaders are trained in the humanities, those disciplines are not without influence upon the great mass of the people. It is necessary only to cite the prodigious influence upon Americans of the recorded utterances of the Founding Fathers to understand this. If the right persons are trained in the humanities, the fact means something, nay much, to the common man although he never heard of them.

Apparently, then, the question reverts to the effect of the humanities on the uncommon man, the highly cultivated individual who is in the minority in all societies. But this is not quite true—or, perhaps, one should say, it is not the whole truth. It does touch the effect of these disciplines on the uncommon man, but only in his role of transmitter, not in that of an absorbent. There are intelligences, some of them extremely acute, that absorb learning as sand absorbs water, without apparent effect. Their inner lives are enriched, no doubt, but the outside world is not affected.

It is impossible to cite the perfect example of this type because the perfect example must inevitably remain unknown and unsuspected. An imperfect example is Henry Adams, who did, indeed, make a generous return to society for his education in his *History of the United States,* but who was so exasperated by the cold reception of that work that he thenceforth devoted his energies to the cultivation of his own intelligence without any further effort at leadership. The classical antitheses, no doubt, are Desiderius Erasmus and Martin Luther; historians are pretty well agreed that Erasmus possessed the more powerful intellect and by far the better training, but as to the effect on history of the two men any comparison is ludicrous.

What the humanities mean to the common man in the United States is, therefore, to be determined by examination of what those who are acquainted with the humanities—and they are uncommon men—have done with their training. If the survey is confined to recent history, an adequate answer is pretty hard to find. If one goes back to an earlier day the case, of course, is different. One need do no more than mention the names of Jefferson, Hamilton, Madison, Marshall to illustrate the prodigious effect that the humanities, as reflected by those minds, have had upon the thinking of all Americans.

But if the question is confined to, say, the last fifty years, the answer is by no means so simple. Within the last fifty years, in fact, the uncommon man has been by no means as strongly affected by the humanities as he was a hundred and fifty years ago. The scientific method had been so extraordinarily effective during the previous century that the man of unusual intellectual attainments was overwhelmed and, as a rule, carried away. Investigation had been incomparably more fruitful than reflection; so it was natural, perhaps, indeed, inevitable that alert minds should turn to investigation exclusively. It may have been equally inevitable that reflection should fall not into disuse only, but also somewhat into contempt.

Minds of a certain type, it is true, adhered to the old order, but it is impossible to call them first rate. Study of the humanities has been relegated too much to the authoritarians. To some extent this was true long, long ago. Jefferson's contemptuous remark that he was worried by his inability to understand the Platonists until it occurred to him that no rational man can understand nonsense is evidence of it. The Platonists were simply authoritarians. To them, the fact that Plato said it, or plainly implied it, was proof that it is wisdom. The fact that there is a great deal of nonsense in Plato they were unable to admit without abandoning their whole intellectual system.

Unfortunately for them, though, it is a fact. Plato wrote a great deal of nonsense, not because he was a fool but because he was ignorant. He was the most learned man of his time, but in his time the whole world was ignorant. Plato carried reflection to the extreme limit it could attain with the body of knowledge then available as a basis for reflection. The disgrace of our age is that with an immensely enlarged body of knowledge we have been unable to extend philosophy much beyond the mark that Plato reached.

For three hundred years this has not bothered the scientists. To them it was simply an indication that reflection had exhausted its resources more than twenty centuries ago, leaving no method of extending the boundaries of knowledge save that of investigation. To this they were committed anyhow, so as long as it continued to produce results, why should they worry? They didn't worry. They went along happily, industriously, and so successfully that they ended by establishing an absolutism over the world of ideas that not only deposed philosophy but almost erased its memory from the mind of the common man. For the last two generations he has hardly been aware that there exists or ever existed any body of learning other than scientific learning.

But of late the evidence has been increasing that the scientific method is approaching the point at which its investigations threaten to become as sterile as the most abstruse speculations of the later Greeks. When modern physics announces the conclusion that all that exists is no more than a curve in space it has produced a statement that may be as true, but certainly is as useless as the theories of the early atomists. Truth that is incomprehensible is valueless to a practical world.

This is somewhat less than reassuring to the common man. His control over his environment has been vastly extended, but it is still so far from complete that his survival as a species is by no means guaranteed even for the predictable future. Yet if philosophy reached the extreme limits of its usefulness two thousand years ago, and if science is plainly approaching the limits of its usefulness now, what is left to encourage him to continue to rely upon the aid of reason for the betterment of his condition? Science and philosophy are the only two intellectual instruments he has ever possessed. If one is worn out and the other beginning to fail, in what direction is he to turn?

The answer is not difficult. In fact, it seems to be staring us in the face. When reason fails, the common man is not left without recourse. There is always superstition, always the reversion to the belief in magic. It served humanity after a fashion for thousands of years before either science or philosophy appeared. It served in a very poor fashion, to be sure, but it served to prevent men from falling into complete despair.

Any doubt that so-called civilized men are capable of reverting to it should be dispelled by one look at Germany. Nazism is necromancy undisguised except by the substitution of "fuehrer" for "necromancer." Moreover, for a while it worked. It proved ruinous in the end, but momentarily it did lift Germany from despair and did develop in the nation an energy that very nearly ruined the world.

But no official magician can tolerate any rival wonder-workers. Hitler's assault on the German intellectuals was inevitable because superstition is never passive; hence the reversion of the common man to trust in magic rather than in mind would not mean merely the neglect of science and philosophy, but the waging of relentless war upon them. The German attack, being localized, could not mean the extinction of science and philosophy; but it could, and it did mean the extinction of scientists and philosophers in horrifying numbers. What a more widespread attack of the same kind would mean one shudders to think; but it is a matter of which all men who still prefer to be guided by reason rather than by emotion should think. And they, like the celebrated Captain Flagg, should think fast.

For it is nonsense to assert that it can't happen here. In this country and in England for twenty years people who were generally called "intellectuals" comforted themselves with the strange delusion that the madness of Germany had a purely material basis—the alleged injustices imposed upon that nation in the Treaty of Versailles. It is incontestable that the treaty did include some injustices, although by no means as many as the intellectuals asserted; but as peace treaties go, it was far from a bad one. For example, by comparison with the peace imposed upon the Southern states of this Union after the Civil War, the Treaty of Versailles was a monument of magnanimity.

Between 1865 and 1869 a vigorous effort was made literally to extirpate the civilization of the South; between 1919 and 1924 even more vigorous efforts were made by her late enemies to re-establish and rehabilitate the civilization of Germany. Yet Germany went mad and the South did not.

From 1919 to 1939 it was not convenient for the intellectuals to remember this. It was much more comfortable to lay all the blame on the vindictive old men at Paris, or on Woodrow Wilson, or on Lodge and the Senate. For if the steadiness of the South under far worse material conditions was in any measure attributable to the intellectual climate of 1865, then the intellectuals themselves must bear some responsibility for what happened after 1919. A science that leads only to war and a philosophy that doesn't lead at all are not preferable, in the eyes of the common man, to a superstition that may lead to ruin eventually, but that at least affords a tremendous, if temporary, vitality, an enormous lift of the spirit, such as Germany experienced for ten years.

> Man, being reasonable, must get drunk—
> The best of life is but intoxication—

The Byronic cynicism may be deplored, but its truth is not to be denied when the common man finds himself living in an arid intellectual climate which is, for him, a climate in which neither science nor philosophy furnishes leaders who can speak boldly and plausibly of the meaning of existence.

There is endless chatter about the social, political, and economic reforms essential to prevent the spread of fascism—probably, as Huey Long predicted, under the name of anti-fascism—to this country after the war. A good deal of it is directly to the point, no doubt, for our system can certainly stand a great deal of reforming. But next to nothing is said about intellectual reforms, perhaps because it is intellectuals who do most of the talking and who discuss raising themselves by their own bootstraps.

The fact remains, though, that it is more than doubtful that political and economic breakdowns alone account for the rise of fascism in Germany and Italy. Spengler began to write before the First World War and the despair he reflects had prevailed long prior to the outbreak of hostilities. It prevails elsewhere than in Europe; Brooks Adams fell a victim to it a generation ago in this country, and it is to be doubted that it has ceased to spread.

Is there any force in the humanities to immunize us against it? That is not for the common man to say. He does not know the humanities; he knows people who have cultivated them and it is through the people that he judges the disciplines.

But he is keenly aware that in some of the ways in which they have been presented there is no antitoxin against despair. Textual criticism, no matter how rigorous, and ancestor-worship, no matter how eloquent, are of no avail. What Plato actually said is not of the smallest importance to the common man. Neither, indeed, is what Plato actually meant, unless he meant something apposite to the life of today.

Rhetoric is listed among the humanities, but in recent years it has borne such a bad name that its very presence there is regarded as something of a scandal and nice minds ignore or slur it over, much as nice people ignore or slur over great-grandfather's bastards in discussing the family tree. That is because rhetoric has become known as a device of tub-thumpers, the use of flowers to conceal the absence of thought.

There was a time, though, when rhetoric meant the science of clear and persuasive statement, which indubitably is a thoroughly respectable study. It is not beyond the power of imagination to conceive that perhaps the humanities might have more effect upon the life of the common man today if this, the least reputable of their number, had not sunk to such low estate. For it is characteristic of the scientific age that it requires more than textual accuracy and an appeal to authority in a statement it is prepared to accept as clear and persuasive. In order to be clear, a statement must be attuned to the mental habits—if you prefer, the mental mannerisms—of the hearer. In order to be persuasive, it must interlock with his experience.

To what extent has the teaching of the humanities for the past fifty years satisfied these requirements? To a pretty small extent, in the opinion of the common man. Investigation, body and soul of the scientific method, has proceeded with giant strides. Never in history have scholars possessed such admirable texts of ancient sources. Never has the world had finer transcripts, translations, comparative analyses, and critical studies. Better, perhaps, than any previous generation since his own we know what Plato actually said; perhaps we know with equal accuracy what it meant to him.

But does anyone dare maintain that imagination, body and soul of the philosophic method, has advanced at anything like an equal pace?

The geocentric universe of Plato's time is gone—definitely wiped out, abolished, eliminated, never to be restored. But it was not destroyed by mere denial. It was replaced by a theory that, confusing as it may have been when it was first propounded, is essentially clearer and more persuasive. The anthropocentric world of Plato's time has also been demolished, not by denial, but by the substitution of a theory that is better attuned to the mental habits and interlocks better with the experience of the common man.

But the teleological basis of Plato's thinking has been largely abandoned without the substitution of any clearer and more persuasive theory. As far as the scientists are concerned, the abandonment was justifiable because questions of purpose and design are irrelevant to the investigation of phenomena, and science has neither time nor energy to waste on irrelevancies. In the opinion of the common man, however, it is the main business of philosophy to deal with such questions. Geocentricism and anthropocentrism could be and have been investigated by the methods of science. In both cases science has offered something clearer and more persuasive; therefore, as far as the common man is concerned, those concepts are dead, and science, incidentally, is vindicated. When called upon it delivered the goods, and that is that.

Teleology, however, is a concept not open to investigation by the scientific method. That method has, indeed, destroyed some of the bases on which Plato established his argument, so it is evident that the Platonic concept is no longer tenable in every detail. Nevertheless, it has not been altogether demolished because nothing clearer and more persuasive has been offered by philosophy to replace it. Philosophy, called upon, has not delivered the goods and the common man accordingly holds it in low esteem.

His estimate of it is not raised by his discovery that it is men working on the extreme range of scientific thought who now seem to be most interested in teleology. The mathematicians exhibit a tendency to edge over into philosophy; and why not, if nobody else is working there? Still, they do not greatly impress the common man. For instance, Sir James Jeans's announcement that God is a mathematician astonished the commoners immeasurably—not the announcement, but the mathematician's evident belief that it is a new and daring idea. The common man's reply is, naturally God is a mathematician. He is so by definition. If He weren't the supreme mathematician He wouldn't be God. By definition He is also the supreme chemist, architect, physicist, astronomer, physician, artist, philosopher, and everything else.

But the question in the common man's mind is, why is it necessary for mathematicians, or mathematical physicists, to express any opinion on the present direction of the movement of the human spirit as long as we have humanists who have devoted their lives to study of this very question? History is one of the humanities, including the history of ideas and the history of aesthetics. Why should anyone else feel the need to form an opinion, if that of the historian is sufficiently clear and persuasive?

It is the belief of the common man that while the science of history—and for "history" you may, with reasonable adaptation, read music, drama, epic poetry, or any of the rest of the liberal arts—has advanced by leaps and bounds, the philosophy of history has hardly moved since Thucydides. It is probably an erroneous belief. Such a man as Toynbee, for example, knows many things, and important things, that Plutarch didn't know about the nature and meaning of history. But as long as the belief prevails it tends to keep the common man's interest in the humanities at a low and languid level.

But if the belief is erroneous, how did it arise? It is at least arguable that its rise had some connection with the decline of the humanists' interest in rhetoric, in the old sense, that is, the science—or art—of clear and persuasive utterance. About rhetoric in this sense there is nothing authoritarian, no set of rules that can be learned once and for all. To speak clearly and persuasively one must know, first of all, the hearer, because what is clear and persuasive to A may easily be confused and dubious to B. That is to say, the student of rhetoric is primarily a student of man, specifically of contemporary man. The modern humanist may be steeped in the lore of the ages, but if he knows none of the lore, nor even the language of this week, he knows no rhetoric and cannot speak clearly and persuasively to the common man.

I hold no brief for this person. I do not contend that it is right for the common man to be what he is. I merely report the facts. One fact is that to the common man humanity consists of himself and his contemporaries, such persons as are walking about the earth today, all of them talking, most of them acting, and some of them thinking at this particular moment in time. Plato? Well, he will concede that Plato was a part of humanity once, but he isn't any more. What he thought and said, therefore, is irrelevant *unless* it can bear translation into the verbal and mental idiom of today without becoming nonsensical. Please note that the verbal idiom is not enough; it must be translated also into the mental idiom, which is affected by all that science has accomplished since Plato wrote.

This has been done with no more than indifferent success; hence the attitude of the common man toward the humanities is indifferent when it is not critical. The trouble with the humanities, in his estimation, is that they are not human. In this he falls into the fallacy of assuming that because they say nothing to him, therefore they have nothing to say about the meaning of human existence. It is possible, of course, that this is true; but it is also possible that they have plenty to say but do not know his language.

This explanation is a slight improvement over the other, and for that reason optimists will prefer it, although it has no lack of both comic and tragic elements. It is tragic that philosophy is ineffective at the moment when science seems to be approaching the limit of its effectiveness, for if both fail the field is left clear for superstition. But it is comic to explain the ineffectiveness of the humanists by attributing to them ignorance of one of the chief elements of humanism, to wit, the ability to communicate with humanity. Yet there is room for optimism in the reflection that the humanists can learn when they choose to study; perhaps even now some genius among them, bored with easy triumphs over the intricacies of Sumerian and Mayan, may be turning his attention to the vastly more difficult language of today, preparing to reveal to the common man a new heaven and a new earth.

Part IV

THE FUTURE OF THE HUMANITIES IN
STATE UNIVERSITIES

Chapter XVII

THE FUTURE OF THE HUMANITIES IN STATE UNIVERSITIES

Norman Foerster

1. Human Values

AMERICA ENTERED THE war to defend democracy against fascism, civilization against barbarism, the humanities against the inhumanities. It was not to be a meaningless war of things, of machines and material resources, but a war of men against men, of mind against mind, of will against will. It was to be a war of human values.

The values believed in by the enemy were all too clear; the values we believed in, all too vague. The Four Freedoms were essentially negative—freedom from religious intolerance, controlled opinion, fear, and want. If freedom could be won and extended, what positive aims were to direct the use of it? No clear affirmations came from our political leaders, or even from those peculiarly responsible, leaders in the fields bearing the proud name of "humanities": historians, men of letters and art, philosophers, churchmen. In the war of values they promptly went on the defensive. They called upon us to "preserve" our way of life, the liberal arts, the humanities, often in a tone that implied only "business as usual." They appeared not to realize the seriousness of the failure of the modern world of science and democracy to achieve new values or to deepen the vitality of old values. They spoke as if unaware that the modern world, interested in multiplying the instruments of living and in distributing them more equitably, has been living upon the spiritual capital of the past, and that this spiritual capital has steadily depreciated. While professing to despise the wisdom of the ages, indeed the past and all its works, we have continued to use our heritage of values, or rather to use it up. The human values that we have taken for granted are nowise different from those of the past, the values founded for Occidental civilization by Greece and Judea, but they have grown more and more attenuated, surviving in ever feebler forms. The coming of the war did not reverse this process. To the crude naturalistic aims of the enemy we were unable to oppose any clear aims of an affirmative and commanding sort. We derived strength adequate for the conduct of the war from our negative aims: our hatred of the painfully clear aims of the enemy, our determination to destroy the menace of those aims. The forces of darkness and indecency must first be halted—then we would set about the advancement of light and decency. And we were clear, at least, that the winning of the war must somehow be followed by the winning of the peace.

Before us lies the long, hard task of winning the peace and keeping it won. This we cannot do by force alone. We shall need courage to use force if occasion demands, a courage lacking after 1918, and we shall need wisdom in the establishment of high purposes, a wisdom lacking after 1918. The burden laid upon our intelligence, our idealism, and our moral character is stupendous. I do not see how any man can reasonably predict our success. Nor do I see how any man of good will can refrain from the effort to do his part to bring about success. Everywhere we shall need men of intelligence and character, both leaders and followers, in industry, in politics, in journalism, in law and medicine, in scientific and humanistic research, in the church, in education. Nowhere do responsibility and opportunity lie more plainly than in the field of education, as modern democracy has always understood even if it has left full demonstration to the totalitarian nations. As never before, we must place our hopes and our striving in education, the education of children, of youth, of adults. Within the field of education, nowhere do responsibility and opportunity lie more plainly than in the public or state universities.

In the pages that follow I shall be concerned with higher education in general and with the state universities in particular. Begun in the South, they have spread throughout the nation, taking on their most definite patterns perhaps in the Middle West. Universities of the people, they have prided themselves upon their service to democracy. In truth they have done much for democracy. They are now called upon to do far more. How much will they do, in the crucial years before us, for the advancement of human values? I shall not venture a prediction. It will be more profitable to consider rather what the advancement of human values entails, what we may understand by a humanistic spirit guiding the life of the state university, and what the conditions are that make for and against that spirit.

2. The Spirit of the Humanities

A state university is or should be dominated by a general intent, a permeating and unifying ideal, however precious the minority opinions that oppose that intent and test its validity. The intent should not be specific—sectarian or partisan—but general: it might be naturalistic, religious, or humanistic. For decades it has been in fact, I would say, naturalistic. It cannot be expected, in the present spiritual situation, and in view of the separation of church and state, to become a religious intent. But it could become humanistic.

What does this mean? To define the humanistic spirit acceptably is as impossible as to define the democratic spirit acceptably. Despite academic literalists hot for the tangibles, it seems necessary to tolerate the vagueness of such terms in order not to lose contact with truth. The two terms, as we use them today, have much in common. In contrast with fascism, the democratic and the humanistic spirit today agree in emphasizing the development of the individual. They agree in emphasizing the human as opposed to the racial or national (despite the fevers of nationalism, democracy has placed first the rights of man). They agree in demanding a society of free men. And they agree in conceiving of authority as internal, a free inner consent or dissent.

The humanistic spirit flourished, of course, long before modern democracy, flourished variously and splendidly—if not in its political aspect—under the absolute monarchy of Louis XIV, in the aristocratic Renaissance, in imperial Rome, under various polities in Greece, where it first came to fruition. Percy

Gardner has stated very simply the several stages in the development of our civilization. "Three great discoveries," he says, "lay open to the awakened spirit of man when he first began to realize and reflect upon his surroundings. The first was the discovery of God, which was mainly the work of the Prophets of Israel, though no doubt Greece added much on the intellectual side; and the religions of both Judea and Greece were carried to a higher point by Christianity. The second was the discovery of man himself, which was in all essentials the great work of Greek thinkers and writers. The third, begun in Greece, has been carried very much farther in modern times, the discovery of nature and her laws." Today the humanistic spirit cannot forget that it was Greece that not only discovered man but gave the fullest demonstration of man's capacities. It was Greece that most splendidly realized the dignity of man as man, as a being essentially different from the rest of the animal order, including, in Plato and Aristotle, an adumbration of the spiritual dignity upon which Christianity staked everything.

In the long history of the humanistic spirit, what has been the fundamental aim? From Socrates and Plato to Goethe and Emerson and persons today who are in the tradition, the aim has been self-knowledge and self-realization. The nature of the human self has been variously conceived, without doing violence to the large area of consensus within the tradition. Man is a creature, it would seem, who recognizes in his constitution a power of command, whether this is regarded as rational or ethical; a power of command over his thronging desires and passions, by means of which he shapes his desires and passions in harmonious expression. Life for him is action, external action and, even more, internal action, an inner working upon himself. The good life comes not by nature, but is an achievement based on progressive self-knowledge and habituation to what is good for his constitution. He realizes the good life not apart from men but among them, with the help of all men of good will, co-operation meaning primarily the relation of example and imitation. From the inner life flows the outer life, action taking the form of deeds, works of speculation, works of fine art, works of useful art, all institutions. The measure of all things, man himself as a complete, symmetrical being, is more important than nature, which gives him materials to work with, or the instruments of living which he fashions (such as the products of what we call technology), or any collective entity such as society, state, or folk. While perceiving that life is full of variety and change, he rests his hopes in personal and social values that are constant and enduring.

For Americans, perhaps the most suggestive expression of the humanistic spirit in relation to education is Emerson's address, "The American Scholar," happily remote from the heated debates of our own day. The marks of a changing world are in it: passages in which the humanistic spirit is given a romantic accent. But Emerson speaks mainly of and from the unchanging world of principles sound at all times. He points out how the ever-growing division of labor, while it has made man more helpful to himself, is threatening to destroy man, that is, man as a complete, symmetrical being. Man tends to become a mere tool, a thing, many things. "The tradesman scarcely ever gives an ideal worth to his work, but is ridden by the routine of his craft, and the soul is subject to dollars. The priest becomes a form; the attorney a statute-book; the mechanic a machine." (Emerson was spared the spectacle of many universities, especially state universities, more and more blithely dedicating themselves to this vocational deformation.) He goes on to describe a generous education worthy of the idea of man. In a threefold curriculum he proposes, first, the study of nature, the field of natural science—the learning of observed facts, the attempt to formulate laws of nature, the suggestion of a relationship between the laws of nature and the laws of the human mind. Secondly, he calls for the study of the human past, the field of the humanities, specifically literature, art, and institutions. Addressing the Phi Beta Kappa Society, Emerson finds it necessary to attack "the book-learned class, who value books as such," meek scholars resting in accepted dogmas as well as "the restorers of readings, the emendators, the bibliomaniacs of all degrees." But books came into the world not dead but as "quick thought," and should beget quick thought, spurring the scholar to fresh creation. "The one thing in the world, of value, is the active soul," which, however obstructed, is contained within every man. Books must be so read, so taught, that they will speak to the active soul. And thirdly, Emerson demands that the scholar recognize action, direct experience in living, as an indispensable means to vital truth. "Only so much do I know, as I have lived," he says, and, perhaps thinking of college faculties, "Instantly we know whose words are loaded with life, and whose not." Living is essential to thinking, and in the end more important. While thinking is a partial act, living is a total act. The scholar cannot afford, whether as scholar or man, to be a recluse.

Having considered the education of the scholar by nature, by books, and by action, Emerson turns to the scholar's duties, summing them up in self-trust. "In silence, in steadiness, in severe abstraction, let him hold by himself; add observation to observation, patient of neglect, patient of reproach, and bide his own time—happy enough if he can satisfy himself alone that this day he has seen something truly." He should be free (academic freedom); he should be brave, not deriving his tranquillity from his position in a protected class (security of tenure).

Nowhere does Emerson speak more plainly in the humanistic spirit than when, in recurrent passages, he asserts the unity of man. He shows his awareness, to be sure, of individual differences, "that peculiar fruit which each man was created to bear," but these differences do not contravene, for him, the essential sameness of men. The great books he finds always contemporary, or rather timeless, because "they impress us with the conviction that one nature wrote and the same reads." Again, the scholar is conceived as finding that his insight is not personal but universal: "In going down into the secrets of his own mind he has descended into the secret of all minds." Like the orator—like Emerson himself in this famous address— he begins perhaps in self-distrust and then, "the deeper he dives into his privatest, secretest presentiment, to his wonder he finds this is the most acceptable, most public, and universally true." "For a man, rightly viewed, comprehendeth the particular natures of all men." The end of a generous education would seem to be, consequently, the transformation of the young and unformed, not into adjusted members of an unsound society, nor into tools for service in ever multiplying vocations defined by the division of labor, but into mature human beings, men and women of understanding and integrity.

Emerson's conception of an education dominated by the humanistic spirit was in harmony with the great tradition from Socrates to the middle of the nineteenth century. It differed, to be sure, in omitting the authoritative sanctions generally applied by European classicism and Christianity, and in recognizing the scientific tradition of "improving natural knowledge" which had developed amazingly since the seventeenth century. Regarded by contemporaries as a forward-looking utterance, his address was heralded as America's intellectual declaration of independence, and rightly enough, since in scholarship, science, and letters the New World soon vied with the Old. But Emerson did not look forward—perhaps did not choose to look forward—to the triumph of the forces of naturalism that occurred within a few decades. Today, more than a century since his address, the humanistic view of life and of education has been almost completely displaced, for the first time in the history of the Occident, by a naturalistic view of life and of education. In theory, our break with the past is all but complete. In saying this I do not forget that in the realm of values we are, in practice, still living on our inherited capital, having acquired no other. We are daily assuming, for example, freedom of will, moral responsibility, human dignity, perhaps even ideal causes or ends more important to us than life itself. We are doing this unconsciously; we are continuing humanistic assumptions and practices because we are human. But they are in the background. In the foreground, in deliberate thought and speech, in the books, the articles, the classroom lectures, in our official philosophy that we seek to promote and put to use, our conceptions are overwhelmingly naturalistic.

3. The Naturalistic University

That this is so may be seen by drawing up a list of beliefs current in American state universities today. The beliefs stated below represent the kind of thinking which some universities have reached, others have approximated, and many others are drifting toward. Flourishing most in the Middle West and least in the South, these conscious beliefs are everywhere resisted by more or less unconscious humanistic assumptions and traditional humanistic practices. From the humanistic point of view, they constitute a set of half-truths and errors which threaten educational disaster and hence social disaster.

It is believed, as a foundation for the entire creed, that man is simply an animal, though not a simple animal. Man's place in nature has been found, and he has no other place. The difference between him and other living beings is purely quantitative. He is an organism in an environment, a bundle of drives seeking expression. Generally he is held to be "good" by nature. Evil is then the result of environment, of faulty political and social systems, probably in the last analysis economic systems. In the understanding of human nature we may safely ignore the pre-scientific "wisdom of the ages"—the humanistic wisdom of Plato and Aristotle and Confucius, the religious wisdom of Buddha and Jesus. Our view of man in the universe must come from the latest correctors of Copernicus, Newton, Darwin, Marx, Freud. Our view of human nature will somehow combine the realistic theory of Hobbes that man is characterized by "a perpetual and restless desire of power after power" with the sentimental theory of Hume that he is characterized by sympathy for his fellows, an original capacity to share in their happiness or misery, or, as John Dewey would put it, a natural desire to serve. In this humanitarian version of naturalism it is hoped, despite the evidence, that when the desire of power and the feeling of natural sympathy conflict, natural sympathy will restrain the desire of power.

It is believed, if not always asserted, that the good life of man consists mainly in the pursuit and possession of material advantages, the machinery of life, the instruments for convenience and comfort and pleasure, the economic and social mechanisms that aid in the manufacture and ever wider distribution of ever new inventions. Living and the standard of living are virtually synonymous, since the program in view consists not in living but in always preparing to live by always raising the standard of living. If our age is reproached with being dominantly utilitarian and materialistic, the answer is that we are *really* concerned for the "opportunity" for higher values in the future—a future that appears ever near but never nearer. An economy of abundance will for the first time in the story of man make possible the more abundant life. We still believe, if less ecstatically, in the "law of progress." Progress may be slow at times, and there may be setbacks, but the human race is marching on, with plenty of time to march. Guided by the sentimental naturalism of the eighteenth century and the utilitarian naturalism of the nineteenth, the modern world is on the right track to a paradise on earth. Those who are assailed by doubts can take refuge in the law of change, which calls for less commitment than belief in progress. The past is "the dead past." "We live in a changing world." "Change is the only constant."

It is believed, despite the fixed views and militant attitude suggested in the foregoing paragraphs, that among the prime virtues of the life intellectual is the virtue of neutrality, the impartiality we have learned from science. It is the duty of the scholar and teacher to show his exalted objectivity in all things by never taking a stand. In that case I am afraid he is not doing his duty. The neutrality so much bepraised in our universities is only a fiction. The same may be said of the insistence on relativity, the scorn of all absolutes. Professing to cast out all absolutes, to believe that all truth is purely relative to time, place, and circumstance, that it is silly to speak, for example, of "eternal values," the professor really means all absolutes save his own. His very relativity is an absolute.

It is believed that the universities, in an age of science, should be dominated throughout by scientific methods and concepts—actually, it turns out, by a distortion of scientific methods and concepts. Now, if science is above all a disinterested search for knowledge of nature, it manifestly has a large and honorable place. Yet even in the departments of natural science such a conception is often subordinated to a narrowly technological interpretation of science. And in other departments what is alleged to be scientific turns out to consist mainly of an indiscriminate transfer of scientific methods and concepts to fields of inquiry in which they are not suitable. There is usually a kind of parody involved in the application of quantitative methods, for example, to the humanities and the new social studies. It is not true that the universities *really* scientize all their subjects, though it is believed that they can and should.

It is believed, in our universities thus dedicated to science and pseudo-science, that the humanities have a significant place only insofar as they are "creative." This is the view of departments outside the humanities. As the scientist is creative in discovery and invention, so the humanist should be creative in the writing of poems and novels, the writing and production of plays and musical compositions, the making of pictures and sculpture. While the great function of science is knowledge and utility, the lesser function of literature and art is the pleasant exercise of aesthetic responses ("beauty feasts," in the phrase of Sir J. Arthur Thomson). They have nothing to do with the quest of knowledge and truth, which belongs to science alone. Criticism of literature and art is parasitic and all but futile. Indeed, the critical spirit in general (which is in fact at the heart of all the humanities, being only another term for the search for values) is a welter of subjectivity in sharp contrast to the objectivity of science. I like this, you like that; I find this true, you find that true. This makes philosophy an unreal battle of mere logic or words, a harmless pastime for those who still care for this sort of game. Theology is like philosophy, and religion is a social science. As for history, there is not much to be said for chronology, in any university subject, and, since all subjects have a history and the specialists in the various subjects are best qualified to deal with it, there is perhaps no place in a university for a department of history. The other social studies are sciences, albeit backward sciences, to be approved in proportion as they are pursued in the naturalistic spirit.

Such is the trend of opinion outside these subjects. Within the subjects is a similar distortion. Literary and artistic studies are regarded by the majority of those who engage in them as primarily historical, or even antiquarian, not creative and critical. History is largely the study of documents and the discovery and organization of facts, the massing of materials for historiography; there is scant interest in the using of the materials in the interpretative and imaginative re-creation of the past by the historian as critic and artist. In the other social studies the aim has been to proceed as scientifically as possible, regardless of the humanistic aspect of these studies, with the result that fundamental concepts and methods are in great confusion. (The same, by the way, is to be said of psychology.) Philosophy, scorned by an age of science, has sought refreshment in the methodological implications of the natural sciences and the naturalistic interpretation of current political and social movements. Religion has often been content with its new role as a social science, sometimes conceiving of campus life as a sort of laboratory.

It is believed, again, that the whole effort of the university should be directed upon the interests and problems of contemporary life. If the humanities do not play their part in this effort, so much the worse for the humanities: they will be a side show. In many quarters there is almost a hatred of the past, which is conceived as the main hindrance to progress. Its achievements are usually minimized (surely John Dewey is an improvement upon Plato), and when they are freely granted are found to be irrelevant to modern experience. Ours is a different world, the beginning of the endless age of science and democracy, the endless age of true enlightenment. It is a living world of experience, not a dead world of records and books, though, in practice, the student must be guided into it by books—our dead and deadly textbooks. The great books of the past are demonstrably full of error, and in any case do not much concern us, who are not Greeks or Elizabethans but modern Americans. If we need belles-lettres let them be not

Homer and Dante and the other classics but contemporary literature, which grows out of and reflects our environment, deals in a "meaningful" way with our problems. Human nature changes, and ours is ours. So strong is this attitude that it is tactically unwise, in many universities, to use in academic circles such words as "the past," "tradition," "heritage," "classical," "medieval," save in a tone of studied contempt.

It is believed that the university should serve the high ideal of research at the frontiers of (scientific) knowledge. Every professor should be active in original investigation and publication. His prestige depends upon this, and consequently his advancement by the administration, which especially honors outside evidence of prestige in the form of "calls." The obligation of research is accepted by most professors, though a large proportion resent the emphasis placed upon it, both those who have no talent for it and those who have the talent but are deeply interested in the liberal education of undergraduates. Teaching is relatively neglected by faculty and administration, sometimes in the comforting belief that the men who are best in research are also best in teaching. There are some qualms about the time and expense allotted to research in a people's university, so that it is given little publicity and then only in its practical or dollar-earning service to the state.

It is believed—despite the notion that research should animate the state university with a high ideal—that a high ideal is *not* suitable in a state university. A state university is a people's university, of the people, for the people, and, in the end, by the people. It must offer them what they spontaneously want, or what they are supposed to want, not what they need and might be taught to want. Of course it is hard to say what they need, or even what they want, but as a working hypothesis we will assume that they want what is useful and practical, not in a remote and indirect way but immediately, something tangibly marketable. To attempt to stuff culture down the throats of *hoi polloi,* to aim at changing raw youth into well-rounded men and women, would be at the least inappropriate. The published catalogue should doubtless state some such general objective, since everyone wishes to be well-rounded, but the curriculum, teaching methods, and adviser system, it should be understood, will be based on the realities of the situation. A faculty of utilitarian specialists, having no horror of one-sidedness, will know how to change raw youth into utilitarian specialists.

It is believed, more specifically, that what the people of the state want is a job-centered education. Frankly, this is what our "student-centered" education comes to. We must prepare the students, who are also people of the state, for employment in a vocation and pecuniary advantage over the unprepared. We must open opportunity to them through a generous variety of curricula, adding one program after another according to a demand imagined if not real. We must include training not only for the professions but also for many lesser vocations among the more than 25,000 recognized by the national census. We need not be deterred by snobbish distinctions between dignified and humble vocations, nor between "education" and "training." Train we must, if our students are to land jobs and hold them. To some extent we must also train them for other "adult activities" and "life situations," such as disease prevention, marriage, and leisure, indeed for a "total adjustment" to contemporary society. To the fact that no one can say what life will be like during the half century our students will span after they leave us, we regretfully close our eyes. To the fact that about half of our students never graduate, and that of those who do half either do not pursue their chosen vocation for more than three or four years or do not pursue it at all, we regretfully close our eyes. We are doing the best we can under such circumstances.

It is believed that the foundations of education, which are biological and psychological, lie in motivation and individual differences. The strongest motive is vocational; the student's desire to enter a freely chosen kind of work provides the motive that enables him to study with the maximum interest and profit. Many students are happily "self-motivated," know at the start what they want to prepare for. The rest "find themselves" more or less slowly or not at all. It is the business of the personnel service and the faculty to prod them into finding themselves, that is, into learning what occupational groove they could be made to fit, what sort of tool they were created to be. It may be noted in passing that to fit men into vocational groupings is a strange way to recognize their *individual* differences. Yet all the faculty talk is of individual differences. The old declaration of independence, which affirmed the half-truth that men are created equal, has been supplanted by the new declaration, which affirms the half-truth that they are created unique. A leading psychologist who pushes the concept of differences to the extreme has ridiculed the liberal and social view of education by saying, "Where the Great Maker created all human beings different, it is the function of the teacher to make them all alike." Apparently the psychologist would have this read: "Where the Great Maker created all human beings different, it is the function of the teacher to make them as different as possible." Another reading, quite out of favor, is to the effect that all men are at once the same and different, and that liberal and social education should develop their samenesses, leaving the differences mainly to special education.

It is believed that no common knowledge may be regarded as essential. The uniform requirement of any particular subject would not be in harmony with the concepts of motivation and individual differences. Besides, there is no specific knowledge agreed upon which every educated person must acquire, and even if he acquired such knowledge he would forget it before or soon after graduation. And what department dare assert that all students should be required to take a course in that department, unless it is prepared to grant the same privilege to every other department? From this political situation two or three required courses may, in practice, emerge, since some departments are strong through numbers, through leadership, or merely customary recognition, and furthermore some subjects do seem to be very important if not altogether essential. The general opinion remains, however, that prescription is psychologically unsound and perhaps undemocratic as well. Subjects, if not men, were created free and equal.

It is believed that knowledge is not its own end but merely a means, an instrument for use, and that the use contemplated in education should be the development of abilities. Apparently the assumption is made (without justification) that abilities learned in college will last, while knowledge will not. Abilities do not involve prescription, since they can be learned in any subject. Thus, the ability to use scientific method may be acquired in physical education, the ability to perceive aesthetic properties may be acquired in mathematics, etc. Or, to shift the point of view to the teacher, any subject, whether Latin or radio broadcasting, may be taught liberally or narrowly, according to the kind and range of abilities that are promoted. The old theory that abilities may be "transferred" from one field to another has been exploded. To be sure, transfer is possible under favorable conditions, when the student or the teacher or both seek to establish relations between subjects and progressively integrate the abilities learned. But apparently we are not to assume or assure these favorable conditions.

It is believed, in view of the preceding doctrines, that a student-centered college must provide the "tailor-made curriculum," that is, a different curriculum for each student. Faculty regulations concerning courses should have great flexibility. This does not argue a return to an unlimited elective system and its attendant chaos. There should be a "core" of courses required in the three great divisions of learning, the natural sciences, the social sciences, and the humanities, permitting, however, "options" within these divisions. And the core should be kept as small as possible, between say twenty-four and thirty-four semester hours. In addition to all options within the core, the entire remaining program of eighty-six to ninety-six hours should be open to selection according to individual differences in aptitude and interest. Who is to do all the opting and selecting? The individual student? the Greek letter houses and the dormitories? the parents? the faculty adviser? Although no system based on any of these sources of wisdom has worked well, a system of faculty advising is usually relied on: the cause of liberal education is entrusted to the specialist. He will know the student and know what is good for him. If persuasion is too time-consuming or ineffective, he will have recourse to "strong talk across the desk" (or else surrender his responsibility to the student). Since the "uneducated specialists," as Mr. Hutchins terms them, have their individual differences and not always the purest motivation, we again face chaos. And chaos will have to be accepted, unless we are prepared to have advisers for the advisers—presumably the administration. In this case the faculty will surrender its responsibility to the dean, or master-tailor.

4. Educationists

Such is the naturalistic conception of life and of education widely prevalent in state universities and many other institutions as well. Most of it reads curiously like a summary of the notions associated with teachers' colleges and with departments, schools, and colleges of education within the universities. In truth there is no great gap between the mentality of professors of "subjects" and professors of "Education." (The conventional terms are unfair, since education is also a subject and a better one than many another.) The naturalistic interpretation of man leads logically to a naturalistic theory of education agreeable alike to both groups. Professors of the various subjects have been deeply indebted to the same line of thought as that which the educationists have used, a line that runs through such men as Bacon, Rousseau, Darwin, Spencer, and Dewey. They may not know but would read with sympathy the works of the successors of John Dewey, men like William H. Kilpatrick, who aimed to establish a science of education, beginning with a dissertation on "Animal Intelligence," and Harold Rugg, author of *The Child-Centered School*. The most vital bond between the two groups is perhaps that of modern psychology, which both have applied in a spirit more zealous than critical.

In view of this close kinship, it is at first glance surprising that professors of subjects, along with a few professors of Education, look upon educationists as a whole with disdain and hostility. For this attitude there are several main reasons. One lies in the conflict between concern for "content" and concern for "method," that is, the belief of professors of subjects that prospective teachers must know as thoroughly as possible the subjects they are to teach, and the belief of professors of Education that teachers must learn how to teach and must therefore include in their preparation a considerable amount of Education. This conflict is heightened by the observation that the science of Education is not yet impressive, that professors of Education are not themselves superior teachers (though one would expect men in "professional education" to surpass those engaged in amateur education), that students required to take courses in Education show, despite vocational motivation, so little of that interest which is held to be requisite, and that the results of the many hours taken in Education are so disappointing when tested by actual practice in the schools.

A second reason for hostility is the belief of professors of subjects that professors of Education have indulged in a bewildering succession of fads. This general opinion is shared, here and there, by prominent professors of Education, such as Edgar W. Knight and I. L. Kandel. As the latter has put it in an article on "The Fantasia of Current Education," "Ever since some educational theorists made the profound discovery that we live in a changing world, that authoritarianism began to be undermined by Galileo and that life is precarious and the future uncertain, experimentalism has run riot and education has been bombarded with a chaotic welter of theories." This welter has characterized the Progressive Education fathered by John Dewey, a contemporary application of the ancient Sophistical rejection of all permanent values and all tradition. Among the advocates of Progressive Education have been both moderates and radicals. Many university professors of subjects, moderates without knowing it, associate the movement with radicals who have reduced its half-truths to quarter-truths and made them ridiculous.

Finally, the hostility is more and more due to fear of the power educationists are already exerting and may exert disastrously in the future. Primary and secondary schools are securely in their control, owing largely to the political protection they have built up, and colleges and universities are increasingly feeling their influence. Faculties of higher education, engrossed in subjects and in the promotion of departmental interests, are in danger of losing by default the battle for control of educational policy. They have in their midst a large group, the professors of Education, who devote full time to the advancement of their cause. When the war came, and with it an inevitable tendency to regimentation directed from Washington, the education experts were naturally in request, and the academic hostility toward them grew. It was not only academic. Writing in *Harper's*, Bernard DeVoto, for example, espoused the cause of the scholars and teachers, who feared that "the accident of war has delivered teaching and scholarship into the hands of their mortal enemies." The professional educationists, he said, "have the charts, the graphs, the gadgets, and the pretty machines, the programs and gospels and theories, the pretentious and half-lunatic philosophies which will convince Congress (as they have always convinced legislatures).... The future of higher education in America will be at the mercy of the Teachers College mind."

A similar alarm was voiced by Dean William C. DeVane of Yale. What have the secondary schools, under the leadership of teachers' colleges, actually accomplished? The high school pupils graduate "unable to write, read, or speak English; unable to cope with mathematical problems which require algebra and trigonometry in a time when we are in dire need of these commodities; unable to read or speak fluently any foreign language in a time when to be provincial is to be only partially alive; unable to remember, much less to understand, a few facts about the history of their country; unable to think clearly, and too undisciplined to behave considerately; ungrounded in the intellectual virtues." What, then, would happen if the Federal government gave the professional educationists an equivalent opportunity in the colleges and universities? "The government would put our institutions into the hand of political-minded professors of education and educational bureaucrats, and that would reduce higher education to a mediocrity which it has not yet reached in America."

Even if the fear of Federal control turns out to be exaggerated or baseless, the fear of educationist control will remain. And not without reason. If all knowledge is the province of the subject faculties, all education would seem to be the province of the Education faculty. As experts in a new science inspired by an age of science, as supporters of the philosophy of democracy which they conceive to have been the gift of John Dewey to the world, the educationists naturally regard themselves as destined to shape higher education as they have shaped the schools below. There need be no sudden change. The state university of today largely conforms to their views; the state university of tomorrow may conform wholly. The danger is real. Yet signs are not wanting, as Leonard Carmichael admitted in his inaugural address at Tufts a year before the war, that "the naturalistic tradition of American education". has been "shaken almost in its day of victory." When the war came it was shaken violently.

5. New Forces

"The twentieth century was cradled in great, not to say stupendous hopes—hopes as to man, as to history, as to the universe itself. Whereas the old-fashioned religion had taught that 'there is no health in us,' that human nature is evil, even sinful, and has to be crushed, we, of the twentieth century, have believed in human nature, holding it to be essentially sound. So much so, in fact, that we have used human nature as our norm and have defined the highest good as the satisfaction of human needs. We have looked to no far-off Kingdom of Heaven, but to the cure of human evils on this earth. And we have believed such a cure to be concretely attainable. Enlighten the mind, spread education through all the classes of society, conquer disease, overcome poverty by a reform of economic institutions, raise the standard of living by the application of science to human needs, advance the front of democracy—has not this been the program of liberalism everywhere? Along with this faith in human nature has gone a belief in a universal law of progress—that somehow humanity is irresistibly marching to its goal and that the very cosmos is conspiring for its success. The faith in progress was really no part of the new scientific mentality—indeed it was hostile to it, being a relic of deism; but still there it was radiating a glow of hope upon the human scene. We were not only confident; we were complacent and arrogant, feeling ourselves Promethean rebels, conquerors both of nature and of the gods.

"But now something has happened—a halt has been called; the two wars—or rather the one war in its two phases—with their attendant economic disasters and political chaos, have shattered our simple faith. Our optimism is proved to have been not only shallow but false. Human nature has disclosed unsuspected depths of irrationality, brutality and barbarism; history is not an upward-onward march. Obviously something is very wrong with human nature and with the nature of things."

These are the words of Raphael Demos in his sober review of Niebuhr which appeared in the *New Republic* (of all places!) in 1943. The new mood here described, the growing suspicion that our optimism has been sentimental and unrealistic, has not yet fundamentally altered the public mind, at least in America; still less has it disturbed the great majority of comfortable intellectuals in our universities. Whether the new mood will become affirmative and will serve as the starting-point for a humanistic revival, depends largely on the political prospects opened by the peace. Yet in any case there are forces, both without and within the universities, which offer some hope for the future of the humanistic spirit in American civilization and hence in American state universities.

There is in our society an increasing disillusionment with the results of naturalism. Many persons have abandoned the naïve optimism inherited from the last two centuries and at the same time are resolved not to succumb to the merely negative disillusionment that paralyzed mind and will after the last war. They perceive that democracy is neither a panacea nor a mistake but a great hope demanding great effort. They perceive that science as a priceless means of attaining knowledge and organizing effort cannot itself provide the ends toward which effort should be directed. They perceive, in particular, that the gifts of technology are only instruments of living and leave untouched the problem of what to live for. They are aware of a vast imbalance, in our type of civilization, of the elements that seem necessary in life, an imbalance which strikes them most forcibly as one between man's tremendous capacity for controlling nature and his tremendous incapacity for controlling himself. They reflect upon the imbalance, again, between the hope that materialistic humanitarianism would give a basis for the good life and the bleak and stubborn failure of the good life to rise spontaneously on this foundation. They see, above all, that naturalism, having broken down the old faith of the Occident, is now losing confidence in its ability to offer a substitute that can cope with the realities of experience. As Geoffrey Crowther, editor of *The Economist*, has put it: "The western democratic world is perilously close to a vacuum of faith. . . . But the trouble about a vacuum is that it gets filled, and if there are no angels available to fill it, fools—or worse— rush in." We have seen them rush.

There is an increasing perception that without faith the modern world will never solve its mundane problems, and that the quest of faith must mean, first of all, a revival of belief in values, the special province of the humanities. More and more this has been the burden of forthright statements by men in varied fields of thought and action.

For example, in the words of Edward Hallett Carr, professor of politics, "The esential nature of the crisis through which we are living is neither military, nor political, nor economic, but moral. A new faith in a new moral purpose is required to reanimate our political and economic system." Almost the same words have been used by Theodore M. Greene, professor of philosophy, who finds the crisis to be not military, nor political, nor economic, but in the stratum beneath these, "the stratum of cultural values and modes of thought," and beneath this again the level of "spiritual commitment and religious faith," and who concludes that "the humanities, having to do so essentially with man's cultural and spiritual life, should make, and can make, and must make a unique contribution to our national welfare." Or, as Raymond B. Fosdick, president of the Rockefeller Foundation, puts it: "Particularly must we rely on the humanists—the historians, the philosophers, the artists, the poets, the novelists, the dramatists—all those who fashion ideas, concepts, and forms that give meaning and value to life and furnish the patterns of conduct." And again, President Seymour, historian, along with the Corporation of Yale University, issued a statement warning of the "impoverishment of the nation's mind and soul" and called for concern, even during the war, with "the less tangible values of our culture." President Conant, less fearful of the neglect of humanistic studies during the war, predicted for them a new period of growth after the war. Boldly sustaining "the thesis that universities are concerned fundamentally with the eternal verities," that theirs is "the guardianship of eternal values," he held that "a general education must be based on a study of the arts, letters, and the various aspects of philosophy," since "in these fields of study, and in these only, the true nature of the exercise of a free choice of values by a civilized man can be understood." Lawyer and political leader, the late Wendell L. Willkie, in one of the best educational addresses of recent years, justified the humanities in terms of democracy—the equality of minds enfranchised. "When you range back and forth through the centuries, when you weigh the utterance of some great thinker or absorb the meaning of some great composition, in painting or music or poetry; when you live these things within yourself and measure yourself against them—only then do you become an initiate in the world of the free. It is in the liberal arts that you acquire the ability to make a truly free and individual choice."

Opinions of this sort, rare a decade ago, have in the last years multiplied. They acquire a special significance when held by natural scientists. It used to be the habit of many scientists to assume (not of course as scientists but as naturalistic philosophers) that science is about all that mankind needs, that its abstractions cover all of reality that is of real concern for man, that its method is competent ultimately to solve the problems of the good life, and that philosophy and religion have been mostly wishful thinking, private or social dreams. Today this uncritical scientism is rapidly declining. I have already quoted a distinguished chemist who speaks of eternal values, and who holds that general education should be based not on science but on the humanities. Let me add the views of some biologists and physicists.

Sir J. Arthur Thomson has clearly stated the limited enterprise of science. "Science," he says, "is a particular way of looking at the world, but it is not the only way.... We learn by feeling and living as well as by scientifically knowing. Science is one of the pathways toward the truth, but there are other pathways. *Vivendo discimus*. By certain methods, determinedly abstract and partial, methods of weighing and measuring, analyzing and reducing, science formulates the fractions of reality which it grips. But by hypotheses it only gets at fractions of reality, since it is too daring a postulate to suppose that scientific methods are always able to exhaust the manifoldness of a situation." Science leaves wide open, for others than scientists, the entire range of human ends. "It is impossible for us," says Robert A. Millikan, "to get along without the aid of certain people who can be trusted to speak with authority on the vitally important questions of human ends. The scientist provides us with extensive enough information regarding what *is*, but unless we have those among us to tell us also *what makes for*, and what does not make for, our more fundamental well-being, we are lost." That we are indeed lost is suggested by Albert Einstein, who remarks that whatever scientific method in the hand of man will produce "depends entirely on the nature of the aims alive in mankind. Once these aims exist, the scientific method furnishes means to realize them. But it cannot furnish the aims themselves. The scientific method itself would not have led to anything, it would not even have been born at all without a passionate striving for clear understanding. Perfection of means and confusion of aims seem, in my opinion, to characterize our age."

Thus in field after field, and by men of the most varied mentality, the humanistic spirit has spoken, in America as abroad, against the intellectual bewilderment and spiritual apathy of the twentieth century. "On every hand today—in the press, the radio, the school—we are called upon to defend 'the Humanities,' the more human arts and human values, against war abroad and against socio-economic and scientific-naturalistic fatalism at home." This observation by Lennox Grey of Teachers College, Columbia (in his editorial foreword to an "impartial" thesis on *The Revival of the Humanities in American Education*) will serve to remind us that the only group who, when called upon to "defend 'the Humanities,'" have failed to respond to the call are the faculties and administration of the teachers' colleges of America.

As for the public at large, a significant portion of it is aware of the essential aimlessness of modern living and is looking round for guidance. It is responsive to newspaper columnists who unjustly berate science and economics for taking us on "The Ride to Nowhere" and who offer philosophy or the great books of the past as better approaches to happiness. It has shown itself ready for a book on liberal education written in the humanistic spirit, a book by Mark Van Doren which went through several printings in rapid succession. It is prepared to listen to the view that vocations were made for man, not man for vocations, that the education called Progressive was really digressive, and that if we learn by doing we also learn by being done. You cannot fool all of the people all of the time. There is in the public a sense of humor, the corrective and sanative aspect of the humanistic spirit, which manifests itself negatively as a kind of skepticism and positively as a desire for proportion. It rises to clearness in our cartoonists and our homespun philosophers (like Will Rogers), not in our university specialists, who are strangers to the comic spirit of Erasmus.

In terms of ideas, perhaps the best hope for a revival of the humanities lies in a conception which has in recent years appealed both to intellectuals, such as those I have quoted, and to much of the public. It is the dignity of man. The phrase is rarely defined, in modern or any other terms. It conveys a vague affirmation that man, whatever his beastliness, possesses some inherent excellence or nobleness. When some effort is made at analysis, man's dignity is likely to be found in his freedom, though what is meant is rather liberty, the absence of outer constraint. Thus, the dignity of man is violated by any form of exploitation, bodily or mental. According to Bruce Bliven, of the *New Republic*, "The conception of the dignity of the individual, of freedom and fairness for all, is a startlingly new one." This amazing remark suggests how completely the naturalist mind, immersed in the contemporaneous and obliged to discover everything for the first time, has broken with the traditions of civilization. As all educated persons know, the conception of the dignity of the individual goes back through the entire history of America to the heritage which Europe received from its cultural foundations in Greece and Judea. Only in comparatively recent times has the conception become vague. In its present form it has little potency. In proportion as this is recognized, we shall doubtless witness efforts to infuse into it some degree of dynamic meaning. Those who have broken with the traditions of civilization will sooner or later wish to find a new reason, perhaps a "startlingly" new reason, for believing in the dignity of man. If the effort is honest, it will merit encouragement, not scorn. Meanwhile we shall do well, surely, to revitalize the old conceptions of human dignity which are at the very foundations of our civilization and its democratic institutions.

It is increasingly recognized that this task, while it concerns the whole of our society, is a special obligation of our intellectuals. Our academic intellectuals, under the pressure of a crisis growing more and more acute, are aware that a humanistic reorientation of the higher learning calls for the united efforts of entire university faculties. At Princeton, for example, a group of eight distinguished professors representing astronomy, chemistry, economics, history, classics, philosophy, and religion collaborated in a statement presented at the 1941 meeting of the Conference on Science, Philosophy, and Religion held at Columbia University. That the opinions I have expressed are nowise novel, but representative of a trend, may be suggested by a series of quotations which may serve as a summary of the argument I have so far advanced:

"Democratic institutions and cultural activities rest upon the assumption that man, while a part of nature, is a spiritual being....

"Spiritual life and its laws... are not identical with any of the phenomena of laws of nature described by the natural sciences; and whatever description of them the natural sciences may be capable of giving cannot affect their reality and their values.

"The human spirit, of course, is dependent to an undetermined extent upon the natural processes of the body and its environment. But, though it is thus conditioned by biological and physical processes it cannot be identified with them and can be fully understood only by means of distinctive methods and categories suitable to its distinctive nature....

"The capacity of man to relate himself to an ultimate source of meaning and worth and to value things and persons for their intrinsic worth is thus essential to a true conception of the human spirit. There have been, however, different ideas about the ultimate source of meaning and worth and the practical implications of man's relation to it. The two major conceptions of the spiritual life which have dominated Western thought are the intellectual and contemplative conception derived primarily from the Greeks and the Hebraic-Christian moral and religious conception....

"Naturalism denies both man's relation to an order of ultimate values and his dependence upon a cosmic spiritual Power. It thus divorces him from the moral and spiritual order to which he belongs and upon which he depends for strength and direction....

"Many who hold to this naturalistic view in democratic countries are unaware of the dangers in their position.... They act as if they still believed in the spiritual conception of man which they have intellectually repudiated. They try to maintain their feeling for the dignity of man, while paying homage to an essentially materialistic philosophy according to which man is simply a highly developed animal. They are loyal to their democratic society and culture, but by their theory they deny the spiritual nature of man and his values upon which it has been built. In short, they are living off the spiritual capital which has come down to them from their classical and religious heritage, while at the same time they ignore that heritage itself as antiquated and false.

"Since this contradiction will prove to be intellectually intolerable, scholars and teachers must recover and reaffirm the spiritual conception of man and his good which we have derived from Greek and Hebraic-Christian sources. If they fail to do this, not only religious reverence and moral responsibility, but also the scholarly activities with which they are directly concerned, will be gravely endangered. Already, under totalitarian regimes, and to a lesser extent in the democracies, these activities are being undermined."

6. The Heritage of Freemen

Our Occidental civilization derives its strength ultimately from the Great Tradition, which is the conflux of our humanistic legacy from the pagan world and our religious legacy from Judaism and Christianity. This twofold tradition may be approached in terms of American experience. In the seventeenth century we had in America an inadequate Christianity, in the eighteenth century an inadequate classicism; only in the late nineteenth century did a corrosive naturalism finally give us our vacuum of faith. If today educators would concern themselves with values, they must begin by acquainting the youth of America with the values which America has shared with the rest of the Occident. This is not a proposal for turning back the clock, for trying to go back to the Middle Ages or Greek antiquity, for attempting to confine the human spirit. It is a proposal of an emancipation from the provincial dogmas of the day, and from all the forms of indoctrination and regimentation which threaten to bedevil our education. To avoid these dangers the best way, in the end, is to give students access to their essential heritage. Burn the books (or ignore them, which is the same) if you would make slaves. "Open the books," as Willkie said, "if you wish to be free" and to make free men.

The books opened most often by Thomas Jefferson, who

assuredly had no desire to turn the clock back, were not contemporary works, though he knew these too, but the classics of Greece and Rome. "By a strange anomaly," as Professor Chinard observes, "the son of a pioneer, the young man supposedly brought up under frontier influences, felt more kinship with Greece and republican Rome than with the philosophies of London, Paris, or Geneva." He preferred to read Homer, Epictetus, Cicero, Tacitus, and he read them not merely for aesthetic satisfaction but rather for knowledge of man and society. When vice-president of the United States, he testified that "to read the Latin and Greek authors in their original is a sublime luxury.... I thank on my knees Him who directed my early education, for having put into my possession this rich source of delight; and I would not exchange it for anything which I could then have acquired, and have not since acquired." Jefferson was not alone in having occasion to thank Him—and those—who directed his early education, as James J. Walsh made clear in his book on the education of the Founding Fathers. They were disciplined in the arts of free men and possessed the knowledge most useful in establishing the institutions of free men, whereas their descendants in our time, as Walter Lippmann and the late Walter A. Jessup have argued, are ceasing to be free because they have lost the discipline and knowledge of their great tradition. If we are to return to the tradition, we shall have to do so mainly through translations. As readers of Greek and Latin know, this will entail a serious loss. Yet the power of great books is so strong even at second hand that translations have again and again proved a fructifying and dynamic agency in the development of national cultures in Italy, France, Germany, and England.

The great tradition is Christian as well as classical. A deist, not a Christian in any orthodox sense, Jefferson had pondered earnestly, as perhaps few of our political leaders have done in recent years, the doctrine of Jesus, as well as other religions and philosophies which have had an important history. But another American president, Abraham Lincoln, serves as a better symbol of the sustaining and ennobling power of Christianity. It is true that he too held aloof from orthodox creeds.

Yet he read the Bible as few read it today, and found in it patterns of what life should be, of what life would be so far as he could guide its course for himself and his people. He learned to feel and speak like the authors of the Bible and the Book of Common Prayer. He was our foremost Christian president. If government by the people is not to perish from the earth, it can ill afford to base its concept of human dignity on anything less than a religious sense of the spiritual worth of each person, as opposed to the naturalistic view of the individual as a mere social unit. The inhumanity of the fascist tyranny brought this home, for example, to a novelist who had won his reputation in the school of naturalism—Thomas Mann. Democracy and Christianity, as he declared in an address at Hobart College, "are united to such an extent that democracy may be called the political expression of our Christian feeling for life, of Christianity on earth. And we may conclude from the close relationship of democracy and Christianity, not that they will disappear together, but that they will survive together." If this is true, effort will be needed to restore the vitality of the Christian faith, and in this effort higher education must have a role. Experience has shown that it is possible to have a school of religion even within a state university. Without such a school it is still possible to present in the course of study the history of Christianity, and to include much of the King James Bible in the reading of every student, if only because this translation is one of the masterpieces of English literature.

Open the books if you wish to be free, above all the books central in Occidental civilization. Democracies have at last begun to realize what is at stake, says I. L. Kandel in *The End of an Era*, and they will maintain themselves only by continuing "the heritage of Athens and Jerusalem, whose possession made men free." This is a large task for secondary and higher education in the humanities. Yet circumstances may soon force us to be concerned with Oriental civilization as well, with at least some knowledge of the history and tradition of China and India. What is most modern in these countries is Occidental (a mixed blessing!) and familiar enough to us. But their national cultures are powerfully shaped by the past, resembling in many ways in China the humanism, and in India the religion, of the West. Confucius and Buddha will take on a new importance for us if the tradition of civilization is to be seen, in the phrase of Ordway Tead, "universally and not merely occidentally." Nor can we rest content here. Outside the central stream of the humanistic and religious tradition are many Western works which have so profoundly affected the course of civilization that they might well have a place in the course of study, the works of men like Machiavelli, Rousseau, Darwin, Marx, Nietzsche. They must be represented not only because of their historic importance but for reasons even more compelling: because they will protect us against too firm and assured guidance of the young, and because the young have a right to access to greatness of whatever kind. We shall keep *all* the books open.

7. Liberal Education

An education inspired by the humanistic ideal will be a liberal education. It alone is fully worthy of the dignity of man. Its object is clear: to liberate the young from ignorance, prejudice, foolishness, and the like; to aid them to attain freedom through realization of their capacities as men and women. An education aiming at something less than the human is in so far barbarous, for example the slavish education of the totalitarian state, or a vocational education which degrades men to tools. To be sure, men must have vocations, and therefore preparation ranging from a few weeks or months to a term of years, according to the calling selected, but such preparation, whether narrowly or broadly conceived, is not what we mean by liberal education.

When liberal education arose in ancient Greece, it was the discipline of free men—the unfree learned the vocations. Today the division is not between classes but within the individual. To make a living he works forty hours a week, more or less; to live he has all the rest, to live freely, as he chooses. Only a relatively few men can have vocations that exercise their full humanity. The vast majority can feel free only in their free time, and they want more and more free time. Whatever the value of their vocational work to themselves and to the state, the value of their free time is even greater both to themselves and to the state as well. For the state needs citizens even more than it needs shopkeepers, carpenters, bankers, lawyers, needs men who are more than instruments in the work of the world, who experience life in many ways, develop many interests, play a role in the formation of that public opinion which is the real government of the democratic state, and attain a morale high enough to sustain the state in peace and war. The most civilized state will, if resources and manpower are equal, be the strongest, happiest, and most memorable.

From the point of view of the American state, therefore, the function of liberal education, as President Roosevelt said at Jefferson's alma mater, is that of "training men for citizenship in a great republic." "This," he went on to say, "was in the spirit of the old America, and it is, I believe, in the spirit of the America of today. The necessities of our time demand that men avoid being set in grooves, that they avoid the occupational predestination of the older world.... Every form of cooperative human endeavor cries out for men and women who, in their thinking processes, will know something of the broader aspects of any given problem." Clearly, the states of the Union cannot afford, in their public universities, the multiplication of occupational curricula that offer what Edmund Burke somewhere calls "tricking short-cuts and little fallacious facilities." Even in the professions liberal training is gravely hindered by the motivation of the student, who, as another of our presidents—Woodrow Wilson—put it, "will be immersed in the things that touch his profit and loss, and a man is not free to think inside that territory."

Liberal education is one thing and vocational education another, and no amount of sophistry about liberal education "in a new sense of the term" will alter the fact. That they differ in principle has been recognized from ancient times to the present. As they were apart in ancient Greece, so they were in the Middle Ages, when an education in the seven liberal arts was prescribed for every student before he turned to his professional preparation. They were apart again in the Renaissance. In the Mantuan school of Vittorino, for instance, which merits a few words here because it blended so well the classical and Christian traditions, the aim, as stated by W. H. Woodward, was "to lay foundations in liberal culture to serve as the necessary preliminaries to specific training for careers." As a humanist educator, Vittorino da Feltre sought to create "the complete citizen," or, to say the same thing another way, "to secure the harmonious development of mind, body, and character." The curriculum was limited by the meagre scientific knowledge then available, but it supplemented the humanities with mathematics and some natural science (astrology was discarded for astronomy). Ancient culture was not pursued in abstraction but focused earnestly on the needs of the present. As for individual differences, Vittorino considered, "almost with reverence, the tastes and bent of each of his pupils." Before going on to professional study his pupils stayed with him "until they had passed their twenty-first year." On the whole, his school might well serve as a fruitful source of suggestion for the liberal college in modern America, as it has served for secondary education in modern Europe. Our high schools accomplish something in liberal education and could accomplish more, but under our system it is the responsibility of the college to complete the program, postponing occupational training till it *has* been completed—if necessary till the student has passed his twenty-first year.

But the beguiling hope persists: Could not liberal education be attempted *through* vocational education? Many persons, like John Dewey in his article in *Fortune* in 1944, have argued that liberal education as we have known it from ancient till recent times is a relic of the pre-democratic and pre-scientific past, and that today the appropriate education must be technical and vocational. It is frankly admitted that our job-centered training has been too narrow and mechanical. So we should set about "liberalizing our technical and vocational education." How this is to be done has not been made very clear. One might suppose, to take a concrete example, that a course in

Advanced Clothing would be so taught as to lead the student back to earlier conceptions of costume, eventually to Greek costume and hence to Greek art and hence to the whole Greek view of life, perhaps attracting the student to an elective in ancient civilization which he would "feed into" his vocational preparation. But this is not what Dr. Dewey means. His great object is to make the student modern, that is, scientific. The past, lingering in our conceptions and standards, is only a clog that prevents our going forward with undivided zeal toward "the scientific way of life." Vocational education must be liberalized by showing how modern industry rests on scientific processes. What this would seem to mean, in our course on Advanced Clothing, is that the student would be brought to "awareness of the scientific processes embodied" in designing, constructing, and preserving clothing and in relating contemporary clothing to contemporary social forces. Whatever it means the net result might be the improvement of vocational education but could not be the improvement of liberal education.

If liberal education is not concerned with vocational skills, it is profoundly concerned with other skills and abilities. There are many things which the student, as a human being, should be able to do. He should be able to care for his body, his physical welfare. He should be able to speak, to read, to write, on a plane suited to his college years and later life. He should know how to think: how to think in the concrete terms of science, how to think in the abstract manner of mathematics and philosophy, and how to think (and feel and will) in the humanistic realm of value-judgments. He should be able to relate his growing abilities and knowledge in the gradual development of a philosophy of life to which he is willing provisionally to commit himself. He should be able to relate his developing philosophy to active experience in living, to complete the revolving circle of thought and action. Through the discipline of his entire nature he will come into ever fuller possession of himself as a human being and as a particular person.

Something like this set of skills and abilities is agreed upon by virtually all who profess belief in liberal education. The list may never be altogether the same, and differences in emphasis will appear, but on the whole the objectives are sufficiently agreed upon. There is a fundamental cleavage, however, between those who assert that liberal education is concerned only with abilities and those who assert that it involves both abilities and knowledge.

The tendency has been especially marked among educationists to limit the objectives to abilities, using knowledge only as means. What sort of person, they ask, do we want the student to be when we are through with him? What do we want to have happen to him in consequence of his education? Once we have decided upon the end-product, it will be easy to plan a curriculum and hire and fire teachers according to their success in changing the student as we want him changed. The student is to be conditioned, the teacher is to be approved or purged. This totalitarian parody of liberal education—I have stated it crudely because I have heard it stated crudely—shows some signs of becoming a menace in a society floundering for lack of assured values. America today has more reason than England had in 1935 to heed the warning then sounded by John Murray, principal of University College, Exeter. "Any dictator," he cried, "might see his chance in the present state of the universities that have sold themselves to utility. If the universities have lost their humanism, or the prophetic and magisterial tones in preaching it, need a dictator hesitate? From him that hath not shall be taken away even that which he hath."

Protection against this perversion is offered by those who assert that liberal education involves not only abilities but common knowledge, common knowledge not of anything at random but of the liberating best that man has said and done. Even if the goal were allowed to be abilities alone, it could be attained most effectively by the use of the best materials. After all is anyone so crass as to maintain that the history of Peru would do as well as the history of modern Europe, the literature of the Philippines as well as the literature of England, an African dialect as well as French, the science of numismatics as well as the science of biology? The knowledge to be learned may obviously be more or less relevant. Is there, then, a most relevant knowledge? Is there an indispensable best? If so, who shall say what it is? At this point the specialist professor will break down in utter helplessness. But even he, if he could drop his pose or his politics, would quickly begin a list of essentials, or of things so important that they might as well be called essentials. There is a large area of general agreement as to the best that man has said and done, large enough for the planning of a curriculum. This best will guard the student against conditioning to the intellectual fashions and veering passions of the day, fashions and passions to which the faculty itself is not immune. He will have at hand a standard by which to measure the instruction he is receiving. Even if the knowledge opened to him is not necessarily the best, it will have high value as common knowledge, shared knowledge, tending to unite his and other students' minds in common experience, common duties, common memories. Liberal education based on common knowledge is social education; vocational education separating youth into groups according to special interests is unsocial education.

When a common fund of knowledge has been selected, the liberal college will begin to take on a definiteness of type comparable to that of the professional schools. Once this definiteness of type has been fully established in terms of objectives, curriculum, and teaching methods, the uniform requirement of specific knowledge will seem no more arbitrary than it does today in training for the professions. If something like half of the total Bachelor's program is made common, the other half will be available for election among advanced liberal studies, or for concentration upon a segment of the field of learning, to be chosen according to individual differences in interest and ability and to be studied in the same liberal manner.

8. The Great Curriculum

What should the common studies be? In a humanistic reorientation, it goes without saying, the humanities will take on a new importance. But can we be satisfied with the thesis of President Conant that a general education must be based on literature, the arts, and philosophy, even if we add history, which he has elsewhere predicted will be the most widely required study in the next fifty years? All these are humanities; is the humanistic spirit content to ignore science? The answer must be clear and unequivocal.

Historically, the answer is plain: an education permeated with the humanistic spirit has always included science. In ancient Greece, science—mathematics, astronomy, some natural history—was a part of liberal education. In the Renaissance, in the school of Vittorino, for example, it was likewise included. That science was sometimes disparaged by the humanists of the Renaissance is not surprising, in view of the scant knowledge of nature then existing. Science was little more than a promise or a hope, while the humanities had attained a dazzling achievement as far back as the fifth century B.C., indeed still earlier in the greatest of all poets, Homer. By the late nineteenth century this contrast had disappeared: science had arrived, it too had attained a dazzling achievement, and it claimed and won its place in education. If the zeal of its opponents was occasionally excessive, so was the zeal of its proponents. One must regret the mutual hostility of the two sides that attended the arrival of science in education and that lingers with us to this day, because it was not and is not justified.

The hostility is the result of mistaken attitudes. On the one side, scientists have often depreciated the humanities as not concerned with knowledge, on the assumption that there is only one kind of knowledge, scientific knowledge. They have believed that science is competent, and alone competent, to deal securely and fruitfully with everything natural and human. All fields of knowledge should be freed of unvalidated guesses, armchair philosophizing, the drag of superstition, and be duly scientized. "What knowledge is of most worth?" "The answer is always—Science." This attitude, as I have already suggested, comes not from science but from philosophy, the philosophy of naturalism. On the other side: humanists have often depreciated the sciences as materialistic, as if they were responsible for the sordid world of the machine, of big business and little living, a world in which things are in the saddle and ride mankind. When this has been their attitude, humanists have forgotten that the source of what they term materialism is, as Michael Pupin rightly declared, not in "any material structure raised by the genius of man," but "in the deepest depths of the human soul where selfishness and greed, hatred and fear" have displaced "beauty and goodness." The evil from which we suffer lies in the realm of the humanities. It was not caused by scientists and engineers and will never be destroyed by them.

Between a naturalistic philosophy reducing man wholly to the flux of nature and a humanistic philosophy emphasizing his distinctive humanity the conflict is real and, in the end, irreconcilable. But between science and the humanities there can be no real conflict whatever. That men in these two broad domains can come together in mutual respect was indicated, for instance, a number of years ago in a public statement. Fifteen distinguished American scientists (including such names as Walcott, Osborn, Conklin, Pupin, Mayo, Millikan) issued a joint statement with a similar group of religious leaders and men of affairs, regretting the antagonism between men in the domains of science and the humanities, specifically religion. They declared: *"The purpose of science is to develop, without prejudice or preconception of any kind, a knowledge of the facts, the laws, and the processes of nature. The even more important task of religion, on the other hand, is to develop the consciences, the ideals, and the aspirations of mankind."* The province of the one is natural knowledge; the province of the other is human values. So long as each stays within its bounds there can be no conflict. They are complementary, and should be co-operative. We need to know *what is*, we need to know *what ought to be*, and we need to know how they may be related.

To say that science is concerned with judgments of fact and not with judgments of value is not, however, to deny that implications of value enter into science. It is precisely because of the value implications of science that the humanistic spirit wholeheartedly supports science. The human values implied and presupposed by science are twofold.

First, it is animated by the passion to know, the quest of knowledge for its own sake. There is no science save as men produce it, and men produce it because they value it as men. Among the "aspirations of mankind" mentioned above, we must assign a high place to the desire for knowledge, including knowledge of nature—the physical and biological constitution and environment of our species. To this aspiration science owes its existence, as Dr. Einstein reminds us in a passage I have quoted. To this aspiration science also owes its capacity to survive. Whenever the aspiration for truth for its own sake declines, science also declines. This happened, for instance, when a Nazi leadership sought to evoke the miracle of a "German science." American men of science were revolted by this perversion not as scientists (science revolts at nothing) but as humanists. The humanistic spirit has, as one of its first and finest attributes, a passion for the disinterested, impartial pursuit of truth. In the process of education it is communicated with difficulty, and demands time and hard work. Yet innumerable college graduates can say of some scientist what one of them, for example, said of his beloved teacher of zoology, Henry V. Wilson, who "first revealed to my hazy young mind the fact that there was a vast field of knowledge where Truth, within certain recognizable limits, was not a matter of opinion, nor of taste, nor a recollection of historical facts, but a thing of demonstrable law.... He is the embodiment of the scientific spirit which seeks Truth always, without prejudices, without preconceptions, not caring where the search leads but careful always that in the utmost detail the distinction be preserved between that which is known and that which is supposed." Now, this distinction is one which is nowhere so impressively communicated as in the sciences of nature, which consequently merit an important place in liberal education.

Secondly, science is animated by the desire for use. Knowledge is not only an end in itself, but a means to further ends. As Francis Bacon taught, knowledge is power, and may be aimed at "the relief of man's estate," "inventions that may in some degree subdue and overcome the necessities and miseries of humanity" and also, we may add, contribute to man's chances of happiness. Science is thus instrumental in the achieving of values already defined by the humanistic spirit. For a hundred years the instrumental service of science has tended to obscure its intrinsic value, so that T. H. Huxley complained, as long ago as 1866, that science had been degraded to "a sort of comfort-grinding machine." On the intellectual plane the same tendency has led to a whole philosophy of instrumentalism, associated with the name of John Dewey. The motivation of this philosophy is human purpose, action, advantage, working experimentally in the overcoming of difficulties, and by a strange inversion truth itself is conceived as serviceability. This conclusion is not acceptable to the disinterested pursuit of truth which we call science. As W. T. Stace has said, "The ideal of the scientific mind has been, throughout the history of the west from Greek times to the present day, not to appraise theories by their capacity for helping human beings, but by their correspondence with the facts of the objective world. Of course science has sought, among other things, to discover truths which shall be of service to men. But it is a monstrous perversion to suggest that the quality of being serviceable to men is what, in the opinion of science, has rendered its discoveries true."

The humanistic spirit, believing in the pursuit of truth as an end in itself, believing also in the use of truth as a means to further ends, must hereafter give unstinted support to the great sciences of nature set in motion by the Hellenic mind and accelerated enormously by our own age. What is to be said of the so-called sciences of man?

The social sciences are relatively new and undeveloped subjects. With the exception of political science, heir of a political philosophy already mature as far back as Plato and Aristotle, the sciences of man in society came into being only a century or two ago—economics in the eighteenth century, anthropology, sociology, and social psychology in the late nineteenth century. As a distinct group or academic division comparable to the natural sciences and the humanities, they date from the present century. They owe their existence, in the form in which we have them, mainly to a belief that the objectives and methods of the triumphant natural sciences should next be applied to the study of human society. In the words of a committee report, "in social science, as in other sciences, an attempt is made to describe, rather than to evaluate, the subject matter. The goal is to understand the social order, to discover important concrete facts, and to find regularities that may be assumed to obtain beyond the cases observed and described." A social scientist, emulating the impartiality of the natural scientist, is not in a position to choose, for example, between democracy and fascism, either in his studies or in his teaching. He is permitted no preferences, no fixed standards, no absolute values. "As a scientist," says Robert M. Mac Iver, "he must be content with his world of relative values. Whatever his own convictions may be, he must be constantly alert not to impose them on the changeful order of things."

The impulse is admirable, but the results have been disappointing, and the suspicion is growing that methods and concepts drawn from natural science will not suffice for social science. The "wavering and incalculable behavior" of man, in the phrase of F. W. Taussig, suggests the enormous difficulty of a true science of man. The concept of cause and effect, as it appears in natural science, seems not to carry over to social science. Unlike other animate beings man is purposive, with a will that seems like the wind's will of the poet. Besides, while social behavior may be observed with a good deal of precision, the attempt to generalize the facts in the form of hypotheses cannot lead to positive results because the scientific method of controlled experiment and verification is not available. The result is a prevailing haziness and sense of frustration. "Twenty years hence," said Torrens in regard to political economy, "there will scarcely exist a doubt respecting any of its fundamental principles." Twenty years passed, one hundred and twenty years passed, and today the air is filled with more doubts than ever. Perhaps the best summary of the struggle of the social sciences to find themselves is that of Roscoe Pound, who begins by saying that he has no quarrel with them, having taught jurisprudence for forty years from the sociological standpoint. "But I do not deceive myself," he says, "as to those so-called sciences. So far as they are not descriptive, they are in continual flux. In the nature of things they cannot be sciences in the sense of physics or chemistry or astronomy. They have been organized as philosophies, have been worked out on the lines of geometry, have been remade to theories of history, have had their period of positivism, have turned to social psychology, and are now in an era of neo-Kantian methodology in some hands and of economic determinism or psychological realism or relativist skepticism or phenomenonological intuitionism in other hands. They do not impart wisdom; they need to be approached with acquired wisdom.... They are not foundation subjects. They belong in the superstructure."

How the social sciences are eventually to find themselves and to establish themselves as an essential part of liberal education, I shall not venture to suggest. One thing, however, seems very clear. They will have to derive their methodology from their own subject matter, rather than from the natural sciences. Since their subject matter is man, they may be expected to draw closer to the humanities. Even the "dismal science" of economics—dismal in its vicious circle of "producing wealth to produce more wealth"—is capable of taking on a profound human relevance in the hands of a man like John Ruskin, who does not look so foolish as he did in the good old days of classical political economy. A university professor wrote to me: "We economists too often stress some mechanical adjustment of prices or production when the real need is men of character and insight who can direct and enlighten us." Is there any reason why economists should not themselves be men of character and insight? In point of fact, the researches of our social scientists are largely directed by concepts of human values, despite professions of innocence. But the values are casually assumed, derived from the climate of opinion rather than earned by study and hard reflection. The social scientist of the future, one may venture to predict, will be obliged to bring his subject into more fruitful relation with the humanities, perhaps even to restore it to its humane matrix.

The curriculum of foundation studies, then, will be drawn mainly from the natural sciences and the humanities: the physical and the biological sciences, history, literature, art, and philosophy. It will offer, not hasty encyclopedic surveys of these fields, but a rich and intimate knowledge and experience of the best that man has learned and said and done in them. It will address the student, not as a future technician and specialist, but as a human being interested in understanding himself and his world. In this new task it cannot be expected to succeed until scholars in each subject have reconceived their aims and methods in the manner proposed, for one subject, by a recent collaborative book on *Literary Scholarship: Its Aims and Methods.* Only then will it be possible for us to undertake profitably the search for the concrete program of subjects and courses which will constitute the modern Great Curriculum equal in solidity and authority to the great curricula of past ages.

Reform within the subjects, if it has not advanced far, has at least begun. While it continues, we may welcome serious reflection upon the more general problem, as in the article by William C. DeVane on "American Education After the War," the book entitled *Liberal Education Re-Examined* by a committee appointed by the American Council of Learned Societies, and the book on *The Rebirth of Liberal Education* written by Fred B. Millett for the Rockefeller Foundation. We may welcome the ferment of curricular thought working everywhere today in our colleges and universities even though so much of it seems only frivolously modish and leads only to a meaningless tinkering dictated by political motives. Yet there is a danger that our preoccupation with curricula and organization and teaching procedures, in a word with machinery, will obscure the real problem. That problem, as I have tried to show, is the spirit and aim of the men who do the teaching, the faculty's philosophy of life and of education, which should give direction to all the practical decisions that must be made. A naturalistic philosophy has led the modern world, in totalitarian and democratic nations alike, toward a materialistic chaos and a resurgence of barbarism. An age of science has become an age of the misuse of science. Whether the forces of darkness will be halted no man can say. But this one can affirm: that if America is to play a high and civilizing role in the rest of the twentieth century, it will need a humanistic philosophy of life based on the concept of the dignity of man, and a humanistic philosophy of education that will supply our democratic society with men and women of intelligence and character.

9. The Great Faculty

Curricular legerdemain is no substitute for a change of heart and mind in the professoriate. What we are suffering from today is not so much a trivialized curriculum as a trivialized faculty. The only fundamental way to improve the curriculum is to improve the faculty which designs the curriculum. What William Penn said of government may be said, by paraphrase, of education: "Education rather depends upon Men, than Men upon Education. Let Men be good, and the Education can't be bad; if it be ill, they will cure it." No educational institution is any better than the men who do its work. This is why, in a report to the Carnegie Foundation on graduate school education, Marcia Edwards cancelled out most of her data by admitting that no plans or procedures can take the place of a competent staff in its eventual effect on education. This we have always known, or should have known. Even an egregiously bad procedure in graduate education, such as that in the field of English and comparative literature at Harvard before the First World War, achieved a large measure of success because the staff included such men as Kittredge, Babbitt, Neilson, Perry, Baker, Briggs, Rand, who transcended the procedure. In Harvard's undergraduate education the procedure was equally bad, the elective system being still in full swing, but again these great teachers, and others like them in other departments, saved the situation. Today, instead of proliferating procedures, plans, experiments, and disappointments, we would do well to begin by reforming the faculty.

The quality of the faculty depends, in the unwritten constitution of the state university, upon the administrators who appoint the professors. When a vacancy arises, what sort of professor do they look for? They look, sometimes hastily, more often persistently, for a specialist of high repute, i.e., high repute among other specialists. Incidentally, they inquire whether the specialist scholar is also a good teacher or at least not a bad one. Incidentally, they consider his personality, being satisfied if it is superficially agreeable. They display no concern for his character so long as he has done nothing scandalous, and they have no interest whatever in the values he lives by. A good professor is simply a good specialist in his particular field.

The results are deplorable. Administrators are not pleased with their own handiwork, students can admire only a few of their teachers, and even the faculty of specialists is aware that specialism is not enough. In its 1933 report on the state of teaching, the American Association of University Professors acknowledged that their own profession is failing to attract to itself "a sufficient number of broadly cultured young men and women," because faculty members are not "portraying by their own careers and example to the younger generation of scholars the kind of profession which strikes the youthful imagination in a favorable light when compared with other callings." The examples are so bad that they are not worthy of imitation.

The examples offered by the state university faculty are mainly of three types: pedants, dilettanti, and career-builders. It goes without saying that the types are not always distinct from each other, nor without some of the admirable traits of a fourth type, the relatively few examples of "Man Thinking." The first type, the pedants, have often been publicly exposed. They have knowledge without the power of it. Their interest in facts and technique is fussy, their results are mostly trifling. In their dull and honest incapacity, they do not well know the difference between the important and the unimportant. They often base their claims for promotion on the number of pages they have published. They impress some administrators, but generally they are regarded as dead wood, of which, it must be confessed, a large part of the academic forest is made up.

Smaller in numbers but more conspicuous are the dilettanti. Some of them are dabblers pure and simple, but as a rule they maintain respectability by publishing as pedants or scholars while teaching as dilettanti: charmers, entertainers, showmen, even clowns. Too often they are swindlers, offering education, in their easygoing way, at cut prices and thus cheating both their students and their employers; or else sentimentalists, pitying the dull and harried student and grading him well above his deserts. By such meretricious practices the dilettanti manage to be "popular," which, according to Emerson, "is to go down perpendicularly." In academic rank and salary they are more likely to go up.

Most successful of all are the career-builders. These are the specialists who "play the game." They are not the dedicated spirits, the absent-minded and unworldly professors, of popular myth. They have no vocation in the fine old sense of a call or summons to a particular occupation. They show with painful clearness that faculty members can be all too "human," that is to say, "natural." Emerson knew them: "Men, such as they are, very naturally seek money or power." The career-builders may be subdivided into two further types. One type comprises the go-getters, the Machiavellians, who subordinate principle to politics. Aggressive party men with a cynical view of human nature, they support the administration of set purpose and shoulder their way ahead of scrupulous colleagues by evasion, treachery, defamation, and the like. They are gifted in cooperation with each other but are quite ready, when need arises, to cut the throat of a fellow go-getter who gets in the way. The other type comprises the more passive yes-men, who, suppressing inner dissent, seek to advance themselves by appeasement: by hypocritical flattery, or a timid and time-serving acquiescence, or an unnatural silence. Emerson recognized them when he charged that "the scholar is decent, indolent, complaisant." Protected by security of tenure, this type of professor is nevertheless too timorous to avail himself of his academic freedom, though only academic freedom can justify security of tenure. In general it is the career-builders, the mass of go-getters and yes-men, who determine what goes on in the university and who are most richly rewarded by the administration.

The admirable exceptions are far too few: young men whose inner resources are such that they will risk much rather than merely play the game, and older men who have learned that life without principle is not really life. In every university faculty there is a minority of dedicated scholars and teachers, who have not permitted their specialties to rob them of their manhood, who are persons as well as instruments, who are devoted to whatsoever things are true and elevated and just, who are laboring in behalf of liberal education and humane scholarship in the hostile environment of a materialistic institution. They are examples of Man Thinking, man devoted to ideas. They are lovers of knowledge ("science," in the old general sense) and lovers of wisdom ("philosophers"). They are "academic" in the sense that they would have been able to hold their own in Plato's Academy. They have the independent mind, the critical spirit, being above their knowledge not beneath it. They are thus, on a higher plane, like the liberally educated student. Combining broad understanding and concentrated knowledge, they relate their special subjects to tangent subjects, to all subjects. They relate past and present, and make both live. They deal thoughtfully with the whole of life, and with life as a whole, having committed themselves to a philosophy—and perhaps a religion as well—worthy of the dignity of man, though there is great diversity among them in doctrine. They are men of character as well as intelligence—men of integrity, not conflicting pieces of men, acting in all things (within the limits of human frailty) with sincerity, fairness, friendliness, and courage. Free and brave, they can say with Emerson, "We will walk on our own feet; we will work with our own hands; we will speak our own minds."

Such are the exceptional scholar-teachers, at their rare best. With them we must be content to subsume admirable types wanting this completeness. Some are admirable because of their personal character, the fine quality of their actual living, though their minds may not be speculative. Others are admirable for the depth and richness of their inner life, or spiritual insight. Others, again, are exceptional for their highly vitalized intellectual life, their energy in forming and relating ideas, or in using erudition for high ends, or in applying standards of value. All of these types, without trying to be exemplary, are aware that values are "caught" more than taught, that the best teaching is always teaching by example, that what motivates students, and motivates them in the right direction, is excellence of mind and character in the teacher. This is not too much to ask of a university professor. He need not be a "great man" or a "genius." He need be great only in what he represents—the humanistic spirit in action.

Every faculty, as I have said, contains a minority of such men. In the eyes of a naturalistic administration, they constitute a sort of opposition party. Sometimes they are viewed intolerantly as a barrier to be forced down, sometimes tolerantly as a means of stimulating intellectual virility in the faculty as a whole. Their numbers are few. But the reform of the faculty will not be in sight till they are many.

The head of a department can do something to increase their numbers. A humanistic head, in one department or another, can assist the dean in the appointment and promotion of the right sort of men, because the dean, as likely as not, will not know the difference between the right sort and the wrong sort. Many a dean, concentrating upon a man's competence as a specialist—his reputation in "his own field"—will accept recommendations of men who, it will turn out, will enlarge the minority. A humanistic head, while giving due weight to specialized competence, will not let himself be misled by "fields." For example, he will prefer an enlightened specialist in Renaissance history to a narrow specialist in American history, even when the so-called vacancy is in the latter field, for what he seeks above all is to gather a group of humane scholars. He will remember that, beneath a scholar's knowledge, guiding the use of that knowledge in teaching and productive scholarship, is his outlook on life, his scale of values. Like William James (at the opening of the first lecture on *Pragmatism*) he will number himself with those who believe, with Chesterton, that "The most practical and important thing about a man is still his view of the universe. We think that for a landlady considering a lodger it is important to know his income, but still more important to know his philosophy. We think that for a general about to fight an enemy it is important to know the enemy's numbers, but still more important to know the enemy's philosophy." In the same way an intelligent department head, considering a scholar and teacher of youth, will find it important to know the man's achievement in learning but still more important to know his underlying philosophy—not so much his formal opinions but rather the values he actually lives by as man and scholar.

In recommending new appointments the department head will desire the fullest evidence of ability, taking into account repeated interviews, the testimony of judges carefully selected for their humanistic standards (not for their names or high place), the quality of publications when closely analyzed, the test of an actual lecture or series of lectures or a temporary summer appointment. He will spare no effort, because he knows that a department, like a university, is not courses or procedures or books or laboratories but men. Once he has found and brought the right men, he will spare no effort to keep them. He will try to assure a wide opening for their talents by dropping the untalented—

> Enow of such as, for their bellies' sake,
> Creep, and intrude, and climb into the fold!

As he comes to know his best men intimately, to understand their natural interests and capacities, he will assign them to tasks which will call forth their creative endeavor. He will give them the courses, committee duties, administrative functions, most likely to develop their abilities, and then let them alone in the spirit of the Middle English proverb: "Send the wise and say no thing." If they have a special gift for productive scholarship, he will do everything possible to protect their time and energies. Since the tasks of a department are numerous, he will welcome diversity in excellence, never seeking to mold the staff to his own image. Free of envy, he will be glad if some of his professors are better than he. In a few state universities where heads have more responsibility than deans, the head will encourage the right men by promotions in salary and rank. In the great majority of institutions, he will do all he can to see that merit, as he understands it, is recognized and rewarded by the administration.

10. THE GREAT ADMINISTRATION

An occasional department head, guided by some such ideal, can do something to increase the humanistic minority. But the general complexion of the faculty is determined, of course, by the administration, by the deans and president who select the department heads and hold the purse strings involved in all appointments and promotions. In a naturalistic university the deans and president are nearly always themselves naturalistic in outlook. To a large extent the university is naturalistic because its leadership is. If it is to become humanistic its leadership will have to be humanistic. We must consequently go on to ask, What sort of leadership is worthy of the place of power in a university?

The qualifications would appear to be closely similar to those of the faculty. The administrator in a humanistic university is, like a sound leader in a political democracy, one of Jefferson's "men of intelligence and character." He will have the type of intelligence appropriate to a university: himself liberally educated, he will have taught with success in a college or university faculty, and will have had, preferably, experience in a lesser administrative position (there is an old saying, quoted by Bacon, that "A place showeth the man"). He will have the traits of character ascribed, above, to the professor, together with consideration and patience in dealing with a faculty which contains his equals and perhaps superiors. He will wish to lead and not drive. He will never use democratic processes as a cloak for the use of force. Courage he will need more than the professor, since his tenure is insecure. Justice may prove costly to him, but in the end injustice would be costlier. He will be mindful of the warning that power corrupts, the more because his position carries great power.

So great is the power lodged in his hands, according to the American system, that a university president can easily become a dictator. If he assumes all the responsibilities implied by his office, he is likely to turn out either a benevolent autocrat or the builder of a sinister power machine. If he prefers to neglect his responsibilities and to become a decorative nonentity ("stuffed shirt," as the elegant phrase goes), his subordinates will be dictators. If he believes in democracy and uses democratic processes as much as the system permits, because he knows that the Great Faculty is a free faculty, he will find the logic of the system against him. The basic fact in the university constitution is that he, the president, ultimately controls the entire budget. How much independence would the United States Senate have if every senator's salary were fixed by the will of a Vice-President appointed by the President? If it is easy for a university head (or his delegates) to play the role of dictator, it is exceedingly hard if not impossible for him to play the role of democratic leader.

Such a system is not in harmony with American democracy, nor is it necessary. University government was highly democratic in Europe, before the New Order, even in countries whose polities were largely autocratic. Sooner or later we shall have to reconsider our system. But till then, under the existing system, the president of a university will continue to have the responsibility of guiding its development through the officers and teaching staff that he appoints. This responsibility he cannot avoid. If, in derogation of his duty, he delegates professorial appointments entirely to his deans, he must still appoint the deans, or, which is the same thing, accept those he has inherited. Whether he attempts much or little or nothing, he cannot avoid exercising an influence so strong that it determines the character of the institution. The character of the institution, we have said, depends on men. He selects the men. As they are, so will the university be. Thus through the president, the university is, as William Ernest Hocking has said, "authoritative in a peculiarly indirect, difficult, and dangerous manner; namely, in the choice of the teaching staff." There is something less than candor, for instance, in the motto heading a department of the *Record* published by Teachers College, Columbia: "Teachers College, as an institution, holds no position, advocates no theory of education. It selects its faculty and, as every such institution must, permits each member untrammeled to present whatever his reflections and his researches lead him to believe." The disarming piety of tone in this statement does not conceal the vital phrase which destroys the piety: *"It selects its faculty."*

Even Thomas Jefferson, father of the State University of Virginia, was obliged to recognize the indoctrination implied by the selection of a faculty, and was willing to accept the responsibility for sound indoctrination, according to his lights. Writing to Madison, he said very frankly: "In the selection of our Law Professor, we must be rigorously attentive to his political principles." Blackstone, as Jefferson conceived, caused the legal profession "to slide into toryism, and nearly all the young brood of lawyers now are of that hue. They suppose themselves, indeed, to be whigs, because they no longer know what whigism or republicanism means. It is in our seminary that that vestal flame is to be kept alive; it is thence to spread anew over our own and the sister States. If we are true and vigilant in our trust, within a dozen or twenty years a majority of our own legislature will be from one school, and many disciples will have carried its doctrines home with them to their several States, and will have leavened thus the whole mass." Was this a fascist zeal for *Gleichschaltung?* Or was it a desire to accept responsibility to "make reason and the will of God prevail" through the orderly process of appointment? Should Jefferson have chosen a law professor of the hue of toryism—especially if the best tory was abler than the best whig? If a number of law professors were to be chosen, should they have been tories or whigs, or dominantly one or the other? or should the selection have been neutral, without regard for hue? In the last case the selection might have been neutral but the result would not have been: since nearly all the young brood of lawyers were tories who supposed themselves to be whigs, Jefferson would have had a tory law school.

Jefferson's problem was difficult, more difficult than that which confronts the president of a state university today in the situation I have indicated. It is not imperative for him to know whether a professor he is considering is a Republican or a Democrat, an Episcopalian or a Methodist. A state university is not committed to any particular party or denomination. What I have termed the general intent of the university is not a particular intent. The general intent involves, broadly, a philosophy of life, and the choice lies between a naturalistic and a humanistic philosophy. Toward which of the two is the president to guide the university through his appointment and promotion of officers and teaching staff? Like Jefferson, he cannot be neutral, since the great majority of the old brood and the young brood in the American academic world are naturalists, even when they suppose themselves to be humanists. To try to be neutral means to side with the naturalists. If the president closes his eyes to all qualifications except ability and reputation (and that is what he commonly does) he will continue to have a naturalistic university.

Let us suppose that the president wishes to change the complexion and intent of his university, to encourage the growth in it of a humanistic spirit. Has he any chance of success? As President Conant has rightly said, "Over a period of years the new appointments and promotions to permanent positions determine the fate of any college or university." If the direction of change is to be humanistic, this statement applies above all to the arsenal of the humanistic spirit, the university's college of liberal arts. First must come the appointment of a suitable dean of the college. Then, in a period of say ten years, there will be an opportunity to refill many headships and other key positions, to promote many men to full professorships, to promote many assistant professors to permanent positions, to reconstitute the large group of assistant professors, and to try out perhaps hundreds of instructors and assistants. Above all, the president and the dean will study closely the younger men, who are in the main the university of the future. At the end of ten years, if the administration has made the faculty its main business and has reached its innumerable decisions wisely, the result will be a university dominantly humanistic.

This is not a proposal of uniformity, which has no place in a state or any other university. Men who have the humanistic spirit are anything but alike; they enjoy disagreeing with each other as much as disagreeing with the naturalists. Nor will the faculty be made up of them alone. "Dominantly humanistic" is not exclusively humanistic. If uniformity became a danger, the administration should of set purpose introduce professors who would assure a healthy difference of outlook. But the danger is unreal. The old guard of naturalists would remain, by virtue of permanent tenure, and would be tolerated because the humanistic spirit is itself tolerant. Besides, it is far from easy today to find men who are of the kind desired, and even if it were not, many mistakes would be made, and many men would turn out to be other than was supposed, or would gradually alter their outlook. All of this the administration would accept with the best grace because the humanistic spirit is not only tolerant but humble, never too sure of its rightness.

A grave difficulty remains. Granted that a good president could bring about a reorientation in this way, how is a state university, unless it already has such a leader, to acquire one?

The choice of a president, under the American system of university government, is made by a governing board of trustees or regents. This is the most important action for which the board is responsible. In theory, to be sure, according to *A Manual for Trustees* by Raymond M. Hughes, "the control of policy is a function of the trustees," who "'should determine what sort of an institution they control." But in actual practice the functions of the board appear to be twofold: directly guiding the life of the university in its business aspects, and indirectly guiding the life of the university in its intellectual and spiritual aspects by the selection of a president. In carrying out the former function the board is usually astute, because it is made up largely of business men; in carrying out the latter function it is usually inept, for the same reason.

The trustees of a state university, it is true, are recruited from the best citizens of the state. They are successful men and women—intelligent, alert, earnest in behalf of the public good, hearty in their belief in democracy and in education. But their experience of life, while it has qualified them for understanding the complexities of business and legal affairs, has not qualified them for understanding the very different complexities of higher education. When, usually but once during their tenure, they are confronted by their responsibility of naming a president, they find themselves sadly unprepared. Their criteria in making a selection are as inadequate as those of a university faculty would be if called upon to name the president of a great industrial corporation. They often look for the "business man" type, which they understand, or an effective "money raiser" (but will he spend the money wisely?), or a man with a good "front" and ability in public speaking, or an "expert in education"—i.e. a man with the Teachers College mind. The net result is that they are likely to choose more men from "Education" than any other field, and more men from outside than inside the liberal arts faculty. The one type which they almost never look for and hence almost never come upon is the type I have described, the man of intelligence and character who understands liberal education and is imbued with the humanistic spirit.

However ill qualified for their task, governing boards could do better than they have done. Busy though they necessarily are with their private affairs, some of the members of a board might give more serious thought to the problems of education. If the humanistic tradition interested them, they could seek to understand the essential principles of humane education by reading, toward this end, *The Republic* of Plato, *Aristotle on Education* (edited by John Burnet), Elyot's *Book of the Governor*, Newman's *Idea of a University*, Arnold's *Culture and Anarchy*, and then some recent American books such as those by Flexner, Hutchins, Van Doren, Greene *et al.*, Millett, and the essays by seven writers which I have brought together in a little volume entitled *The Humanities After the War*. It is perhaps a fair guess that few state university trustees are really familiar with half the books in any such list. Then, for advice, they should go to the best judges they can find, e.g., alumni whose standards can be respected, administrators and professors in small colleges who appear to be genuinely liberal in outlook, and men of breadth and understanding in various occupations, such as scientists, churchmen, authors, editors. If only two or three members of a governing board made an earnest effort to comprehend what is at stake, to determine the right criteria, and to seek advice in the right places, they would be able to exert a strong influence upon their less active colleagues. They might succeed in getting the board to name a president who was, at least, not hostile to the humanistic spirit.

But in fact most governing boards will continue to name presidents as they have been doing. Naturalistic and utilitarian boards will give us naturalistic and utilitarian presidents. Only occasionally and by chance will they select a man competent to lead the way toward a university whose general intent is humanistic. What foresight failed to do a happy accident may do. Here and there we may expect a president to be chosen who will see his opportunity to demonstrate what such a university is and what it can accomplish for society. He will attract plenty of attention. Puzzled and rudderless as they are, our institutions of higher education turn with the keenest interest to any demonstration or experiment, such as the Meiklejohn experiment, the General College at Minnesota, the Chicago College Plan, St. John's College, in which somebody (*mirabile dictu*) seems to have a clearly defined purpose. One or two demonstrations of a humanistic state university would be a wonder among wonders in the eyes of those who are without standards and are looking for possible "trends" to adjust themselves to. It might even start a new trend.

In the long run public opinion will determine whether we shall have the humanistic university. If there is to be a great curriculum, a great faculty, a great administration, there must be a Great Society. Broad movements of thought and desire, rising to clearness in our society as time goes on, will decide whether the naturalistic philosophy of life and education is the wave of the future, or whether a humanistic philosophy will give a new direction to life and education. The formation of public opinion, in a democracy, is an exceedingly complicated matter. But one thing is plain: universities need not wait passively for its formation. They are themselves formers of public opinion. They not only reflect trends, they also start and accelerate them. University faculties contain a majority of the intellectuals of this country, and certainly the intellectuals are agents in shaping the public mind and will. They originate doctrines and attitudes, pass them on to their students, and, through the students as well as directly, reach the general public. University thinkers, writers, and scientists have had an incalculable influence in the making of the world we live in today, and can have the same influence in the making of the world of tomorrow. Are they prepared for this high responsibility? More and more of them are being stirred to creative thought by the crisis of our times, but the great majority have not yet emerged from the apathy of the period between the wars.

Are the designated leaders of the faculties, are the presidents of the state universities, prepared any better? Unhappily they seem to be lagging behind both the faculties and the public. With few exceptions they stand helpless and bewildered, devoid of critical and creative thought, unable to imagine a revitalized university, repeating the clichés of yesterday's education. This is the impression given, at all events, by the report on Postwar Educational Problems, issued in 1944, by a committee of the National Association of State Universities. The report frankly admits that the state universities, in the depression crisis of the 1930's, "failed to do what they should have done": failed "to consider the fundamental questions." For this discreditable reason, "the problems that confront us today are essentially the same problems that confronted us a decade ago.... Are we going to miss our second opportunity to face these problems squarely?" Apparently we are, judging from the report, which can only be called a model of futility. It is devoid of intellectual virility. It proposes the old conflicting objectives and the old impossible means of attaining them. It abounds in the old claptrap about motivation, individual differences, student advising, teaching methods, measurement of achievement, and the like. It is written in a manner self-conscious, pretentious, complacent, and condescending. And it contains fantastic passages, phrased as if for low IQ's, such passages as those on the dictionary definition of "to plan," on glaciers and mastodons, on hospital patients and their trays, which one might enjoy as satire of administrative inanity were they not offered in all seriousness. At the close the report reminds us, quite rightly, that state universities depend for their support upon public taxation and hence upon public opinion. "We must therefore subject education to critical analysis before less skillful persons invade our province." But the way to invasion is left wide open. One can only hope that the persons invading will be not less but more skillful.

One can hope this with some confidence, for public opinion is today sounder than administrative opinion. It is more likely to ask the fundamental questions and face them squarely. It has a stronger feeling for the essentials of education, for a "common core" of knowledge and abilities as a means of self-realization and social unity. Less swayed by the relativities that obsess the academic mind, the public is inclined to the belief that essentials are always essentials, good at all times. Despite its seeming inertness it looks for leadership, in education as in politics, which can inspire it with purposes a little above its ordinary self. It contains many thoughtful citizens who will demand better state universities as soon as the period of emergency is over. What sort of period will follow, no man can say. At the worst it will repeat the disillusionment that came after the First World War, but it will hardly repeat the blindness and apathy. The second and greater war has shown that America is in the world, in a very dangerous world. If the American public is realistic enough to accept universal military training if it seems necessary as a measure of safety, it may well be realistic enough to accept a solider education for the same purpose. For it seems clear that, whether the new era is to be one of international co-operation or international anarchy, we shall need a stronger democracy than we have had, better disciplined in body and mind. Such a program will necessitate a more liberal education, in which the humanities will be regarded as "builders of morale," once these subjects have got themselves ready for such a role.

To underestimate the public is a more serious blunder than to overestimate it. Let those who are planning the state universities of tomorrow remember this. An educational leadership of cynicism and fear will solve nothing. An educational leadership of faith and courage may be defeated in the end, but it is better to be defeated in the end than at the beginning.

www.ingramcontent.com/pod-product-compliance
Lightning Source LLC
Chambersburg PA
CBHW021121300426
44113CB00006B/235